More praise for

It Was a Very Good Year

"Many books dealing with financial history are accurate, far fewer are illuminating, and only a small handful are entertaining. In *It Was a Very Good Year*, Merrill Lynch's Martin S. Fridson has accomplished a triple play. This is financial history at its best. Must reading for anyone interested in how bull episodes develop and the people who make them move."

—ROBERT SOBEL
Lawrence Stessin Professor of Business History
at Hofstra University, and author
of *Panic on Wall Street*

"Marty Fridson has captured the 'good times' with perception, skill, depth, and humor. It's a great read for anyone interested in the past, present, or future of the U.S. stock market. Also, the book confirms that the four most dangerous words in the investment profession remain 'this time is different.' "

—R. CHARLES TSCHAMPION, CFA
Managing Director, Investment Strategy & Asset
Allocation, General Motors Investment
Management Corporation

"Fridson's lyrical tour of the best years in stock market history has profound implications for what we can expect from stocks for the remainder of the twentieth century."

—TED ARONSON
Managing Partner, Aronson & Partners

∾ *It Was a Very Good Year* ∾

Other Wiley Investment Books

Merton Miller on Derivatives
Merton Miller

Cyber-Investing: Cracking Wall Street with Your PC, Second Edition
David L. Brown and Kassandra Bentley

*The Investor's Anthology: Original Ideas from the
Industry's Greatest Minds*
Charles D. Ellis with James R. Vertin

Mutual Funds on the Net: Making Money Online
Paul B. Farrell

Independently Wealthy: How to Build Wealth in the New Economic Era
Robert Goodman

REITs: Building Your Profits with Real Estate Investment Trusts
John Mullaney

The Art of Short Selling
Kathryn F. Staley

It Was a Very Good Year

〜

EXTRAORDINARY MOMENTS IN STOCK MARKET HISTORY

〜

MARTIN S. FRIDSON

JOHN WILEY & SONS, INC.

New York • Chichester • Weinheim • Brisbane • Singapore • Toronto

This book is dedicated to Dr. Irving Sisman,
whom I have been privileged to know
for seventeen very good years.

Copyright © 1998 by Martin S. Fridson.
Published by John Wiley & Sons, Inc.

All rights reserved. Published simultaneously in Canada.

Library of Congress Cataloging-in-Publication Data:
Fridson, Martin S.
    It was a very good year : extraordinary moments in stock market
history / Martin S. Fridson.
      p. cm.
    Includes index.
    ISBN 0-471-17400-9 (cloth : alk. paper)
    1. Investments—United States—History. 2. Stocks—United States—
History. I. Title.
HG4910.F788 1998
332.64′273—dc21   97-28866

∾ *Preface* ∾

Every once in a while, stock market investors enjoy a spectacularly good year. In 1933, for example, the Standard & Poor's 500 Index produced its highest total return (reflecting both dividend income and price appreciation) of the twentieth century—53.97 percent. As recently as 1995, the performance was a gratifying 36.89 percent. Eight times since 1900, the market has generated an annual return in between those two figures.

Imagine how simple investing would be if you could tell when another sensational year was about to begin. You wouldn't have to worry about picking the right groups or the right stocks. There would be no need to jump in and out of the market, hoping to capitalize on minor fluctuations. Instead, you could lock in a fabulous result by simply buying an index fund and placing your investment strategy on automatic pilot for the next 12 months.

Unfortunately, absolute certainty about the market's future isn't a realistic goal. But examining the past may turn up valuable clues for determining when stocks are set to bust loose again. *It Was a Very Good Year* is a quest for those clues. I began the research for the book with no preconceived notions. It turned out, however, that certain themes were indeed common to the century's 10 best years.

My investigation didn't focus primarily on economic or financial statistics. Instead, I paid careful attention to the observations of well informed commentators who were on the scene during the Very Good Years. Invaluable insights turned up in the musty pages of *Barron's*, *Business Week, Forbes, Fortune,* and the *Wall Street Journal.* Other periodicals, now largely forgotten—including the *Literary Digest, Munsey's Magazine,* and the *Magazine of Wall Street*—likewise yielded exquisite treasures. I profited as well from the observations of economists and historians who studied the outstanding years with the benefit of hindsight.

In the course of seeking to explain exceptional market performance, I uncovered useful evidence about other investment chestnuts. It turned out that wars haven't been invariably regarded as boons to business. Hollywood did not thrive on the public's desire for escape during the Great Depression. Also in the realm of fiction was Joseph Kennedy's tip-off about the Great Crash from his shoeshine man. These myths live on, however, along with the timeless delusion of a "new era" that has invalidated all established valuation standards.

To anticipate a possible criticism, let me acknowledge that calendar years are not the only valid units of time for analyzing investment returns. Wonderful books remain to be written on bull markets that either covered a portion of a year or overlapped two consecutive years. And although I strove to assess the U.S. experience in a global context, more extensive cross-border comparisons would be invaluable. Sacrificing breadth that would have pushed the page count into the thousands, I opted for depth. I focused on a single country's stock market, concentrating on a few years selected by a simple criterion. My modest goal was to tell the story of the great bull years in an interesting manner.

The story would be incomplete, not to mention duller, without a few biographical digressions. I hope that single-minded wealth seekers will forgive my providing some flavor of the times through personality sketches. The subjects include not only financiers, journalists, and politicians, but also notables from other fields who wandered into Wall Street's view. It's no great trick to identify other luminaries who never appear in the book yet influenced the market more profoundly than Roger Babson, Lucille Ball, William Jennings Bryan, Phil Carret, Charlie Chaplin, Ben Graham, John Raskob, Walter Winchell, or Cecelia Wyckoff. But there's little point to such carping, because I make no representation that the cast is complete.

In a similar vein, readers shouldn't get carried away in tracing the Tin Pan Alley motif that gives this book its title. Many of the in-chapter subheadings are *not* lyric fragments. And those that are do not necessarily appear in chapters corresponding to the years in which the associated songs made the hit parade.

None of my attempts to enliven *It Was a Very Good Year* should divert investors from the serious business. I genuinely believe that by closely studying a few particular slices of time, I've managed to develop a fresh perspective on the stock market. For the record, here are the century's 10 top years, in order of total return:

1933	53.97%
1954	52.62%
1915	50.54%
1935	47.66%
1908	45.78%

1928	43.61%
1958	43.37%
1927	37.48%
1975	37.21%
1995	36.89%

For 1908 and 1915, which preceded the introduction of the Standard & Poor's 500 Index, the returns derive from the Cowles Commission indexes. (This series was originally compiled on a primitive Hollerith computer, much like the equipment that figured in Ben Graham's failure to capitalize on one of the twentieth century's greatest stock plays.) My thanks to Jim Bianco of Arbor Trading Group for his help in assembling these returns.

Acknowledgments

I am grateful to John Dean Alfone for his many hours of arduous research, as well as for his contagious enthusiasm. My wife, Elaine Sisman, aided me in countless ways to complete this book. In addition, I thank Myles Thompson of John Wiley & Sons for giving the green light to the project, as well as Mina Samuels, Jacqueline Urinyi, Mary Daniello, and the staff of Cape Cod Compositors for working tirelessly to bring it to fruition. A special debt of gratitude is due Ervin Drake, who wrote a song entitled "It Was a Very Good Year."

Others who helped to turn my idea into reality include: Moosa Aziz, Dolores Colgan, Norman Currie, Christopher Garman, Jim Golden, Linda Greenberg, Jack Kavanagh, Rebecca Keim, Howard Kelting, Lorrie Langella, Ann Marie Mullan, Dorothy Nelson-Gille, George Nitschelm, Henry Postema, Fred Siesel, Gerald Stanewick, and Stephen Wheeler.

Thanks finally to my children, Arielle and Daniel Fridson. Their industry and idealism sustained me while working through the stacks of material that became *It Was a Very Good Year.*

MARTIN S. FRIDSON

New York, New York
November 1997

About the Author

Martin S. Fridson has worked on Wall Street since graduation from Harvard Business School in 1976. He received his undergraduate degree in history from Harvard College. Currently a managing director with Merrill Lynch & Company, Fridson was dubbed "the dean of the high-yield bond market" in conjunction with being voted onto the *Institutional Investor All-America* research team. Fridson serves as a trustee of the Institute of Chartered Financial Analysts, as well as a governor of the Association for Investment Management and Research. The latter organization awarded him a Graham and Dodd Scroll for Excellence in Financial Writing in 1994. Fridson's 1993 book, *Investment Illusions: A Savvy Wall Street Pro Explodes Popular Misconceptions about the Markets*, was among the 22 books published since 1841 that *Worth Magazine* in 1997 included in its investor's core library.

~ *Contents* ~

∾ 1908 ∾

It is not to be expected, or even hoped, that our industries will at once, or in the very near future, rebound to the dangerous height where they were when the recent crash came. And it is not necessary that they should reach this high-pressure point in order to give employment to our workers and good business to our factories, our merchants, and our transportation lines.
—FRANK A. MUNSEY, *Munsey's Magazine*

*O*nce more, as in the "boom times" of 1901 and 1906, Wall Street began to hear of a group of enormously wealthy financiers engaging in speculation on an extensive scale, and of obscure speculators who had made sudden fortunes.
—*The Nation*

*C*onfidence returned gradually during the past year and its first sign was naturally a long rally in the stock market. This was a result and not a cause, although some observers seem to think that an advance in stocks by itself can be used as an instrument to create real wealth. It need hardly be said that you cannot create summer weather by warming the bulb of the thermometer.
—*Wall Street Journal*

Crash and Burn

On the theory that markets always swing back from extremes, an investor might try to catch the Very Good Years by buying stocks whenever a Very Bad Year has just ended. History doesn't endorse such a strategy, however. For example, the Dow Jones Industrial Average's 17 percent decline in 1929, the year of the Great Crash, was followed by a 34 percent drop in 1930. The index lost 53 percent of its remaining value in 1931. Then, after three consecutive bearish years, investors were punished yet again for assuming that whatever goes down must go up: In 1932, industrials plummeted by 23 percent. Nor is it the case that upswings are invariably preceded by downturns. For instance, 1928 was one of the twentieth century's 10 best years, but so was 1927. Like all simple trading rules, buying on big dips is far from an infallible approach.

That being said, an utter collapse in prices can create a lot of upside. Had the Great Panic of 1907 not occurred, 1908 probably would have been a good but not an extraordinary year for stocks. Instead, 1908 began with a huge potential performance bonus in the form of severely depressed prices. From December 31, 1906, to December 31, 1907, the Dow industrials lost 38 percent of their value. Railroads, which figured more prominently in the investors' activities than in later decades, dropped by 32 percent.

Actually, the massive decline of 1907 consisted of two distinct events. March's stock market crash was followed by a money panic in October, which spilled over into further declines in share prices. Neither incident inflicted fundamental damage on the longer-run growth of the U.S. economy. Merchants and industrialists shrugged off the March episode as a Wall Street affair with little relevance to general business activity. Astute market watchers correctly perceived that the repercussions of the October crisis would be temporary. "This panic did not come about from a congestion of manufactured articles, as has been the case on other recessions," wrote Frank Munsey, in *Munsey's Magazine*. "WE HAD NOT overdone our manufacturing. Our warehouses were not glutted with stocks of unsold goods. On the contrary, most manufacturers were running overtime, and turning out products to the limit of their capacity, and even then could not meet the demand." One indisputable effect of the 1907 upheavals, however, was to eliminate high stock valuations that would have precluded a sensational bull market in 1908.

The events of both March and October ultimately derived from a worldwide credit shortage. It was the heyday of the gold standard, which continued until 1914. Under that system, expansion of the world's money supply was limited by the physical supply of the yellow metal. New discoveries enabled the annual production of gold to grow sharply during the 1890s, but after the turn of the century the volume began to level off. Meanwhile, demand for credit grew vigorously. Increasing prosperity sparked ambitious investments in transportation and in manufacturing capacity. Great business combinations, such as the formation of U.S. Steel in 1901, required vast sums of capital to pay the entrepreneurs who sold out to the consolidators. Furthermore, the Boer War (1899–1902) and the Russo-Japanese War (1904–1905) resulted in massive governmental borrowing. On top of all these bidders for a finite supply of credit, speculators took out loans to buy securities as stock markets boomed all over the world. As Frank Munsey put it, "There isn't money enough in the world today to do the world's work."

By 1906, the strains were apparent. The cost of loans backed by stock market collateral ("call loans") fluctuated wildly. At times, the annualized rates soared to 20 percent, 30 percent, and even occasionally to 100 percent. Level-headed analysts considered it foolhardy to borrow at 20 percent or more to buy stocks with dividend yields (at the prevailing high market prices) of only 2 percent or 3 percent. But speculators counted on making up this "negative carry" and more through continuing price advances. Capital gains fever ran high and the *Wall Street Journal* noted parallels to the conditions that led up to the Panic of 1857.

The first cracks appeared when high-quality American railroads began finding it impossible to float new long-term bonds in Europe. Faced with insolvency if they failed to roll over their maturing debts, some railroads eventually settled for domestic short-term funding at exorbitant rates. Others were wise, in Frank Munsey's view, to enter bankruptcy rather than pay whatever rate the banks demanded.

Stock prices broke on March 13. The Dow railroad index plunged from 112.53 to 107.52, then to 99.71 on the 14th. Industrials declined by 12 percent over the same two-day period. No startling event precipitated the fall, which prompted widespread margin calls and brokerage house failures. Then, as abruptly as it began, the crash ended. Stock prices didn't fully recover to their February highs, but in the case of railroads, the market was 12 percent above its March 25 low by the end of April.

Investors who peered a bit beyond the current price quotations saw that the financial strains hadn't disappeared. A series of shocks occurred during the spring and summer of 1907:

- The city of San Francisco failed to float a loan in New York, indicating that credit remained tight.
- Egypt's Alexandria Stock Exchange crashed. When London came to the rescue by shipping $3 million of gold to Alexandria, the Bank of England was left in a vulnerable state. A run on the pound ensued.
- Stocks fell sharply on the Tokyo Exchange and Japan was struck by a wave of bank failures.
- Fearful French investors began buying gold, draining huge amounts from the United States.

- President Theodore Roosevelt's administration stepped up its antitrust activities. Charging that Standard Oil of New Jersey held a near monopoly of the petroleum business, the government disclosed plans to seek its dissolution.
- Bond offerings for the cities of Boston and New York, as well as a stock offering for Westinghouse, were undersubscribed.
- The Metropolitan Traction Company, created as America's first holding company to control New York City's streetcar lines, went bankrupt.
- New York's money center banks were strained by the customary seasonal migration of funds to America's agricultural regions. This was a recurrent pattern, but the U.S. Treasury could never figure out how to use its vast gold reserves to neutralize the impact. As a consequence, interest rates invariably rose violently in autumn.

The panic began on October 15 with the collapse of a scheme to corner the stock of the United Copper Company. In a superb account of the 1907 travails, historian Robert Sobel reports that the Standard Oil interests were widely suspected of undermining the attempted short squeeze in United Copper. One of the corner's architects, Frederick Augustus Heinze, had run afoul of the group a few years earlier, when it was in the process of creating a copper trust.

United Copper's free fall from 60 to 10 brought down the financial empire of Heinze and his partner, Charles W. Morse. Investors knew that they had used depository institutions under their control to finance their failed corner. First, a run on the Mercantile National Bank forced the institution to shut its doors. Shares of Morse's ice companies nose-dived, creating wide anxiety in the market.

Westinghouse, although not tied to Heinze and Morse, was still shaky after its recently failed share offering. The electrical equipment company's stock declined from 103 to 79⅝ on October 18, was suspended from trading, then opened the following day in over-the-counter trading at 35. Two brokerage houses failed as a direct result, while hundreds of speculators were ruined. Continued withdrawals worsened the banking crisis. By now, the crisis was too great for even the U.S. Treasury to contain. It was time to refer the matter to a higher authority, namely, J. Pierpont Morgan.

When My Ship Comes In

The preeminent banker of his day, Morgan had masterminded the formation of U.S. Steel and other leading industrial concerns. He had also gained a commanding position in Eastern railroad lines, which caused him to clash with Edward Harriman, the dominant Western player. Nevertheless, Harriman was among the Wall Street lions that Morgan assembled in the nation's dark hour.

Under Morgan's leadership, the group set about determining which financial institutions could still be saved, while consigning the rest to oblivion. Most immediately in danger were the trust companies. These depository institutions, later outlawed, exploited a loophole in the New York state law in order to operate without material reserves. Seen as rivals by New York's banks, most of the trust companies had been effectively banished from the Clearing House, the institution that customarily provided liquidity during banking crises. Because the New York Clearing House didn't monitor the trust companies' financials, it wasn't able to determine quickly whether it was prudent to extend credit to them when the 1907 panic hit. (In Chicago, where trust companies had always remained within the clearinghouse's surveillance, no trust companies or banks failed during the Panic.)

Morgan quickly concluded that it was pointless to try to rescue Heinze and Morse's Knickerbocker Trust Company. This judgment about New York's third largest trust company came from Benjamin Strong, who was destined to receive a large share of the blame for the 1929 Crash. When the Knickerbocker failed, amidst allegations of malfeasance, panic gripped depositors at other trust companies.

At that point, Morgan was assured by his associates that the collateral was adequate at another Heinze-Morse entity, the Trust Company of America. Replied Morgan, "Then this is the place to stop the trouble."

Curiously, the collateral in question included a controlling interest in the Tennessee Coal & Iron Company, a major U.S. Steel competitor. The investment banking house of Moore & Schley had posted the shares as security for loans it had taken when the stock market began its plunge. Morgan capitalized on the opportunity to capture Tennessee Coal & Iron for U.S. Steel, paying with bonds worth less than the already-depressed price at which Moore & Schley had been trying to bail out.

The Tennessee Coal & Iron maneuver required Theodore Roosevelt's acquiescence to a merger that he opposed on antitrust grounds. But with the President envisioning a complete financial debacle, Morgan knew he was indispensable. And he meant to be rewarded for his trouble. According to associates, he vowed, "I won't take all this on unless . . ." and concluded with a gesture that they took to mean, "unless I get what I want out of it." To convince the President that the situation remained grave, Morgan withheld the news that London was prepared to ship gold to help relieve the crisis. Roosevelt consented to U.S. Steel's acquisition of the country's lowest-cost steel mill and a half-billion tons of iron reserves.

Meanwhile, the Trust Company of America was saved by a typical Morgan stratagem. The U.S. Treasury was willing to help, but wasn't authorized to make deposits in trust companies. Morgan therefore induced Treasury Secretary George Cortelyou to deposit $35 million in the New York banks, which immediately relent the sum to the nearly insolvent Trust Company of America. Additional heroics followed. In just five minutes, Morgan arranged a $27-million emergency bank loan to save the New York Stock Exchange. When the tight money conditions persisted, he persuaded the banks to accept scrip, redeemable in bona fide money at the conclusion of the panic. Along the way, Morgan rescued the New York City government from insolvency and even prevailed upon the municipality's leading clergymen to preach bullish sermons.

On November 6, $7 million of gold arrived from London. With it came news that another $10 million worth was headed to America aboard the *Lusitania*. J. Pierpont Morgan had ended the panic, while picking up immensely valuable assets on the cheap. Most other investors had to wait until 1908 for their bonanza, which consisted of a one-year total return of 45.78 percent.

Small Fry

Among the many small investors whose margin accounts were wiped out during the Panic of 1907 was Dorothy Grossbaum of New York. To compound the disaster, her bank failed.

After a bric-a-brac business left by her late husband disintegrated, along with proceeds of his life insurance, the young widow had turned to keeping a boardinghouse and eventually to speculation. Her modest-sized account was carried by a member of the Consolidated Stock Exchange, where round lots consisted of just 10 shares, rather than 100, as on the New York Stock Exchange.

Dorothy Grossbaum's son, Benjamin, was just 11 years old in 1907. Each day, he inspected the financial pages to see whether his mother's favorite stock, U.S. Steel, had risen or fallen. It was a humble launch of the brilliant career of the Dean of Wall Street, who became known to the financial world as Ben Graham.

Big Shot

Most contemporary readers won't recognize the name of Frank Munsey, who's quoted several times in this chapter. During his lifetime (1854–1925), however, the onetime Maine telegraph operator achieved several distinctions.

One was to revolutionize the magazine publishing business by cutting the price of his flagship monthly, *Munsey's Magazine*, from 25 cents to a dime. That 1893 innovation launched the mass circulation era. Munsey parlayed his magazine profits into a fortune in real estate and grocery stores. He also speculated successfully in stocks, becoming for a time the largest shareholder of U.S. Steel.

Munsey's second distinction was being called "probably the most hated publisher that ever lived." He earned the title by firing reporters and editors on such capricious grounds as being too young, too fat, or left-handed. Perhaps owing to his peculiar management style, Munsey's dailies lost money. As a consequence, he either killed or consolidated New York's *Press*, *Sun*, *Herald*, *Tribune*, *Globe*, and *Mail*, gaining the additional designation of "the executioner of newspapers." Munsey didn't bother telling the *Herald*'s managing editor, George Lincoln, that the paper was being merged until the moment that he handed him the announcement for typesetting. As an afterthought, Munsey asked Lincoln to stay on and run the *Herald-Tribune*. Lincoln rejected the offer, saying that he regretted every moment he'd ever worked for Munsey.

Four years before his death, the lifelong bachelor made out a new will. After rattling off a number of bequests that totaled about one-sixth of Munsey's estate, his lawyer asked who ought to receive the residual. "Well, give it to the Metropolitan Museum," Munsey answered casually.

It's not clear whether Munsey ever set foot in New York's Metropolitan Museum of Art, although he was a member from 1916 onward. Making large bequests to the institution carried immense prestige, however. In addition, Munsey's lawyer was reportedly an art lover, even if Munsey was not. The museum's share of the fortune ultimately came to approximately $10 million, indicating that talk of a $40-million estate was grossly exaggerated. Nevertheless, the hated publisher's legacy was the largest cash gift ever made to any museum up until that time.

On the Road Again

The Dow Jones Industrial Average's low point for 1907 had been reached on November 15. According to *The Nation*, signs of returning credit facilities first appeared on Saturday, November 23. Helped by the revived money market, stock prices recovered by 11 percent during the panic year's final month and a half. The favorable trend was encouraged as the new year began, in typical postpanic fashion, with further easing of credit conditions. On the first working day of 1908, the Bank of England lowered its key lending rate from 7 percent, a century-high level that had arisen from strained credit conditions during 1906.

Although it was too early to discern any improvement in business conditions, the Dow industrials climbed by 12 percent during the first two weeks of the year. Railroads, which finished 1907 at 88.77, hit a short-term high of 95.75 on January 19. At that point, the bears descended, scaring general investors out of the market temporarily. For the moment, the rally stalled, with the railroads plunging to 86.04 on February 17.

Nevertheless, stocks held the gains achieved during the final weeks of 1907. The 1908 low for industrials of 58.62, which represented a negligible decline from the year-end 1907 mark of 58.75, occurred on February 13. Then, after a month-long domination by professionals bent on driving down prices, the recovery resumed.

By that time, a glimmer of optimism was returning. Week by week, merchants' inventories were being reduced or exhausted and scattered factories were resuming part- or full-time schedules. Elbert H. Gary, chairman of the executive board of U.S. Steel, reported that business was increasing rapidly. January's bookings rose by more than 20 percent over the preceding month, which had been the slowest in the corporation's seven-year history. As of late February, Gary reckoned that volume for the full month would climb by another 40 percent. (It's testimony to the magnitude of the 1907 panic that despite Big Steel's sharp rebound in the first two months of 1908, its mills were still running at less than half their rated capacity.)

The fact that the recovery in steel demand was more pronounced in manufacturing than in the railroad sector was taken as a bullish sign. It implied that industrial output was on the rise, rather than indicating a surge in transportation of goods already produced.

Frank Munsey, in *Munsey's Magazine*, thought business would soon be looking up for the railroads, as well. Already, the rails were benefiting from seasonal shipments of citrus fruits and early vegetables from Florida. While the carriers awaited a more general pickup, passenger traffic and mail transportation were generating reasonably steady revenue. On the whole, shareholders had ample cause for optimism regarding the railroads' long-term prospects. Accordingly, Munsey predicted that to keep their roads and rolling stock in good repair, the companies would conserve cash by cutting dividends. This observation helps to explain why the bulls of 1908 weren't discouraged by widespread dividend reductions and omissions.

In fact, from a certain perspective, investors might even have viewed dividend cuts as good news. Prior to the Panic of 1907, according to Munsey, the controlling interests of several railroads had raised dividends excessively for their own enrichment. In a typical scheme, the directors accumulated a large block of stock, then hiked the payout. A quick rise in the share price resulted, but the company was left short of cash to maintain its facilities.

Munsey specifically cited Edward Harriman's August 1906 increase of Union Pacific's dividend rate from 6 percent to 10 percent of par. The maneuver caused Union Pacific stock to jump by 14 percent in just two days. It was "one of the rankest cases of stock-gambling with a legitimate business that has happened in recent years," in Munsey's words, but by no means unique.

Perhaps, as dividends receded to more prudent levels, investors began to perceive the railroads as genuinely improved investments. Alternatively, they may have reasoned that the reduced dividend payouts gave the smart operators a chance to run up the same stocks all over again. If so, their instincts weren't entirely misguided. "No one has lost any money in following the leadership of Mr. Harriman," insisted the *Commercial and Financial Chronicle* in a late-1908 assessment of the financier's career.

To be sure, the optimal balance between dividends and cash retention was a debatable point and it remains so. From Ben Graham's 1926–1928 proxy battle with Northern Pipeline to Kirk Kerkorian's hostile bid for Chrysler in 1995, insurgents have routinely charged management with hoarding cash that could be more usefully distributed to shareholders. Likewise, critics of 1980s leveraged buyouts echoed *Munsey's Magazine*'s accusation that Edward Harriman had drained cash out of Union Pacific at the expense of essential expenditures. Perhaps some of the LBO sponsors did, in fact, cut through fat and into the muscle. No one, however, can accuse them of inventing the idea.

Cold, Cold Heart

Edward H. Harriman and his immediate family shaped events across the span of all of the Very Good Years. The great speculator made his first stock market killing in the Black Friday panic of 1869. His daughter-in-law served as Ambassador to France under President Bill Clinton.

Although less colorful than many financiers before and since, Edward Harriman was a leading celebrity in 1908. "His downsitting and uprising were compassed about with reporters," according to *The Nation.* "News about him and inventions about him were read with absorbed attention by millions of his fellow-countrymen. He stood as one of the chief symbols of his class—a name freely bandied about, abused more than he was admired, yet always a synonym of power, possibly of danger, but unquestionably of social and political importance."

In *The Nation*'s estimation, Harriman was a throwback to the robber barons of the preceding generation. "The imperious and ruthless methods which he too often adopted, used to be endured in a Commodore Vanderbilt, in a Fisk or Gould, but they were obsolete even while Mr. Harriman was employing them."

But even in light of the Union Pacific affair of 1906, Harriman was praised for investing heavily in maintaining and upgrading his properties. "He is admitted to have been as able a railway man as he was stock manipulator," *The Nation* acknowledged. A journalist who admired his intellectual ability said of Harriman, "He would be a wonderful character if he only had a heart."

Certainly, heartlessness was a characteristic commonly ascribed to Harriman. *The Nation* supported the judgment with several specific charges:

- Remorselessly marching over the wrecks of others on his way to power.
- Coldly disregarding the human element in finance.
- Having little patience for criticism.

The Nation also took exception to Harriman's "clutching after and use of political influence to further his business ambitions," yet tried to be fair about the thing. "We say nothing of his charities," added the periodical, "for they may have been much larger than the public knows."

Indeed, aside from such widely recognized philanthropies as endowing boys' clubs, Harriman took great interest in the welfare of everyone on his 7863-acre estate in Orange County, New York. Each Christmas, Harriman bestowed a suitable gift on every man, woman, and child of the manor. One year, Tom, a forlorn boy who lived with his drunken father in a shack some four miles from the big house, was inadvertently omitted from the Christmas list. Accompanied by his son Averell, the future governor of New York, Harriman himself "went to the little shack in the woods, with a sled—a fine sturdy sled, such as every boy longs for." Harriman's biographer, George Kennan, regarded this touching episode as just one demonstration of how grievously the railroad magnate was misjudged by those who observed him only in a business setting.

Incidentally, the remarkably long span of influence of two generations of Harrimans arose from rather unusual circumstances. Edward Harriman was not quite 21 on Black Friday, 1869. At 43, he fathered Averell, who 80 years later married a woman 30 years his junior. Averell's widow was the daughter-in-law not only of Edward Harriman, but at an earlier point, of Winston Churchill. Her appointment as Ambassador to France came near the end of a long and very busy life. Among Pamela Digby Churchill Hayward Harriman's reputed lovers was crooner Frank Sinatra, whose many hits included "It Was a Very Good Year."

Pulpit Bully

"Wall Street is in such a nervous and irrational condition," wrote Frank Munsey on February 25, 1908, "that if the President says anything, it trembles and translates his utterances into some fresh disaster. If he says nothing for a little while, Wall Street regards his silence as ominous, and shakes in its boots." According to Munsey, Wall Street even blamed Theodore Roosevelt for the 1907 panic. An unabashed admirer of the hero of San Juan Hill, Munsey denied that there was "one little bit of truth in this assertion."

In retrospect, certainly, Roosevelt's stepped-up trust-busting in 1907 seems a minor factor in comparison with the mounting strain on the credit system. Inadequately reserved, and therefore inherently unstable, trust companies didn't help matters. On the other hand, the Colonel's overheated rhetoric invited attack from Wall Street.

Hardly anything could be worse, Roosevelt maintained, than permitting America's fate to be determined by "the man of mere wealth, to whom the stock market is everything, and whose short-sighted vision is bounded by the horizon of a material prosperity." Among the many character flaws that the Colonel detected in such individuals was a deplorable lack of patriotism. This failing became apparent to Roosevelt when they questioned the wisdom of war with Spain in 1898. "The big financiers and the men generally who were susceptible to touch on the money nerve, and who cared nothing for National Honor if it conflicted even temporarily with business prosperity, were against the war," Roosevelt later recalled. Might this opposition, as many contended, represent in some measure a principled stand against imperialism? No, explained Teddy, it was all attributable to "the craven fear and brutal selfishness of mere money-getters."

Why, war would be a positive blessing for America, which, in Roosevelt's view, was too complacent about national defense. "I sometimes question," he confided to a future German ambassador to the United States, "whether anything but a great military disaster will ever make us feel our responsibilities and our possible dangers." And it didn't matter much which country provided this valuable lesson, including Germany. "Frankly, I don't know that I should be sorry to see a bit of a spar with Germany," he remarked in 1889. "The burning of New York and a few other sea coast cities would be a good object lesson in the need of an adequate system of coast defenses." By 1895, Roosevelt was all for declaring war on Great Britain over a dispute involving the border between Venezuela and British Guiana: "Let the fight come if it must. I don't care whether our sea coast cities are bombarded or not; we would take Canada." The following year, Teddy's enemy of choice had changed again: "It is very difficult for me not to wish a war with Spain, for such a war would result at once in getting a proper navy." By 1897, he was happy to pick an adversary at random. "In strict confidence," he wrote to an officer, "I should welcome almost any war, for I think this country needs one."

Theodore Roosevelt was surely one of the Nobel peace prize's most belligerent recipients. "He would like above all things to go to war with someone," a college friend wrote of him back in 1885. "He wants to be killing something all the time." And shame on anyone who felt otherwise. "A Quaker may be quite as undesirable a citizen as a duelist," Roosevelt asserted, in the following year. "No man who is not willing to bear arms and to fight for his rights . . . should be entitled to the privilege of living in a free community."

Fourteen years later, campaigning for Vice President among members of the Society of Friends, he backtracked a bit: Without the Quakers, whose "social and industrial virtue" entitled them to "the respect of all people," the American people "would never have been able to make the Republic what it is and should be." In fact, Roosevelt mellowed so much that by the time he published his memoirs in 1913, he conceded that not all proponents of disarmament and mandatory arbitration of international disputes were malevolent enemies of social order:

> Many of them are, in the ordinary relations of life, good citizens. They are exactly like the other good citizens who believe that enforced universal vegetarianism or anti-vaccination is the panacea for all ills.

During his presidency, however, Roosevelt regarded disagreement as sacrilege. It was no exaggeration for former Republican Secretary of the Interior Carl Schurz to portray him as believing all opposition to his reelection to be wicked "and that therefore, those who decide to vote against him—about one-half the voters of the United States—are unpatriotic citizens and bad Americans." Added British journalist George W. Smalley, "He honestly believes it is impossible to differ with him honestly." In castigating his opponents in the Senate as "demagogues" and "crooks," in ridiculing "the limited mental horizon" of those who differed with him, Roosevelt was neither fairer nor more temperate than Wall Streeters who blamed him for market slumps.

The Substance of Things Hoped For

On May 21, *The Nation* cautioned that the second leg of the 1908 stock rally was signaling a business recovery that wasn't actually materializing. In fact, certain business statistics suggested that the economy was worsening. U.S. Steel's March 31 orders for future delivery were below the December 31, 1907, level. Iron ore production in the United States declined in April, while the number of idle railroad cars increased after a promising drop in March.

"Here was apparently a picture of uninterrupted depression," *The Nation* proclaimed. "Yet on the Stock Exchange, a second upward movement began at the close of April, and has continued, with increasing rapidity and violence, ever since." No comparable level of speculation had been observed since the "Harriman Market" of August 1906, when the diminutive financier known as the "little giant" went on a rail securities buying spree and radically increased Union Pacific's dividend. Not only had stocks rebounded to the prices witnessed prior to the October 1907 money panic, but they were approaching the levels attained before the March 1907 market crash.

The bullish case rested on the observed resumption of payments by the banks and restoration of credit. As long as lending was curtailed, investors were not only precluded from buying, but were compelled to liquidate stocks to meet their obligations. It was typical, pointed out the bulls, for stocks to rally after a panic as banks resumed payments. This time around, moreover, the postpanic environment included the atypical blessings of a sound dollar, a well funded U.S. Treasury, and prosperous conditions outside the Eastern financial centers. New York's banks had created a somewhat isolated problem by excluding the trust companies from the ordinary surveillance of the Clearing House. The most optimistic speculators spoke of an immediate revival of the boom that had been rudely interrupted by the traumas of 1907.

Arguing for caution was European skepticism regarding the U.S. stock rally. Not only were the great banking houses of Europe refusing to finance any new American railway loans, but New York had just been hit with a massive gold outflow. And while the initial surge in stock prices may have represented a normal postpanic response to the restoration of credit, *The Nation* saw no precedent for as swift a business rebound as the continuing rally implied. The periodical also noted that the market would have to deal with the upcoming presidential election, "traditionally an unsettling factor in business."

Did You Ever Have to Make Up Your Mind?

In July, the Republicans' noncontroversial choice of William Howard Taft as their 1908 presidential candidate offered hope that the election would be less unsettling than usual. A former governor of the Philippines and future Chief Justice of the Supreme Court, Secretary of War Taft was Theodore Roosevelt's chosen successor. For all of the blustering against the Rough Rider, Wall Street looked favorably upon continued Republican occupation of the White House.

Taft was to be remembered as much as anything for his girth. "He was our great human fellow because there was more of him to be human," said homespun humorist Will Rogers upon Taft's death. "We are parting with 300 pounds of solid charity to everybody." Taft him-

self made light of his heft. He told of a youngster who was warned
that if he didn't stop biting his nails, he'd swell up like a balloon and
burst. The boy believed his nurse and broke his bad habit. A month or
so later, the lad met Taft, eyed him with stern disapproval, and said ac-
cusingly, "You bite your nails!"

If there was any great difference of opinion about the GOP nominee, it was in the views of Theodore Roosevelt before and after Taft
entered the White House. In 1901, the Colonel wrote, with remarkable prescience:

> A year ago a man of wide acquaintance, both with American pub-
> lic life and American public men, remarked that the first Governor
> of the Philippines ought to combine the qualities which would
> make a first-class President of the United States with the qualities
> that would make a first-class Chief-Justice of the United States,
> and that the only man he knew who possessed all these qualities
> was Judge William H. Taft, of Ohio. The statement was entirely
> correct.

Roosevelt went on to rhapsodize about Taft's "absolutely unflinch-
ing rectitude on every point of public duty, and a literally dauntless
courage and willingness to bear responsibility." After the 1912 election, in which he bolted his party to oppose Taft in a three-way race
that handed the presidency to Woodrow Wilson, Roosevelt had a
much different view. Through his narrowly legalistic interpretation of
the President's role, said Roosevelt, Taft put himself in a class with the
lamentable James Buchanan. Roosevelt's own approach to the job, in
his own estimation, placed him in the company of Andrew Jackson
and Abraham Lincoln.

In 1908, however, Roosevelt backed Taft heartily and investors endorsed his choice. Republican victory was all the more imperative in
light of the Democrats' selection of William Jennings Bryan. Although
twice before defeated for the presidency, the "Nebraska Cyclone" had
lost none of his fervor. And the financial world regarded him as no less
of a menace than in 1896, when he ran against the gold standard and
"the Wall Street syndicates which have been bleeding this country."
Other epithets favored by the "Silver-tongued Orator" included:

- "Money changers and the attorneys of the great trusts and corporations."
- "Great combinations of money grabbers."

- "Idle holders of idle capital."
- "The class which owns money, and trades in money, and grows rich as the people grow poor."

This time around, Bryan asked, "Shall the people rule?" His answer, in part, was that they could not, as long as corporations were able to buy elections. He proposed mandatory disclosure of campaign contributions above $100, as well as a prohibition of contributions in excess of $10,000. The "Knight of the West" denounced Standard Oil of New Jersey as "the most notorious lawbreaker in the United States." He advocated a licensing procedure for corporations, designed to prevent the creation of monopolies. In short, Bryan erased any possible doubt in Wall Street's mind about the necessity of electing Taft.

That left a lot of potential votes for Bryan to capture, however. The "Great Commoner" felt confident of victory, based on his undeniable rapport with the disaffected population of the small towns and farms. "He never felt uncomfortable with the poor farmers and laborers with whom he might rub shoulders in town squares," wrote Bryan biographer LeRoy Ashby in 1987. "He had no trouble . . . identifying with even the most deprived residents of village and rural America."

H. L. Mencken looked less kindly on this aspect of William Jennings Bryan's character. "He liked people who sweated freely, and were not debauched by the refinements of the toilet," observed the eminent editor and critic upon Bryan's death. "His career brought him into contact with the first men of his time; he preferred the company of rustic ignoramuses." Nor, in Mencken's judgment, did Bryan merit respect for remaining true to his principles, however benighted: "If the fellow was sincere, then so was P. T. Barnum. The word is disgraced and degraded by such uses. He was, in fact, a charlatan, a mountebank, a zany without sense or dignity."

Biographer Ashby, while making no excuses for Bryan's defense of Southern statutes that denied black suffrage, put a positive spin on the anti-Darwinist crusade of the aging "Boy Orator of the Platte." As an unfailing upholder of the powerless, argued Ashby, Bryan instinctively opposed a doctrine that he saw being used to justify exploitation of the weak by the strong. Once again, H. L. Mencken viewed the matter in a different light. At the celebrated 1925 Scopes "monkey trial," Mencken wrote of Bryan, "He descended to demagogy so dreadful that his very associates at the trial table blushed. His one yearning was to keep his yokels heated up—to lead his forlorn mob of imbeciles against the foe."

The Sound of One Company Merging

During the spring of 1908 representatives of four leading automobile manufacturers met in Detroit's Penobscot Building to discuss an audacious plan. The proposal was to form an automobile trust on the model of the United States Steel Corporation. With their combined annual production of 22,000 cars, the companies would dominate the industry, enabling them to take some of the risk out of an intensely competitive and volatile business. Financing for the consolidation would be arranged by J. Pierpont Morgan, who had masterminded the U.S. Steel deal seven years earlier.

Unfortunately, the four proposed principals had very different plans in mind. Before long, two dropped out—Henry Ford and Ransom E. Olds, manufacturer of the Reo. That left Buick Motor Company, headed by one-time carriage manufacturer William Crapo Durant, and Maxwell-Briscoe.

Benjamin Briscoe had hatched the consolidation scheme and brought the House of Morgan into the proposition. When news of the pending consolidation was leaked to the *New York Times*, however, the House of Morgan angrily yanked its support. Durant in turn dropped Maxwell-Briscoe from his plans.

Herbert L. Satterlee, J. Pierpont Morgan's son-in-law and head of the law firm handling the deal, quite reasonably asked Durant how it was possible to effect a consolidation with only one company. At that point, the Buick chief sprang a surprise: For the past month he had held an option to acquire at least 75 percent of Oldsmobile, a troubled company originally founded by Ransom E. Olds. Durant would now be the unchallenged head of an automobile powerhouse. His inspiration was to produce several different makes, thereby maximizing the chances of having a hot seller in any given year.

Before long, the new company would advance that goal by acquiring the Oakland (later the Pontiac) and the Cadillac. But first, the corporation needed a name. Durant preferred "International Motors," but the Morgan partner who had originally proposed it indicated that he wanted to retain the name for a possible future combination. "United Motors" was scratched when one of Satterlee's law partners uncovered a New Jersey company operating under the name "United Motor Car Company." And so, on September 16,

1908, General Motors Company was incorporated with a token capitalization of $2000. After Durant tendered Buick shares worth $3.4 million to the entity, the directors raised GM's capitalization to $12.5 million. From these modest beginnings emerged the stock that technical analysts came to regard as a bellwether for the entire market.

The Match Game

On the then customary two-hour Saturday trading session of August 22, a curious incident raised fears of stock manipulation. During the week, many large sell orders had arrived on the New York Stock Exchange floor. Market participants attributed the sales to major operators who'd been caught short and were hoping to limit their losses. Aside from mysterious drops in a few railroad names, however, the bear initiative failed. Then came, in the words of Howard Schenck Mott of *Harper's Weekly*, "one of the most remarkable phenomena ever witnessed in the stock market." In the first hour of Saturday's trading, prices rose moderately on immense volume. Turnover remained exceptional during the second hour, as prices broke gently and finished essentially unchanged on the day.

Suspicions were widespread that the huge volume of August 22 consisted largely of "matched orders." With an eye toward rigging the market, it was alleged, a large operator would surreptitiously enter both a buy and a sell order. (Edward Harriman dubbed the practice "selling in circles.") "That these enormous transactions of Saturday were bona fide, that the principals were really prepared to pay for the stocks which they bought and to deliver the stocks which they sold, is inconceivable," commented *The Nation*. "The attendant circumstances indicated that the great activity was a humbug. Brokers were openly declared to have been entrusted with orders for 5,000 or 10,000 shares, orders which they were instructed to execute only with certain other designated brokers."

Outsiders weren't sure whether the maneuver was aimed primarily at covering shorts at artificially depressed levels or at levitating prices in order to take gains. In either case, argued Mott, who later moved on from *Harper's* to become a vice president of the Irving National Bank of New York, the fact that prices scarcely budged was proof that established New York Stock Exchange safeguards precluded successful manipulation. Still, he felt obliged to rebut the popular perception of the exchange as an iniquitous institution. "No widely entertained view could possibly be more fallacious," he wrote. In a similar vein, the

American Review of Reviews, while frankly acknowledging the prevalence of matched orders, reported that the most egregious example during 1908 was a bear effort that failed. "The successful financiers are not those who defy the workings of natural conditions," remarked the editorialist, with obvious satisfaction, "but those who see them first." Never mind that, as *The Nation* pointed out, "By general agreement among brokers, the operations in question constituted a flagrant violation of good faith and the rules of the Exchange."

Fallacious or not, the popular impression of monkey business as standard operating procedure was probably an inevitable result of the frantic speculation that characterized 1908. The public saw clearly that the production of goods and services wasn't recovering at a rate commensurate with the leaps in financial market values.

According to the *American Review of Reviews,* however, this was no indication that speculators were (or were even capable of) pumping up stock prices artificially. The simpler explanation was that with loan demand depressed because of the business slump, lendable bank funds had flooded into New York. There, competitive forces had driven six-month money rates down to the 3 percent to $3\frac{1}{2}$ percent range. Wealthy individuals could hardly be faulted for capitalizing on their strong credit ratings to borrow at 3 percent and invest in bonds with coupons of $4\frac{1}{2}$ percent or stocks carrying dividend yields of 5 percent or 6 percent. Their plan was to earn a couple of points above their borrowing cost for a while, then sell at higher prices when business conditions inevitably improved. There was risk in the strategy, certainly, but these affluent people could stand it, as long as they took care to diversify their holdings.

Realistically, the *American Review of Reviews*'s explanation of the stock market surge was probably a little too tidy. It's hard to imagine that along with the responsible coupon clippers that the author portrayed, there probably weren't some highly aggressive operators in the market as well. And what would happen when the prudent investors decided to take their profits? If their shares weren't absorbed by some other group that had been on the sidelines, prices were bound to fall. Worse still, there's no getting around the fact that a strategy of borrowing at 3 percent and investing at 6-percent-plus-price-change is a leveraging game. It's axiomatic that leverage feels great on the way up, but that in a downturn it creates painful losses, which lead to further liquidations.

But even if the *American Review of Reviews* painted too rosy a picture of speculators, the periodical offered a highly plausible interpretation of the rally. During the Very Good Years of 1927 and 1928, analysts once more hypothesized that because available credit exceeded ordinary loan demand, it was flowing into margin lending. The result once again was a bull market of greater proportions than conventional valuation measures could justify. By then, however, the creation of the Federal Reserve System had made it possible for the game to go on quite a bit longer.

The Real Thing

Ty Cobb of the Detroit Tigers enjoyed a customarily outstanding season in 1908. He won his second of an eventual 12 batting championships with a .324 average. Cobb also led the American League in hits, doubles, triples, runs batted in, and assists by an outfielder.

In the same year, Cobb was photographed on the bench with a carton of soda pop conspicuously displayed at his side. The soft drink was a brand produced in his native state of Georgia, originally marketed as "French Wine Cola Nerve and Tonic Stimulant."

After World War I, Cobb's golfing partner and fellow Georgian Robert Woodruff formed a syndicate to buy all of the rights to Coca-Cola. Up until then, Cobb had resisted Woodruff's pleas to invest in the company on the grounds that the stock wasn't listed on the New York Stock Exchange. But the fleet outfielder was impressed by Woodruff's confidence, evidenced by his entering into the largest financial transaction arranged in the South up to that time. What's more, Woodruff offered to have his bank, Georgia Trust, lend Cobb the money to buy the shares. The loan could be repaid with Coca-Cola dividends.

The Georgia Peach purchased 300 shares for a total of $10,800. Within eight years, his annual income from Coca-Cola reached $350,000. Eventually, with the help of additional purchases, Cobb's yearly dividends reportedly exceeded a million dollars. Fellow Hall of Famer Tris Speaker profited from Cobb's advice to buy Coca-Cola and hold onto it for retirement.

Well before age 40, Cobb was a millionaire, even though his baseball salary never surpassed $85,000 a year. Besides his reluctant, but spectacularly successful investment in Coca-Cola, Cobb also bought into General Motors a year after its founding. Additionally, he profited in commodities, owned a lucrative car dealership, and unsuccessfully tried to buy a major league ball club. But Coca-Cola held a special place in Cobb's heart, as well as his portfolio. He even refused to patronize service stations that didn't sell Coke.

It Never Entered My Mind

Following the nominations of Taft and Bryan in early summer, bull-minded investors seemed curiously unconcerned about the approaching election. In contrast, the Great Commoner's first nomination in 1896 had been greeted by a violent "election scare" that drove prices down through mid-August. Thereafter, warnings were regularly sounded that insulated Eastern speculators were oblivious to Democratic inroads in traditionally Republican Midwestern constituencies. The visitor from Iowa, who'd found that every man he'd met there was planning to vote for Bryan, became a stock figure on Wall Street. Fearful that bimetallism would wreck the currency and with it the nation's financial condition, investors lined up at the Sub-Treasury's redemption window to exchange legal tender notes for gold. On the day before the 1896 polling, the yield on call money soared to 96 percent. Four years later, the specter of Bryanism was still frightening enough to perturb the market throughout September and send money rates to 25 percent on election eve.

Conceivably, the complacency that ensued upon Bryan's third designation as the Democratic standard-bearer was attributable to the absence of an election scare in 1904. In that year, as in the scareless campaign of 1892, well informed investors never had doubt about the outcome. Nor did the 1888 election discombobulate the market, which was equally comfortable with either candidate. At any rate, the 1908 calm was suddenly shattered in September. All five of the most active stocks of the period, railroad names in each case, declined by about 15 points on heavy volume. No explanation was offered on the Street except for a sudden fear that Bryan might succeed at long last.

Precipitating the abrupt shift in attitude were the results of a state election in Maine. The Republican plurality of 7700 was well below the 27,000-vote edge achieved four years earlier. Even in September 1892, two months before Democrat Grover Cleveland recaptured the White House, the GOP managed a 12,500-vote victory in Maine. Never mind that Maine had delivered a record Republican plurality in Cleveland's November 1884 triumph and on numerous other occasions showed itself a less reliable bellwether than Vermont. Shaken by the real possibility of an event they hadn't seriously contemplated, investors momentarily permitted greed to give way to fear.

Incidentally, the claim of East Coast isolation from events in the heartland, noted in connection with the 1896 Presidential race, became a cliché throughout the twentieth century. Despite vast improvements in communications over the decades, New York–based economists were regularly charged with obliviousness to trends west of the Hudson River. High-concept corporations capitalized on the same perception to argue that their shares were undervalued as a consequence of Wall Street's insularity. "If only brokerage house analysts would venture beyond the five boroughs," sighed management, "they'd discover that in other parts of the country, manufactured housing is regarded as a prestigious lifestyle option, rather than the despised 'trailers' they imagine." The story had an undeniable emotional appeal, derived from the same inspiration as the Populist image of a cow eating grass in the Midwest while being milked in New York. It's uncertain, however, whether any investor ever found a systematic method of profiting from the supposed East Coast isolation effect.

Easy Living

The election scare drove the Dow industrials to a low of 77.07 on September 22, representing a 9 percent decline from August's close. A month later, the index stood 7 percent higher. Helping to fuel that resurgence were unexpectedly favorable money market conditions.

Ordinarily, interest rates rose in autumn as farmers borrowed at country banks, draining cash from New York. In 1908, money was flowing in the customary fashion, yet rates remained low. The financial press professed amazement. According to the *New York Sun*, the stock market was benefiting from an unprecedented combination of favorable conditions:

- An abundant supply of money in the United States and around the world: "Not paper money or that proceeding from mere currency inflation, but real money—namely, gold."
- A good crop, with prospects for high prices.
- Continued strong consumer demand in the West, which appeared untouched by the late panic: "Almost half of the country is not aware that Wall Street has been troubled in any way."

To be sure, the U.S. economy wasn't yet back to full speed. Railroad earnings were running about one-sixth below 1907 levels, while bank clearings were roughly 20 percent behind the year-earlier pace. *Dun's Review*, however, could now describe the iron and steel outlook as "more encouraging than at any time this year." The U.S. trade balance had improved, with imports down by approximately one-third, year over year, and exports up slightly. A decline in the number of idle freight cars emboldened bankers and market commentators worldwide to predict a steady improvement in conditions. "It is this anticipation which reconciled disinterested students to higher security prices," concluded the *American Review of Reviews*, "and it was a low money rate which made the rise practicable."

The Ramparts We Watched

In the closing weeks of the presidential campaign, investors grew increasingly optimistic about the outcome. The growing likelihood of a Taft victory was also given credit for an apparent business pickup during October, although subsequently released railroad earnings cast doubt on the perceived recovery. Going into the fourth quarter, the 1908 rally had a good distance yet to run. The Dow Jones railroads climbed from 105.95 on September 30 to 120.05 on December 31, with the industrials registering a more modest ascent from 79.93 to 86.15.

Before the final quarter's upsurge commenced, however, stocks traded off modestly on a European war scare. After a brief and fairly mild reaction within the U.S. market, European selling of American stocks produced an aftershock. The objective was evidently to raise cash in anticipation of possible disruption in the financial system. In the end, the setback proved minor and temporary. Rails, which took the brunt of the sell-off, fell by only 1.6 percent between October 4 and October 10.

The war scare began when Austria-Hungary annexed the Turkish provinces of Bosnia and Herzegovina. Under the 1878 Treaty of Berlin, the Dual Monarchy had been entrusted with "occupying" and "pacifying" Bosnia and Herzegovina, while sovereignty remained with Turkey. The annexation was part of a broader scheme to expand Austria-Hungary's influence, which reportedly included creating a Slavic state to produce a Triple Monarchy. When dispatches from London described the Balkan crisis as the gravest threat to European peace since the Franco-Prussian War of 1870–1871, American investors largely wrote it off to alarmism. True, some speculators tried to stimulate action by circulating rumors that Turkey had fired on a Bulgarian ship or dispatched forces to subdue Crete. But these imaginative tales failed to provoke the intended bear reaction.

As *The Nation* explained, however, the true danger wasn't a conflict between "two second-rate governments" (i.e., Turkey and Bulgaria).

The real threat to financial markets arose from the possibility that major European powers would be dragged into hostilities. Several had claims under the Treaty of Berlin that might be threatened by uncontrollable popular uprisings. Evidence that Europeans weren't taking this risk lightly included sizable price declines in government bonds—6¼ points for Turkey, 3¾ for Russia, 1⅝ for Great Britain, and 1½ for Germany. A sharp advance in wheat prices on the Chicago Board of Trade was likewise seen as a manifestation of war fears. U.S. rumormongers tried to jump on the wider-war bandwagon by whispering that Serbian guerrillas had invaded Austria. In retrospect, fears of a wider war weren't as farfetched as U.S. investors seemed to believe. Six years later, the assassination of Austro-Hungarian Archduke Francis Ferdinand in Bosnia set off the chain of events that produced World War I.

Part of the reason American investors refused to panic in response to the latest attempt to drum up a war scare was that it had been done so many times before. The years leading up to 1908 had been a golden era for belligerent types like Theodore Roosevelt. Market disturbances in advance of actual or potential hostilities included the following:

- 1895: U.S.–British dispute over Venezuela–British Guiana boundary—war averted.
- 1896: U.S.–Spanish dispute over Senate's declaration of Cuban independence—war averted.
- 1897: Outbreak of Greco-Turkish War—wider European war averted.
- 1897: New U.S.–Spanish friction over Cuba—war averted.
- 1898: Explosion of *Maine*—prelude to the Spanish-American War.
- 1898: French–British dispute in Sudan ("Fashoda Incident")—war averted.
- 1899: Dispute between Great Britain and the Transvaal—prelude to the Boer War.
- 1904: Russian–Japanese friction over Manchuria and Korea—prelude to the Russo-Japanese War.
- 1905: French–German dispute over Morocco—war averted.

Howard Schenck Mott of *Harper's Weekly* found that the impact of war scares on U.S. stock prices depended on the prevailing state of the economy and the credit market. For example, instant panic greeted the 1895 Venezuelan crisis because the federal government's finances had been strained for several years, leaving the money market vulnerable. Two years later, by contrast, the market quickly recovered from an initial drop. The first Cuban crisis arrived while the credit market was flourishing and a business recovery was stimulating railroad profits. Rising railroad earnings helped again in 1899, overcoming the combined effect of the Boer War's approach and tight money.

On the whole, Mott concluded, war scares mattered most when there was a chance of the United States getting into the fight. The negative effect did not arise from the fact that wars were bad, per se. Rather, the problem was that U.S. involvement created a bigger drain on the domestic money markets than strictly foreign wars. "The larger the demand for capital," he explained, "the higher interest rates rise, and the higher interest rates rise, the lower the relative return for security investments." As for the latest war scare in the Balkans, Mott was confident that industrial and financial conditions were sufficiently favorable for the market to get by without lasting damage. In fact, while a European war would put upward pressure on interest rates, it would also increase demand for U.S. agricultural products and manufactured goods. "The effect on our trade and industry," he observed brightly, "and ultimately on our stock market as well, would doubtless be stimulating." Of course, he added, a continuation of the ordinary recovery already underway "would be more wholesome."

Getting to Be a Habit

On November 3, William Jennings Bryan lost by the largest margin in his three attempts to capture the White House. But even after this latest setback, his political influence was not at an end. In 1916, Bryan helped turn the tide in favor of granting the Democratic presidential nomination to Woodrow Wilson, who subsequently named him Secretary of State. Eight years later, the Democrats unexpectedly chose his brother Charles Bryan, the governor of Nebraska, as presidential candidate John W. Davis's running mate. Some thought it a ploy to capture votes from William Jennings Bryan's die-hard, but possibly inattentive, supporters. The affair gave rise to a presumably apocryphal account of an elderly Mississippi farmer who sized up the Democrats' 1924 ticket: "Bryan's a good man. I voted for him three times. But ain't Jeff Davis getting kind of old?"

In 1908, notwithstanding the common people's continued affection for Bryan, investors were delighted to see the electorate reject him yet again. On Wednesday following the election holiday, the Dow industrials finished 2 percent above Monday's close.

Finishing Touches

Over the nine sessions following Taft's victory, the industrials rose by
nearly 7 percent, reaching their 1908 high watermark of 88.38 on November 13. Railroads, in contrast, extended their postelection rally
through year-end. Shortly before Christmas, the upturn was briefly interrupted, with a report that Edward Harriman was ill providing the most
ready explanation. "The mere intimation that Mr. Harriman was slightly
indisposed," marveled the *Commercial and Financial Chronicle*, "was
sufficient to unsettle the market and put financial circles on the quiver."
In the following year, the slightly indisposed Mr. Harriman died.

Temporary anxiety also arose over testimony by Andrew Carnegie
opposing tariff protection for the steel industry. The *Commercial and
Financial Chronicle* noted that Carnegie's opinion was out of line
with the view of industry leaders (all dispassionate in their judgment,
no doubt). Perhaps, the periodical insinuated, Carnegie was resentful
over having sold out his steel holdings to the newly formed U.S. Steel
in 1901, only to see the new corporation prosper magnificently. In the
Commercial and Financial Chronicle's judgment, Carnegie's reputed
feeling that he ought to have gotten more for his interests was unrea-
sonable. According to the editorialist, the consensus at the time was
that he received an excessively high price. Now, the *Commercial and
Financial Chronicle* somewhat hyperbolically contended, Carnegie
was spitefully jeopardizing not only the steel tariff, but with it, the
nascent U.S. economic recovery.

Investors, in any event, didn't act as though the situation was as
bad as all that. They saw that the October war scare had blown over
with no lasting damage to the credit markets. A favorable harvest had
eliminated a potential obstacle to recovery. Furthermore, industrial
production had rebounded more swiftly than in past recessions. U.S.
Steel was now operating at 60 percent of capacity, a level that the *Wall
Street Journal* deemed higher than anybody ought to have expected.
With all signs pointing in a positive direction, the Dow railroads index
hit its 1908 peak of 120.05 on the very last day of the year.

Words of the Prophet

Frank A. Munsey's 1908 outlook, published in his eponymous magazine, had been extraordinarily prescient. Prognosticators have produced a decidedly mixed record over the years, but Munsey's
December 1907 forecast is an inspiration to pundits everywhere.

Munsey saw that at the time of the money panic in October 1907 conditions hadn't been bad in the real economy. That is to say, prosperity reigned in every branch of the production of goods and services. There was no unemployment or inventory overhang at the time, he maintained. The only weak point was overextension of credit: "There had been too much high finance, too much highway robbery under the name of FINANCE." Conditions were ripe, Munsey believed, for a rally in stocks.

Among Munsey's right-on-the-money predictions for 1908:

- "Money will undoubtedly get much easier after the first of the year."
- "We shall have a shorter period of paralysis than ever before in our recessions."
- "The price of securities will show a marked advance."

The Big Bounce

Among the 10 best years of the twentieth century, 1908 ranked near the middle of the pack. Total return on the Cowles Commission index (the Standard & Poor's 500 hadn't been introduced yet) was 45.78 percent. By comparison, total return in the top year (1933) was 53.97 percent, while 1995 brought up the rear at a not unimpressive 36.89 percent. While the period's comparatively high dividend yields helped the cause, price change by itself provided a healthy gain. The Dow Jones Industrial Average rose by 46.64 percent in 1908 and the Railroads Average by a highly respectable 35.24 percent.

Like several other Very Good Years since the beginning of the century, 1908 was a bounce-back rally. During 1907, investors suffered a money panic on top of a stock market crash. In that year, the Dow industrials plummeted 45 percent from peak (96.37 on January 7) to trough (53.00 on November 15). The potentially stabilizing influence of the Federal Reserve System, it's worth noting, didn't arrive on the scene until 1914. Nevertheless, the restoration of credit at the beginning of 1908 was widely regarded as the catalyst for the ensuing bull market.

Although credit conditions began to improve early in the year, the stock market ran well ahead of the economic recovery. Earnings on the Dow industrials declined by half from the 1907 level. Numerous dividend cuts and omissions likewise gave investors little to cheer about, yet New York Stock Exchange volume rose slightly in 1908.

Historically minded analysts, however, didn't regard the market's 1908 performance as entirely anomalous. "A practically identical recovery in stocks took place in 1858 after the great panic of the previous year," noted the *Wall Street Journal*. "The rally therefore may be taken as normal and in many striking ways, history has repeated itself."

Late in 1908, the bull market survived a war scare. The concept of a war *scare* may be jarring to latter-day readers, who either recall or have heard about U.S. prosperity during World War II. In the many international flare-ups around the turn of the century, however, investors' first concern was the strain that mobilization would put on the credit market. They reasoned that as interest rates rose, wealthy individuals would sell their securities in favor of safer, yet competitive, returns on short-term money instruments.

Still, analysts recognized that after the initial shock, war could be good for business and consequently for the stock market. If extended further back in time, the list of 35-percent-plus total return years would include both 1862 and 1863 from the Civil War period. Investors didn't have to wait long for the proposition to be tested again. By 1915, U.S. stocks were into the market-friendly phase of a war that began when the worst fears of the 1908 Balkan crisis actually came to pass.

∾ 1915 ∾

If a well-informed Wall Street man were asked to explain the rise to his own satisfaction, he would find no difficulty. We are the greatest neutral state in a world war, and our diplomacy has apparently insured our maintenance of that position, with maintenance also of our national self-respect.

—The Nation

It is the universal experience of investment history that immediately after periods of stress high-class securities sell relatively far better than those of poorer quality.

—Financial News

The war has caused 500 millions of people to begin to save even their potato peelings. It has caused 200 million people in Russia to be sober, all at one time, a thing that never happened in the world before.

—Housman & Company

Over There

The bull market of 1915 had several elements in common with the 1908 rally. Both represented rebounds from sudden, sharp declines. In 1907, prices became depressed by a money panic, while in 1914, the shock was the start of World War I. In a precise echo of 1908, early dispatches from London reported that the situation was the most grave since the start of the Franco-Prussian War in 1870. Once again, the American response was to suspect that the assertion "may have been exaggerated," in *The Nation*'s words.

This time, however, the conflagration made reality of the nightmare that prompted the 1908 war scare. Just as the alarmists of six years earlier had feared, a Balkan dispute now broadened into a conflict involving the major European powers. In lieu of an annexation, the newest pretext was an assassination. Francis Ferdinand, the Austrian archduke gunned down in Sarajevo on June 28, 1914, had been the prime advocate of adding a third, Slavic kingdom to the Austro-Hungarian dual monarchy.

Around the world, investors were extremely bearish about Europe's seemingly unavoidable plunge into World War I. Serbia, which was at the center of the precipitating events, saw its 4 percent bonds fall 5½ points during the first week of the crisis. The French 3 percent issue declined by 4⅛ and British government debt ("consols") dropped by 2¼, all before Austria made it official by declaring war on Serbia. Between the 27th and 30th of July, stock exchanges closed in Amsterdam, Berlin, Brussels, Budapest, Edinburgh, Paris, Rome, St. Petersburg, and Vienna. The London Stock Exchange followed suit on the 31st and remained on furlough until January 4, 1915.

By then, London's reign as the world's center for financing trade was coming to a close. *The Nation* commented that Europe itself recognized America's central role in world finance while the war lasted. When peace finally came, however, New York kept the baton.

On the Outside Looking In

In the United States, which swiftly declared its intention to stay out of the war, the assassination of Archduke Francis Ferdinand sent equity prices into retreat. The 12-stock Dow Jones Industrial Average then in use declined from 79.07 on July 27 to 71.42 as of the July 30 close. At that point, the New York Stock Exchange suspended trading for the first time since the Panic of 1873. When the Big Board resumed activity, on December 12, the old 12-stock index finished the session at 74.56. (Based on a retroactive calculation, the new 20-stock Dow introduced in 1916 closed at 54.63 on December 12. Quotations in the balance of this chapter are based on the expanded index.)

Notwithstanding the sensational returns that the stock market was to enjoy in 1915, American investors' initial, negative response to World War I was not by any means irrational. Certainly, nobody doubted that the belligerents desperately needed the output of America's farms and factories. The tricky part was paying for it. As European countries switched over to a wartime economy, they sacrificed the option of generating funds by exporting their own goods to the United States.

A second means of financing imports, namely, borrowing from American banks to buy American goods, was likewise nixed. In President Woodrow Wilson's view, neutrality was a financial, as well as a diplomatic, policy. Secretary of State William Jennings Bryan declared in August 1914 that "in the judgment of this government, loans by American bankers to any foreign nation which is at war are inconsistent with the true spirit of neutrality."

That left the warring nations the option of floating war loans domestically. To subscribe to such loans, European investors would have to raise cash by liquidating securities, including U.S. stocks. Once again, the implications were bearish for stocks. In the end, the belligerents settled on a third, equally bearish strategy. They sold stocks and used the proceeds to pay for imports from America.

The Europeans' liquidations depressed U.S. share prices during the latter part of 1914. How can we tell, given that U.S. stock exchanges were shut down? (During its suspension of trading, the New York Stock Exchange permitted emergency sales, but only at specified minimum prices, generally equivalent to the stocks' July 30 closes.) The evidence of a fall slump derives from the "gutter" exchange that quickly arose in the New York financial district's streets. In this free market, prices of several stocks sank on news of dividend cuts. U.S. Steel, for example, lost 25 percent of its July 30 value.

There was little comfort in the fact that foreign selling pressure was bound to abate once the combatants had completely liquidated their U.S. holdings. Investors realized that when that point was reached, the belligerents would have no more means of generating cash. The profitable trade with Europe would dry up and America would suffer a depression. What's more, the bleak day didn't appear to be very far off. Europeans had been selling U.S. stocks ever since the Balkan Wars of 1912–1913.

As an indication of the fear created by the prospect of massive European liquidations, here are several suggestions that were offered to a committee charged with establishing policies for the eventual reopening of the New York Stock Exchange:

- Keep the exchange closed until a commission could visit every country in Europe and take an inventory of all U.S. stocks and bonds likely to be sold.
- Induce the federal government to declare it a misdemeanor for brokers to accept orders from anyone but American citizens.
- Require that payments to foreign sellers of securities be made on the basis of 10 percent cash and 90 percent nonnegotiable (except among banks) certificates of deposit.

Opening the Window

Much as in 1908, restoration of credit (albeit in a different form) was the catalyst that launched the 1915 bull market. In the autumn of 1914, Wilson raised no objection when National City Bank extended short-term commercial credit to two countries involved in the war. Gutter market prices bottomed out in the final week of October. The New York Curb (later restyled as the American Stock Exchange) successfully reopened in November, along with bond trading on the New York Stock Exchange. Possibly contributing to renewed confidence as well in that month was the commencement of the Federal Reserve's management of the U.S. banking system. This reform was inspired by the 1907 money panic, but didn't begin to overcome political inertia until Woodrow Wilson's inauguration in 1913.

Notwithstanding its importance from a U.S. foreign policy perspective, the National City Bank financing amounted to a mere $5 million for Russia and $10 million for France. Clearly, if the belligerents wished to continue their heavy purchases of American goods, they would have to raise long-term debt in the U.S. capital market. The Wilson Administration wasn't yet reconciled to such a scenario, but the President would experience a change of heart in 1915.

They Weren't Neutral about Wilson

Woodrow Wilson's firm neutrality at the beginning of World War I enjoyed immense popular support. Even Theodore Roosevelt, who had often hoped for war and viewed any slight of America as a splendid reason to start one, was reluctant to make an issue of German atrocities in Belgium.

To be sure, the rivals in the 1912 presidential race didn't see eye to eye on all matters of war and peace. Unlike Roosevelt, for example, Wilson never suggested that Quakers weren't fit to live in a free society. In fact, Wilson went so far as to offer the position of Secretary of War to a member of the pacifist denomination, A. Mitchell Palmer. (He declined.)

Like all Presidents, Wilson had both admirers and detractors. He distinguished himself, however, in dividing not only political commentators but also literary critics. Contrast, for example, the judgments of Wilson's Secretary of the Navy and biographer, Josephus Daniels, with those of H. L. Mencken:

DANIELS   MENCKEN

The Life of George Washington *(1896)*

"A masterpiece of biography."

"The narrative is one full of charm and the style singularly careful and polished."

"The book is a mass of puerile affectations."

"This incredible work is an almost inexhaustible mine of bad writing, faulty generalizing, childish pussyfooting, ludicrous posturing, and naive stupidity."

Wilson's Prose Style

"His language has all the elegance of classic English and yet it is shot through and through with the phrase and feel of the man in the street."

"He knew . . . how to arrest and enchant the boobery with words that were words and nothing else. The vulgar like and respect that sort of balderdash."

Wilson's Speeches

"Their remarkable literary quality would alone be sufficient to insure their being read by generations yet unborn. His incisive, clear-cut, throbbing sentences and paragraphs helped to crystallize the vague longings of right-thinking men in all nations."

"Reading his speeches in cold blood offers a curious experience. It is difficult to believe that even idiots ever succumbed to such transparent contradictions, to such gaudy processions of mere counter-words, to so vast and obvious a nonsensicality."

Leave Your Worries on the Doorstep

Even before Woodrow Wilson relented on the financing of war-related trade, market pessimism began to recede. One brokerage house estimated that between August 1 and December 1, 1914, while the New York Stock Exchange was closed, investors absorbed $750 million of liquidated securities and took them off the market. During the official suspension of trading, moreover, brokers paid off loans at the behest of their bankers. The brokers in turn encouraged their customers to reduce their margin balances, so the December 12 resumption of trading found investors in a strong financial position.

Stocks rose during January 1915 at a pace that surprised onlookers. For example, the Dow industrials, which opened at 54.63 on January 2, soared to a short-term peak of 58.53 on the 23rd. The *American*

Review of Reviews explained the steep rally by arguing that war fears had suppressed worldwide stock prices for as much as two years prior to the commencement of hostilities.

In February, Wilson raised no objection to a $50 million credit extension to France by J. P. Morgan & Company. To be sure, this wasn't yet a full-fledged flotation on the U.S. markets. Moreover, the size of the financing was small, relative to the total volume of trade with countries involved in the war. On the other hand, the transaction represented a substantially larger credit extension than National City Bank's tentative step of the previous autumn.

Once stocks had rebounded from the lows of 1914, investors moved on from the ultrasafe names to more risky issues. By March, the *American Review of Reviews* declared that buyers had reached the stage of chasing low-priced, non-dividend-paying stocks, just as they had shortly after the Panic of 1907 ended. Even U.S. Steel, which had initially fallen after omitting its common dividend on January 26, now drew intense buying interest. Before long, analysts ceased worrying that European dumping of U.S. stocks would depress the market. Instead of "sudden and overwhelming" liquidations, the *American Review of Reviews* reported that the sales were "slow, quiet, and dragging." The National City Bank of New York commented:

> We have reached the situation where instead of being concerned lest our securities may be returned too fast we are beginning to be concerned because they do not come fast enough to keep the exchanges in normal condition.

Pass the Ammunition

As the first quarter of 1915 began, expectations of huge profits from war orders started to propel stocks upward. Bethlehem Steel, the leading U.S. shipbuilder, soared 70 points in the space of 10 days. During the course of April 9 alone, Bessie vaulted from 88 to 117. Investors stopped doing any detailed analysis once the story made the rounds that Bethlehem was sure to become the top American supplier of guns and ammunition to the warring nations of Europe. Allegedly well informed sources circulated stories of immense contracts, along with colorful accounts of Bethlehem president Charles M. Schwab's business-garnering skills.

American Locomotive jumped 18½ literally overnight. Between the close of one session and the opening of the next, the stock zoomed on rumors that the company had nabbed a $65-million Russian contract. American Locomotive's management ridiculed the figure, but acknowledged receiving an order. That admission sufficed for investors to attribute a $50-million contract to another company, despite its president's laughing protest that he had yet to book a dollar of war orders.

Encouraged by their success in promoting these stocks, Wall Street operators inevitably expanded the war orders story to every vaguely military activity. Not only manufacturers of ordnance and explosives were touted, but also producers of raw materials for those products. Even suppliers of pots and pans were deemed good "plays" in some quarters. Speculators rather optimistically assumed that companies engaged in entirely different businesses could switch over to munitions and still achieve excellent profit margins. In actuality, unexpected production snags ultimately left many war contractors without profits on their war orders. Nevertheless, a wide variety of stocks surged 5 to 15 points on hopes that they would reap millions from the Great War.

The marvelous thing about war orders was that their aggregate size was impossible to estimate. Foreign purchasers of military goods had a natural interest in keeping the information secret, which the manufacturers generally respected. Stock promoters consequently felt free to pull numbers out of the air. One company's shares skyrocketed on a Wall Street estimate that it had raked in $100 million of war orders. Management put the actual number at less than $20 million. Later in the year, the *World's Work* calculated that stocks fully reflected not only all potential profits on war business, but also the entire *sales volume*. Besides which, the magazine pointed out, war profits represented transient gains that logically couldn't add permanent value to the associated stocks. As Paul Clay observed in the *Magazine of Wall Street*:

> In the early days of the conflict we heard a great deal about the destruction of capital and the impoverishment of nations caused by these conflicts; but now it is the fashion to talk about the boom in business based upon European buying which is to occur after the war. The destruction and impoverishment have been forgotten and it appears to be assumed that the gold with which Europe is to do this buying will fall down out of the battle clouds of smoke like manna out of heaven.

Such remonstrances were in vain, however. March's surge in demand for war stocks occurred in the context of a light volume of new issues. Underwriting had been hampered by war-related uncertainty, so there was no large supply to block the rally. Nothing, it seemed, could stop the bull market. Even when the military dispatches briefly created a perception that the hostilities might end quickly, it was taken as good news, despite the bulls' love of war orders.

I'd Let My Golden Opportunities Pass Me By

Among the New York Stock Exchange's new listings of 1915 was Computing-Tabulating-Recording Company. The company leased out Hollerith machines, which rapidly sorted and tabulated complex data through a novel method involving punched cards.

Hollerith machines were used primarily by the Census Bureau. In 1912, however, U.S. Express Company adopted the innovative technology to study a new rate system devised by the Interstate Commerce Commission. Benny Grossbaum (whose family changed its name to Graham during World War I) took a leave from Columbia University to head the project.

The man destined to become the father of securities analysis resumed his studies, and upon graduation commenced his Wall Street career at Newburger, Henderson, & Loeb brokerage. As one of the few financial people to have used the Hollerith machine, he believed C.-T.-R. was an unrecognized and undervalued stock. Despite prospects that seemed promising to Graham, the shares were trading at a modest seven times earnings and only one-third of book value. (To be sure, C.-T.-R.'s assets included some lumped-together intangibles, the value of which was nebulous.)

"Ben," responded his boss, "do not mention that company to me again. I would not touch it with a ten-foot pole." The assets on C.-T.-R.'s balance sheet, explained the shrewd and successful senior partner, were "water." In other words, they had no tangible backup. Companies of this sort had nothing to support their stock prices . . . except for their future earnings prospects. Graham was so chastened by his mentor's excoriation of Computing-Tabulating-Recording that he never bought a share of it in his life, even after the company changed its name to International Business Machines.

Spring Revives Animal Spirits

Between March 15 and April 15, the Dow industrials soared by a remarkable 19 percent. During that interval, on March 31, the New York Stock Exchange rescinded the minimum price rules established in December. The steady drip of European selling explained why the floors hadn't been removed earlier.

As prices escalated, the public leaped into stocks with gusto. A cumulative rise of 100 points in Bethlehem Steel was credited with awakening individuals who had spare cash available for chasing the opportunities they were missing. New York Stock Exchange volume in early April was the heaviest for that time of the year since 1909. Fueling the furious speculation was a reduction in bank reserve requirements under the legislation creating the Federal Reserve System. The change resulted in a surplus reserve of $148 million at New York banks. Had the change not been made, the banks probably would have shown a reserve deficiency, but instead they had considerable capacity to expand credit.

On an international level, incipient inflation may have been contributing to the rise in stock market values. *The Nation* maintained that "prodigious" expansion of the German currency was a matter of common knowledge. The Reichsbank itself had put $761 million of new notes into circulation since the beginning of the war. A secondary currency, issued on pledge of all manner of private property, had added to the supply. The exact amount in circulation was undetermined, but issuance of as much as $750 million of the euphoniously named *Darlehnskassenscheine* had been authorized. French banknote circulation had ballooned by $1 billion over the preceding year, while France, Britain, and Germany had all expanded bank credit dramatically. At the end of 1915, the *Magazine of Wall Street* reported that Austria had issued an estimated $1.5 billion of paper money since the start of the war, while its gold-covered currency had shrunk from $350 million to $150 million. As a result, Austria's paper was selling abroad at a 40 percent discount.

Wall Street professionals vacillated between resisting the rally, which seemed to be getting ahead of itself, and participating on the grounds that it would be futile to fight the tape. The *Financial Chronicle* cast its lot with the skeptics, commenting that the market's "element of artificiality was altogether too patent to be ignored." In the opinion of the *American Review of Reviews*, however, the rally sprang mainly from natural causes, even though the upheaval was "not lacking in reprehensible and dangerous features of excitement and recklessness." Speculation had been held in check for a long period, while stocks had fallen to low valuations by historical standards. The *American Review of Reviews* further explained that an excess of idle bank funds always stirred up speculation, sooner or later.

With the better-quality, dividend-paying names having already risen, speculative interest now focused on low-priced, rumor-sensitive stocks. According to the *Literary Digest*, some of the biggest gainers seemed more likely to require assessments of shareholders than to initiate dividends.

Shot Down in May

On May 7, German submarines sank the *Lusitania*, the very same ship that had brought a critical gold shipment from England to help end the Panic of 1907. Among the more than one thousand killed in the sinking of the British-registered liner were over a hundred U.S. citizens. America's ability to continue its policy of neutrality, while enjoying the benefits of trade, was now in doubt. The Dow industrials declined by 9 percent between May 6 and May 10.

In a May 13 note, signed by Secretary of State William Jennings Bryan, the United States government warned Germany that it wouldn't omit "any necessary act to the performance of its sacred duty of maintaining the rights of the United States and its citizens and safeguarding their free exercise and enjoyment." Finding the German replies unsatisfactory, President Wilson drafted a second *Lusitania* note emphasizing that any further treading on American rights would be regarded as "deliberately unfriendly." Bryan resigned rather than sign the aggressive June 9 dispatch, which instead carried the signature of Robert Lansing, the new Secretary of State. The cabinet had lost a staunch advocate of keeping America out of the war.

Lansing soon challenged the Wilson Administration's application of its neutrality policy in the financial realm. He argued that if the Allies weren't allowed to raise money in capital markets, the United States would suffer a depression. Wilson meanwhile had come around to the view that his original policy of prohibiting loans was inconsistent with the conventional rules of neutrality. Besides, it was pointless to single out money, among all commodities, for an embargo.

As the United States became less hesitant about its financial role in the Great War, stocks rebounded from their May slump. The Dow industrials gained an astounding 40 percent during the fourth quarter. Railroads rose by only 6 percent over the same period, for even the most imaginative touts couldn't pass them off as pure war stocks. (Paul Clay pointed out in the *Magazine of Wall Street*, however, that the most prosperous railroads were carriers of soft coal. The large increase in traffic in that commodity sprang directly from demand on the part of munitions manufacturers and producers of other export goods.)

The message was clear: War had been bad when the United States was determined to remain completely out of the conflict. Now war was good, based on the country's willingness to get involved in a financial way. But war would be bad again if the United States decided to get involved in a military way. Finally, however destructive and indicative of human folly it might be, war was *very* good for selected companies in a position to cash in. And it could be made to *seem* good for many other companies, although there were limits even to the small investor's gullibility.

The Best Part of Breaking Up

Ben Graham missed a great investment opportunity when his boss at Newburger, Henderson, & Loeb persuaded him never to touch IBM stock. But the 21-year-old was soon teaching the Street a few lessons himself.

The 1915 dissolution plan of Guggenheim Exploration Company marked, in Graham's words, "the real beginning of my career as a distinctive type of Wall Street operator." Guggenheim, then trading at 68⅞, owned large interests in four major copper mines. All of the mines were themselves listed on the New York Stock Exchange. According to calculations reported by investment advisers Irving Kahn and Robert D. Milne, each Guggenheim share represented an interest in $76.23 worth of shares of the underlying companies.

Graham reasoned that a relatively easy arbitrage profit was available. By buying Guggenheim and simultaneously selling the shares of the four mines, an investor could lock in a gross profit of $7.35 a share. The risks, which Graham judged minor, were that the dissolution would be rejected by shareholders or delayed by litigation, plus the difficulty of maintaining a short position through the entire process.

Newburger, Henderson, & Loeb decided to play. It put Graham in charge of the arbitrage, with a 20 percent cut of the profits. The Guggenheim dissolution went off without a hitch and Ben Graham's financial position improved dramatically. That year he bought a Model A Ford. Driving lessons were included in the $395 price.

Who's Prepared to Pay the Price?

The United States began removing the last vestiges of trade-finance neutrality in September. In an action that helped New York banks out-flank their London competitors, the Federal Reserve System agreed to rediscount foreign acceptances. (These were evidences of trade debts incurred by foreign parties.) Thereafter, New York definitively overtook London as the financial center for world trade.

In October, the Wilson Administration approved J. P. Morgan's flotation of a $500-million loan to Great Britain and France. Finding the public unenthusiastic, the underwriting banks had to eat the last $187 million of the issue in December. Still, the loan enabled the Allies to continue buying American goods. Meanwhile, the U.S. wheat crop set a record, exceeding one billion bushels for the first time.

With the American banking system continuing to expand credit, prosperity reigned and the stock market soared. Investors indiscriminately rushed into "war-stocks, semiwar-stocks, possible war-stocks, stocks that beyond the range of human imagination could not by any possible metamorphosis be converted into war-stocks," reported the *Literary Digest*. The Dow industrials jumped 13 percent between September 15 and October 15.

The Nation cautioned that stock market booms invariably ended grievously for small investors. The professional traders unobtrusively pulled out, making it just a matter of time until the market cracked. Unfortunately, noted the periodical, it was impossible to foresee exactly when the inevitable break in the 1915 rally would occur. Market timing was especially risky under prevailing conditions, with bank reserves overflowing and with no apparent signs of a tightening in the money markets. Still, *The Nation* saw unfavorable omens. "Sober capitalists" had withdrawn from the market several weeks earlier, while the "professional Wall Street operators" were heading for the exit by early October. The smart money's liquidation was disguised, in customary fashion, through such maneuvers as aggressively bidding up one group of stocks while selling another. Soon, predicted *The Nation*, small investors would be left holding the bag. The *Literary Digest* chimed in:

The International League for the Alleviation of Unnecessary Atrocities, or some organization of similar purpose, will doubtless be formed soon after the close of the present war. Were it in existence at present there might well be laid before the august body a report on the outrages recently perpetrated in Wall Street, in New York City, where for days the gutters have been running yellow with gold and the cries of the tortured "lambs," fleeced to the quick or strangled in coils of ticker-tape, rise even above the tops of the skyscrapers and cause uneasy turnings and quakings beneath the stones in Trinity Churchyard.

Too Hot to Handle

The close of the third quarter brought a surge in New York Stock Exchange daily volume to 1.5 million shares. That was about triple the level then regarded as normal. Comparable activity had been observed previously only on such occasions as the "Harriman Market" of August 1906 and the postelection boom of November 1908.

As a consequence of small investors "buying without restraint at the top of a violent advance," according to *The Nation*, back-office workers at the commission brokerage houses faced physical exhaustion. The idea was floated of declaring a stock exchange holiday to allow them to catch up with their work, a measure resorted to under similar circumstances in 1901. Instead, most firms ordered their order-processing staffs to report for duty on Sunday, October 3. Even with the extra working hours, the brokerage houses had difficulty plowing through the mass of orders in time for Monday's opening. Cashiers suffered fatigue from having to sign two thousand or more checks in a single day.

Quote-Unquote

On October 13, the New York Stock Exchange changed the basis of quoting and trading stocks from percent of par value to dollars. (In the preceding chapter of this book, for example, a stock quoted at 60 was selling at a 40 percent discount to its par value of $100.) While the new practice didn't affect the intrinsic value of the shares, it highlighted a gradual shift in the perception of common stocks.

A contemporary reader of the early-twentieth-century financial press forms a distinct impression that in those days responsible investors regarded a common stock as an inferior sort of bond. Expected growth in earnings wasn't a primary focus of valuation, because price appreciation loomed small in people's thinking. Indeed, the *Magazine of Wall Street* in 1915 defined investment as "the placing of capital in a more or less permanent way, mainly for the income to be derived therefrom." Analysts prepared no elaborate spreadsheets to justify a price-earnings ratio on the basis of long-run earnings prospects. Instead, the trick was to forecast whether issuers would cover their bond interest with anything to spare. Investment experts deemed a stock acceptable if the issuer appeared likely to have enough income left over to declare a dividend. (Corporations weren't having any of that later nonsense about paying dividends even when book profits turned negative.) Under such assumptions, it was perfectly reasonable to quote stocks in par value.

To be sure, the lesser-grade stocks fluctuated in value, presumably because of the machinations of the big operators. The desirable shares, however, were those that behaved like bonds in terms of price stability. Journalists commonly equated the established dividend payout with the return on the stock, giving little thought to possible appreciation. They compared the payout rate directly with prevailing bond yields; total return's day hadn't yet arrived. The prevailing orthodoxy held that dividend yields had to exceed prevailing interest rates on bonds to compensate for the greater uncertainty of payment. Not until several decades after the Big Board stopped quoting stocks like bonds would this mind-set change, as detailed in the 1958 chapter.

Back in the Saddle Again

"Durant Again Holds Control of General Motors," trumpeted the *New York Times* near the end of 1915. " 'Wizard of Automobile' Ousted in 1910 Now Holds a Majority of the Stock." Behind the headline was a dramatic battle for control that pitted bankers against a creative genius with a fatal lack of administrative ability.

Just two years after its 1908 founding, GM fell victim to a sudden drop in car sales. In his zeal to expand through acquisition, founder William C. Durant had stretched the company's finances to the limit and beyond. The many friends he had made along the way proved to be his most valuable resource. Loyal GM dealers began shipping suitcases full of cash to the faltering automaker. They knew that any money transferred through ordinary bank channels would be seized to pay off Durant's overdrafts at Buick.

At long last, General Motors managed to line up a $15-million (face amount) loan, out of which the bankers immediately extracted $2.25 million in fees. The other terms were equally harsh. GM was compelled to shell out a bonus to the lenders of $2 million in common stock and $4 million in preferred shares. Worse still for Durant, voting control passed to a five-member board of trustees, with Durant perennially outvoted by four bankers. Almost as soon as the five-year loan agreement was signed, auto sales turned up, rendering the capitulation all the more galling to GM's creator.

Subjugation to the bankers proved intolerable to the free-spending Durant. He resigned from the management of General Motors and promptly launched the Chevrolet Motor Company. Within four years, Durant had built Chevrolet into a nationwide organization. Soon, Durant began issuing new stock, which he swapped for GM shares. By the time the five-year loan matured, Durant reckoned, he would own or influence enough GM stock to regain control.

Durant had some powerful allies. For one thing, a vast number of General Motors shares were in the hands of former owners of companies acquired during his 1908–1910 reign. Grateful that he hadn't been stingy when he bought them out, they were happy to vote with Durant. Additionally, in 1914 a financially astute executive of E. I. du Pont de Nemours & Company named John J. Raskob had perceived hidden value in the carmaker. The bankers who controlled GM were retrenching and holding off on dividend payments, which limited the marketability of the stock. Raskob bought 500 shares for his own account and persuaded Pierre and Irénée du Pont to invest as well. Although the du Ponts strove to remain above the fray, their holdings helped to turn the tide in Durant's favor.

During the 1915 rally, General Motors shares soared from a February low of 82 a share to 558 in December. To discourage his supporters from selling any of their strategically vital stock, Durant promised to "protect" them. This meant that he would pay them the highest price reached, even if the shares subsequently declined. (One can only wonder how he proposed to finance such a guarantee, if called upon to honor it.)

The drama culminated, according to a story retold many times, when Durant strode into a meeting of GM's board. Flanked by assistants toting bushel baskets full of stock certificates, he intoned, "Gentlemen, I control this company." This account is balderdash, besides which Durant didn't fully consolidate his grip until 1916. The final phase of his reconquest entailed a new exchange of Chevrolet stock for General Motors shares.

As part of a curious series of connections, the dominant figure on the bankers' side of the battle with Durant was Bostonian James Storrow. The lawyer/banker's distaste for Durant's autocratic management accorded with his Progressive political principles. In 1910 Storrow was the nonpartisan Citizens' Municipal League's nominee for mayor of Boston. He narrowly lost that race to John "Honey Fitz" Fitzgerald, whose daughter Rose was already dating her future husband, Joseph P. Kennedy. The son of another local politician, young Kennedy would become one of the most successful speculators during the spectacular rally of the 1920s.

No less prominent in the bull market of Calvin Coolidge's New Era was William C. Durant. Durant shifted his energies to speculation after losing control of General Motors for the second and final time, largely through the efforts of John J. Raskob and Pierre du Pont. Despite all, Raskob and Durant were both participants in the most celebrated stock pool of the Twenties, involving the Radio Corporation of America.

The Days Dwindle Down

The frantic buying of war order shares abated somewhat as October wore on. Helping to calm the frenzy was an increase in required margins on loans against stock collateral. There were also reports of European profit taking. Still, the averages didn't vindicate the financial columnists' dire prophecy of a near-term correction. After dipping from 93.63 on October 13 to 92.56 on October 15, the Dow industrials resumed their climb, finishing the month at 96.02. Railroads performed better still, rallying by 6 percent during the second half of October.

Industrials dipped in the early portion of November, a move that the *Magazine of Wall Street* characterized as a technical correction. All of the good news of 1915 was already in the market, the periodical argued. Nevertheless, the Dow industrials scratched out a small net gain for the month, closing at 96.71. Rails dropped a fraction of a point to finish at 106.36. As of early December, the *Magazine of Wall Street* saw few if any bargains in industrial stocks. Many issues, in the publication's judgment, had been run up too high on war order speculation to be considered safe. Writing in the same publication in January 1916, however, Preston Stewart Krecker predicted that stocks would go still higher, based on market reactions to wars of the preceding 60 years.

In any event, American investors' cash reserves remained ample. The *Magazine of Wall Street* reckoned that only a small percentage of the nation's war booty was being relent to the Allies. A still smaller portion of the inflows was being recycled to Germany. Richard Wyckoff, the *Magazine of Wall Street*'s publisher, suggested that the mix wasn't accidental. Allied victory was generally regarded as a bullish outcome, on the grounds that the status quo antebellum would presumably be restored, in financial and commercial terms. German triumph, on the other hand, would necessitate a complete readjustment.

Perhaps resentment over this bias in America's official neutrality accounted for a German cartoon that appeared around the time. It depicted Lady Liberty, J. P. Morgan (son of J. Pierpont), and John D. Rockefeller, with the caption: "The deeper Europe sinks in gore,/ We only swim in gold the more." U.S. Steel chairman Elbert Gary made a similar point just a shade more obliquely: "The longer the war lasts, the worse it will be for those engaged and the better for this country." At the end of it all, Gary predicted, the United States would be the leader of the world. (Publisher Richard Wyckoff challenged that assertion. "It is one thing to capture a competitor's business while he is engaged in punching the head of his neighbor," he wrote, "and another to hold it when he returns to commercial fields.")

While the *Magazine of Wall Street* was correct in observing that cash remained abundant, investors were directing much of it to new bond offerings by railroads. In December, however, the Dow industrials resumed their rise, gaining 2.5 percent. The December 31 close of 99.15 was just a hairbreadth below 1915's high tick of 99.21, recorded on December 27.

A Picture from the Past Came Slowly Stealing

On Christmas Day, the *Magazine of Wall Street* carried an essay entitled, "Is It Time to Take Profits?" by Scribner Browne. The author noted that conservative investors, who relied on the experience of the preceding 30 or 40 years, had been left at the post during the 1915 rally. As a result, many people now spoke of "new conditions" and "a new kind of market," implying that all lessons of the past must be cast aside. Browne took exception to that view:

> It is true enough that every period has its own distinct characteristics, so that historical parallels are frequently misleading. But there are certain fundamental principles that remain the same. One of these is that every boom is sooner or later followed by a decline.

Essentially the same line of argument has been used countless times in succeeding years. The bull market of the Twenties has become the standard reference point for booms that are inevitably followed by declines. As we shall see in succeeding chapters, many authors of these historical perspectives consciously or unconsciously invoke the nick-name of the Coolidge prosperity, the "New Era." A decade earlier, Browne applied the very same phrase, drawing his homily from a pre-vious boom:

> To those who were watching the markets in 1900 and 1901, this talk about a "new era" has a familiar ring. Almost the whole finan-cial world then became convinced that big combinations of capital were to usher in totally different conditions of business, that the economies of big-scale industry were to permit huge profits previ-ously unknown.

Déjà vu upon déjà vu! Even the flaws that undermined this rosy scenario uncannily resembled the legendary weaknesses in the 1920s system—"cases of dishonest management" and "inside profits at the ex-pense of stockholders." Browne concluded his dissection of the 1900–1901 experience thus: "The final result was that the 'new era' turned out to be very much like the old era on a larger scale." In light of his remarks, it's extraordinary that the term "new era" still carries a positive connotation for many investors a full eight decades later.

How Did the Oracles Fare?

Business executives and financial commentators were upbeat by the beginning of 1915. John Hays Hammond, chairman of the industrial economics department of the National Civic Federation, reported a consensus among businesspeople that the initial, adverse impact of the European war had passed. The gearing up of the new Federal Reserve System also engendered optimism, along with a perception that a large amount of capital lay ready for investment. Hayden, Stone & Com-pany similarly argued that the United States was at an optimal point in the perennial cycle of savings, investment, and liquidation. Thanks to the caution of consumers during the recent recession, said the broker-age house, "The country is probably more thoroughly liquidated than at any time since 1893."

The *Magazine of Wall Street* was bullish on U.S. stocks. Outbreak of a continental war showed that American investments were free of a risk that hung over all European investments. Accordingly, Europeans ap-peared likely to hold on to their U.S. shares, if they were able. This as-sessment was vindicated by subsequent dismay among U.S. brokers over the comparatively small volume of European selling. Publisher Richard Wyckoff of the *Magazine of Wall Street* scored a bull's-eye with his recommendation to buy stocks and buy more if they went lower. He scored again by predicting that the market would soon begin to focus on the end of the war as a reason to rally. Hopes that peace might be at hand lifted stocks in the spring, although they were soon dashed.

Ballar & McConnel of Pittsburgh took a less sanguine view than most about the Great War's impact:

> It seems to us that no one who has yet spoken or written for publication has manifested any real appreciation of the tremendous disturbance that is taking place in financial, commercial, and social affairs as a result of this war. Everybody seems to act as though it were merely a horrible nightmare. We feel that the time for caution has not yet passed and that the investor should not be carried away with the first sign of improvement in sentiment.

Bethlehem Steel's Charles Schwab was correct in proclaiming that the business slump was over. At the same time, a comment by the president of the most prominent beneficiary of war orders looks way off the mark in hindsight:

> There is, I fear, a mistaken impression as to the extent contracts for war supplies play in the upbuilding of our trade. They are scarcely of significance in the bigger prospect that is offered to our view. Their volume is not sufficient to justify serious attention. There are but few materials we are in a position to supply without contravening international law.

Things Are Never as Bad as They Seem

In summary, the first full year of the Great War was a great time for U.S. stock investors. During 1915, the Dow Jones Industrial Average vaulted a dazzling 81.66 percent (based on the new, 20-stock index). Bethlehem Steel, quoted at 46⅛ at the conclusion of 1914, ended the year at 470 after trading as high as 600. The Dow railroads, which benefited less directly than the industrials from the European conflagration, rose by a more modest 22 percent. Total return, measured by the Cowles index, was a robust 50.54 percent, third best in the twentieth century. New York Stock Exchange activity reached its highest level since 1909. Daily trading volume hit the million-share mark 48 times, up from just 3 times in all of 1913–1914.

At the low point following the outbreak of war in 1914, investors worried that the stock market would be crushed by European liquidations. A cutoff of trade was also foreseen, culminating in a U.S. depression. All of these fears proved to be greatly overstated. By the end of 1915, brokers were complaining that the belligerents weren't selling stocks fast enough to keep activity at an acceptable level. Foreign trade boomed to such an extent that Wall Street thought the volume of gold flowing into New York was unhealthy. The U.S. trade balance rose from $324 million in 1914 to $1.7 billion in 1915, producing a bonanza for American industry. Steel capacity utilization climbed from 50 percent in January to 100 percent at year-end.

Financial markets, foreign trade, and the domestic economy didn't make their 180-degree turnarounds on their own. Rather, credit played a key role at several junctures. In the autumn of 1914, the Wilson Administration began to ease its restrictions on lending to belligerents. As the permissible extension of credit to Europe broadened during 1915, stocks gained additional support. A legislated reduction of bank reserve requirements provided yet another boost. Easy credit was further facilitated by European monetary expansion as a means of financing the war. Through a variety of forces, including prosperity arising from war orders, deposits at New York clearinghouse institutions increased by approximately 65 percent. That unprecedented rise helped the banks to increase their outstanding loans by roughly 46 percent. At the end of 1915, six-month money was available in New York at a highly attractive 2¾ percent rate.

Paul Clay assigned credit a less prominent role (to put it mildly) than seems reasonable. At the end of 1915 he wrote in the *Magazine of Wall Street*:

> As to security prices, there does not seem to be the least room for doubt. There is one, and only one, factor which has made the 1915 bull market. That factor is war profits, or profits derived indirectly from the war.

Without financing of war purchases, however, there wouldn't have been any war profits. And Clay himself argued that investors were foolish to bid up stock prices on the basis of profits that would surely vanish when peace came. Perhaps stock buyers weren't really so blind.

It may be that with credit proliferating rapidly, share prices couldn't help but go up.

In 1915, the recently established Federal Reserve System was just beginning to feel its way. A dozen years later, its contribution to the New Era rally would be widely commented upon. Later economists interpreted the back-to-back Very Good Years 1927 and 1928 according to a variety of theories. At the time, however, insightful commentators almost universally emphasized the role of that period's New York–dominated Fed.

~ 1927 ~

*I*s it not entirely possible that conditions at present are so different from conditions in the past that the old standards of comparison are worthless?

—WILLIAM R. BIGGS, *Barron's*

*E*xtensive buying of a stock rarely develops from spontaneous public interest. The mechanism of the market is such that certain individuals or groups first see possibilities in a company and begin buying. It sometimes happens that these are buying for permanent investment, but more often it is a pool that expects to stimulate interest in a stock and then sell.

—JOSEPH P. WHYTE, *Barron's*

A New Era

"We appear to be entering an era of prosperity," said President Calvin Coolidge in his 1925 inaugural address, "which is gradually reaching into every part of the nation." Near the end of the decade, John Moody, founder of the investment research organization that bears his name, wrote glowingly of future economic growth. "No one can examine the panorama of business and finance in America during the past half-dozen years," he asserted, "without realizing that we are living in a new era." Another author predicted that the industrial advances of the preceding quarter-century, which included an increase in U.S. automobile ownership from 4000 to over 20 million, would pale in comparison with the progress to be realized in the new era.

"New Era" became a label for the prosperous years of Calvin Coolidge's presidency. As historian Jordan A. Schwarz has pointed out, the term connoted no government initiatives or philosophy. In this respect, it differed from the earlier New Nationalism and New Freedom and the later New Deal. The New Era, in Schwarz's words, was simply "an enthusiasm that pervaded Washington during the twentieth century's third decade."

All the same, the phrase was ubiquitous during the Twenties. When Henry Ford introduced the five-day workweek, the press gushed that he had inaugurated a new era in industry. More generally, "new era" was taken to mean that the old cycle of boom and bust had been abolished. From now on, people believed, the good times would be permanent.

Among the millions inspired by the notion of boundless opportunity was Russell Dancey, an autoworker at the Dodge main plant in Hamtramck, Michigan. Along with a coworker, he founded the New Era Potato Chip Company. Then as now, salt-laden snack food was a reliable recipe for enticing the consumer. The venture succeeded so well that Dancey came to be known as "The Potato Chip Man." New Era merged with the Frito Company in 1958, another of the stock market's greatest years. Dancey's profits enabled him to create a foundation, named in memory of his wife, Opal, which footed the seminary bills for over 200 young ministers.

To be sure, "new era" was not an altogether new phrase of the Coolidge era. For example, the village of New Era, Michigan, had been founded about a half century earlier. According to lifelong resident Henry Postema, the name derives ultimately from the Erie Railroad. Somehow, the village came to be called "New Erie," which was eventually corrupted to "New Era." Be that as it may, the entire country was caught up in visions of an economic new era during the years leading up to the Great Crash of 1929.

Predictions of permanent prosperity rang hollow when the Great Depression settled in for a long stay. By 1933, the *Magazine of Wall Street*'s "Charles Benedict" (actually the nom de plume of publisher Cecelia G. Wyckoff) wrote of "that false and gilded 'new era' that hypnotized and befooled us." And the memory lingered long afterward. In a roaring bull market six decades later, economist Henry Kaufman drew an explicit parallel with the exaggerated optimism of the late Twenties, then added:

> Some claim that we are in a brand-new era because of many breakthroughs in science and technology and because of political liberalization around the world. According to this view, securities deserve higher valuations.

Yet even though subsequent events mocked the designation of the Coolidge years as the New Era, the term was revived during the 1990s in connection with a noble-sounding enterprise. As we shall see, the story once again ended unhappily. Much as in 1929, a number of supposed sophisticates contracted acute cases of financial embarrassment.

At the Outset

Richard W. Schabacker wrote in the January 1, 1927, *Forbes* that he saw "no reason to expect anything but gradually, though irregularly, rising security prices, despite the high levels already attained." Indeed, the preceding year's rally appeared well justified by a coinciding rise in corporate earnings. *Barron's* calculated that the price-earnings multiple of the 20 Dow Jones industrials had declined during 1926, from 12.1 to 11.7. The value of that index was up by 12.5 percent, but earnings were up by 16.1 percent (based on estimates of 1926 earnings available at the start of 1927).

While Schabacker noted "a very decided feeling that the long bull market is not over," he didn't rule out a flat or modestly down year in 1927. In order for stock prices to continue rising, he said, several conditions would have to continue:

- A high level of business activity.
- Cooperation between capital and labor to produce increased national purchasing power.
- Retention of U.S. gold supplies and the supply of credit.
- Availability of excess capital in pursuit of high-quality investments.

Over the short run, said Schabacker, the father of investment newsletter editor Jay Schabacker, business conditions suggested vulnerability in stock prices. In particular, he observed that the auto industry had suffered its largest short-term decline in several years and that bank clearings had fallen precipitously. Construction activity was lagging in some regions of the United States and commodity prices were depressed. Certain corn- and wheat-growing areas had already fallen into a genuine depression and the South seemed poised to join them. In his concerns about the fundamental outlook, Schabacker was not alone.

Also writing in *Forbes*, editor B. C. Forbes worried about several billion dollars of merchandise that consumers had purchased on installment credit. He regarded these goods as potential excess inventory, a blot on an otherwise good match between factory production levels and customer demand. Forbes noted that heavy reliance on installment credit was a new factor on the economic scene. During the 1920–1921 depression, he recalled, commercial banks rescued manufacturers from an inventory crisis. But bankers were unlikely to bail out consumers who suddenly found themselves out of work and unable to keep up their payments. Still, Forbes took heart from signs that the worst excesses of installment selling had already been curbed.

Another drawback to installment selling, in the view of B. C. Forbes, was that it enabled companies to accelerate orders. Absent ready credit, consumers would have to defer purchases until they had saved up the required cash. On this basis, Forbes predicted that manufacturers would be unable to maintain their brisk 1926 sales levels during 1927. In a similar vein, said Forbes, capital spending by railroads was likely to slow down, simply because they had spent aggressively in 1926. Stiffer competition in foreign exports could also be expected, which could result in a reversal of the preceding year's gold inflows. Certainly, there were offsetting bright spots on the economic horizon. Among others, Forbes listed labor peace, declining public debt, minimal agitation for public ownership of industry, and the Coolidge Admistration's reigning popularity. All in all, Forbes was neither enthusiastically bullish nor hysterically bearish about stock prices, but he inclined toward caution.

As for the market's technical condition, opinion was divided as 1927 began. Then, as now, interpreting the various trend and volume figures involved more subjectivity than one might suppose.

Forbes's Schabacker argued that a correction might occur during the first quarter of 1927. To begin with, prices had risen almost uninterruptedly since mid-October. In addition, daily trading volume had been averaging a comparatively high 1.5 million shares, with occasional surges to over 2 million. Schabacker inferred that a considerable amount of stock had been distributed into public hands. In corroboration of this interpretation, he pointed to a slowdown of percentage gains on high-volume days.

"The Trader" of *Barron's* saw things in a more bullish light. Confidence remained high in the proverbial "well informed circles." The fact that stock yields were only ¼ percent above the cost of money did not indicate to "The Trader" that the risk premium was insufficient. Rather, it was a sign that investors expected further rises in corporate earnings and, as a consequence, in dividends. With call money (i.e., financing collateralized by stocks) readily available at a modest 4½ percent rate, investors had no desire to let go of their shares. Consequently, recurrent fears of liquidation remained unrealized.

Like Schabacker, "The Trader" perceived that the wider public had begun buying. For the most part, though, he thought the action remained dominated by professionals. At prevailing prices, stock investing was an activity for the rich, in his view. Bullish, too, in the opinion of "The Trader" was the exceptionally high short interest. Stock lending was reportedly at an unprecedented level at one of the leading Wall Street houses.

"Easy money, the long-sustained trade activity and all the new wealth in the country produce one of those typical 'eras,' which come every so often in this country," summarized the *Barron's* columnist. "There is the will to speculate in an era like this and an incentive for rich men in lowered taxes and the means in cheap money. And that is why the ferment will probably not die down easily."

Discounting the Future

The stock market was already three years into a bull phase as 1927 began. In fact, equities had been trending upward since 1921. Consequently, many stocks could no longer be bought at their traditionally calculated investment value.

As Joseph P. Whyte explained in a *Barron's* article, conservative investors were willing to capitalize a company's established earnings at double the interest rate on prime-quality bonds. That is to say, with the highest-grade bonds then yielding 5 percent, earnings would be expected to equal no less than 10 percent of a stock's price. Flipping over that earnings-price ratio of $\frac{1}{10}$ produced a maximum price-earnings multiple of 10, assuming normal market conditions.

By early 1927, however, market conditions were not normal. Speculators were banding together to drive selected stocks well above their intrinsic value. The key was persuading the public to discount the future. For the bull operators' purposes, it was fine if investors continued to capitalize (or "discount," in bankers' jargon) established earnings at a conservative interest rate. Somehow, though, the fuddy-duddies would have to be taught to see value also in earnings potential that had yet to be realized. Between the price derived from traditional methods and the discounted value of future earnings, P/E ratios well above 10 were achievable.

Whyte commented that the best vehicle for such a scheme was a company judged "rich in potentialities." Ideally, a recent period of unusually robust economic conditions would provide some foundation for hopes of increased earnings.

In the New Era heralded by Calvin Coolidge, such a multiplicity of optimisms was not beyond speculators' dreams. Early in 1927, for example, cigarette manufacturer Liggett & Myers was selling at a robust 16 times its latest full-year reported earnings of $6.35. The difference between the actual price of 101 and a price equivalent to 10 times earnings (63½), contended Whyte, was speculation predicated on a continued increase in cigarette smoking. He was willing to concede only that the speculation was perhaps based on "the most reasonable probabilities." Clearly, neither Whyte nor investors in general had any inkling of the health concerns that would surround tobacco beginning in the 1950s. That portion of the future, plainly, was not being discounted.

Could the market premium for potential future earnings persist throughout 1927? Whyte, for one, was skeptical. A lucky few companies might reach new earnings plateaus, he thought, but history showed that for the majority the outlook was hopeless. And notwithstanding the widespread belief that the business cycle had been repealed, periods of overproduction had always alternated with periods of underproduction. The prevailing economic boom, in Whyte's view, was fueled by easy credit for consumers. He acknowledged that with half of the world's gold supply within U.S. borders, credit probably wouldn't tighten right away. Eventually, though, a contraction was bound to come. Business activity might then decline by only 15 percent or so from the zenith, but investors would be reminded that peak-to-trough declines in stock prices typically ran many times that figure. Readers who were impressed by Whyte's erudition never would have suspected that the market was on the verge of its first back-to-back Very Good Years since 1862–1863.

The Case for Discarding History

Right about the time that Joseph P. Whyte was defending historical valuation standards in the pages of *Barron's*, William R. Biggs was attacking them in the same publication. Biggs, the father of Morgan Stanley investment strategist Barton Biggs, cited historian James Harvey Robinson's argument that while radical thinkers are usually wrong, ultraconservative thinkers are *always* wrong. Nobody can foresee the future, Biggs explained, but it invariably turns out differently from the past. The conservative erroneously assumes that the future will resemble the past.

In this particular instance, said Biggs, the historically based thinker's fallacy was to presume that stock prices were too high, simply because they were higher than in the past. "The charts tell a plain story," he wrote, "but they do not indicate the future." Several facts suggested that this time was different, contended Biggs, who went on to become chief investment officer of the Bank of New York.

For one thing, *Barron's* had recently published an article demonstrating that U.S. Steel's stock price, adjusted for inflation, was well below its all-time high. In fact, allowing for the corporation's large reinvestments in plant and equipment, the price was "quite conservative," according to Biggs. This despite the fact that by the reckoning of *Barron's*, U.S. Steel had been 1926's second biggest gainer (behind General Motors) among the Dow Jones industrials.

A second reason to downplay the past, according to Biggs, was that America's continuing prosperity had enabled corporations to boost their dividends substantially. Despite the market's run-up, therefore, the average stock yield (annual dividend rate divided by price) was higher than at the conclusion of many previous bear markets. Furthermore, corporations had capitalized on the good times by building up large cash positions. Therefore, a run-of-the-mill business downturn would not devastate them.

Biggs also argued that future market fluctuations would be less pronounced than in years gone by, thanks to the establishment of the Federal Reserve System in 1914. The United States now had a banking system that tended to head off both inflation and depressions. After two years of unprecedented prosperity, noted Biggs, not only was credit easy and cheap, but no serious inflation was in sight.

During both the 1927–1928 bull market and the aftermath of the Great Crash, the Federal Reserve would be harshly criticized for pursuing procyclical, rather than countercyclical, policies. That is, the monetary authorities were accused of fueling reckless speculation, then aggravating the ensuing depression by tightening credit. Subsequent events thus made Biggs a false prophet, but his most dubious argument for ignoring history had nothing to do with monetary policy. Rather, it was his contention that wider participation in the stock market would temper fluctuations. "The small investor is becoming more and more of a factor," he exulted, "not only through his increased resources but also through his greater intelligence, so that less money proportionately is thrown away in unwise speculation."

After 1929, it became a cliché that when even the shoeshine man is trafficking in stock tips, it's time to sell out. During the Very Good Year of 1995, the bears hammered at the theme that first-time mutual fund buyers would panic when they realized that stocks could go down, as well as up. Such fears may have been exaggerated. But no latter-day Biggs could have persuaded many market observers that increased involvement by small investors would be a stabilizing force.

Art Imitates Life

Of all the bull markets dissected in this book, none has acquired a mythic status to rival that of the 1927–1929 episode. That's probably because no other binge has been followed by a hangover on the scale of the Great Depression. It's by no means clear that the 1929 stock market crash caused the economic contraction of the 1930s. Literature, however, requires no more proof of that proposition than it requires a murderer's foul deed to be the cause of the earthquake that destroys him in the final chapter. For writers of fiction, the Depression provides poetic retribution for the perceived greed of Wall Street manipulators during the Jazz Age.

Not every depiction of Coolidge's New Era descends to crude melodrama, however. In W. Somerset Maugham's novel *The Razor's Edge* (1944), a stockbroker ruined by the Crash makes a poor subject for sermonizing about the evils of speculation.

The minor character Henry Maturin is described as one of the richest men in Chicago. Maugham depicts him as a tough negotiator in big financial deals, but devoutly protective of his clients' savings. "To tell you the truth," Maturin says, "I'd rather lose my own money than see them lose theirs." An anecdote follows that indicates that he is indeed telling the truth. It seems that an elderly client recently came to the office intending to invest a thousand dollars in an oil scheme recommended by her minister. Maturin not only refused to take the order, but administered such a tongue-lashing that the woman left in tears. Then, for good measure, he called the minister and bawled him out, too.

Maturin is plainly a believer in Coolidge's New Era. He views the United States as entering an era destined to "make the achievements of the past look like two bits." Nevertheless, writes Maugham, Maturin doesn't countenance speculation. He invests his clients' money in sound securities, yet their wealth nearly doubles between 1918 and 1926, simply because of the general rise in the market. (Maugham's numbers are right on target. The Dow appreciated by 91 percent over that period.)

As the market's rise accelerates, however, Maturin grows exasperated by the sight of his friends raking in fortunes overnight. Egged on by his less cautious son, upon whom he dotes, Maturin abandons his old conservatism bit by bit. He begins to buy on margin, all the while protesting that he's not gambling. Common sense tells him that America's resources are inexhaustible and that there's nothing to stop the country's progress.

When the market breaks on October 23, 1929, Maturin initially dismisses the price drop as a plot by the New York brokers. Berating his fellow Chicagoans for allowing themselves to be stampeded, he pours new cash into the market. Proud that his devoted legions of widows and pensioners have never lost money by following his advice, he covers their losses out of his own pocket.

Naturally, Maturin is wiped out in the October 29 crash, dying shortly thereafter from a heart attack. Maugham isn't enough of a sentimentalist to permit him to escape his fate. But neither is Maturin made a symbol of greed, as he might be in the work of a more self-righteous, but lesser author. The narrative presents a realistic portrait of psychological change induced by a bull market.

Incidentally, the author of *The Razor's Edge* could afford to write about the Crash with a measure of detachment. Maugham might have remarked airily, like a character in the book who likewise escaped the debacle, "Oh, I'm not complaining. God tempers the wind to the shorn lamb."

Somerset Maugham liked the concept of financial independence. "Money," he wrote, "is like a sixth sense without which you cannot make a complete use of the other five." But Maugham was no speculator. Long before the Crash, he had conservatively invested $25,000 of royalties from his plays in debentures. His stated investment objective was achieving freedom from the obligation of having to write for money.

Alas, in 1921 the brokerage firm with which Maugham dealt went bankrupt amidst allegations of misappropriating clients' funds. Although he eventually recovered two-thirds of his investment, he believed he'd been swindled. Thereafter, Maugham made his investments through Bert Alanson, a trustworthy San Francisco stockbroker he'd met five years earlier on a Hawaiian cruise. Alanson not only made the author wealthy, but also became his best friend, all the while waiving his management fee.

Maugham enjoyed telling a story that he'd once given Alanson $15,000 to invest, then not thought about it again. Years later, Maugham recounted, he casually mentioned the investment over lunch, saying he assumed that the money had been lost a long time ago. Not so, replied his broker. He had carefully invested the sum, which now amounted to more than a million dollars.

While the anecdote enabled Maugham to project casualness about money, it had no basis in fact. On some occasions, the novelist told an even more preposterous version. He claimed he'd won Alanson's devotion by tipping him off to an impending fall in the ruble. The incident allegedly occurred in Siberia, where Maugham was traveling on a secret government mission. In this variant of the story, Alanson repaid Maugham's help in clearing a profit of £200,000 by sending him a box of cigars.

Behind the Balance Sheet

Shortly before the beginning of 1927, *Barron's* published a short treatise on financial statement analysis. Its author was a former bond salesman of whom we shall hear more in a later chapter. Philip L. Carret, having graduated from Harvard College in 1917, had already written a book entitled *Buying a Bond*.

Rereading Carret's discussion of the balance sheet sheds light on many financial reporting gimmicks that remain in use today. "The management naturally desires to make the best possible showing in its periodical statements," writes Carret. "A certain amount of 'window-dressing' is the result."

To illustrate the concept, he describes a hypothetical company with $15 million of current assets, consisting of $10 million in inventories, $4 million in accounts receivable and $1 million in cash. Current liabilities stand at $10 million, so that the ratio of current assets to current liabilities is $1\frac{1}{2}$ to 1. Over the next few months, the company sells half of its inventory, using the proceeds to pay off debt. The curtain conveniently drops on the fiscal year with current assets standing at $10 million and current liabilities at $5 million.

Seemingly, the current ratio has risen from a satisfactory $1\frac{1}{2}$ to 1 to a more impressive 2 to 1. In reality, though, management has simply timed its financial reporting to take advantage of a predictable seasonal lull, when inventories are customarily at their low point of the year. Note that Carret's example presumes that the company merely "gets out even" on its inventory. If it instead makes a normal profit on the goods and retains the additional cash, the ratio of current assets to current liabilities will be even greater than 2 to 1. And as Carret points out, a company that lacks an exploitable seasonal pattern can manufacture an improvement in its current ratio by selling accounts receivable at a discount to a lender specializing in such transactions.

Carret also cautions investors against relying too heavily on reported inventory values. Obsolete or out-of-fashion goods may be carried well above their true realizable values. "When a leading wholesale dry-goods house whose name was synonymous with strength in banking circles failed a few years ago," Carret recalls, "it was discovered that it had on its shelves goods which had been out of style and practically unsalable for years."

In an even more alarming real-life example, the author recounts that the treasurer of a leading cotton mill was caught padding the inventory account. The company's president urged investors to take the discovery in stride. He reasoned that "the stockholders had not lost anything, they merely did not own as much property as they thought they had." Shares promptly fell from 40 to 1.

Regrettably, financial misreporting remains a favorite corporate pastime. If latter-day readers were to overlook the dates of the balance sheets in Carret's examples, they might imagine they were perusing a contemporary article. Accounting standards have improved a bit over the years, but companies have not lost their passion for disguise.

A Rally on Economic Weakness

Stocks began 1927 with momentum from a late-1926 rally, led by the autos. As the year progressed, however, the economic situation deteriorated. Part of the problem was that Great Britain's return to the gold standard in 1925 had proven ill-timed. Gold became scarce as large amounts flowed first to the Dutch East Indies, then to Germany. Now the British had hard currency and a depression. The effects spilled over to the United States, which suffered a decline in industrial production in 1927. Output reductions measured 8 percent in steel ingots, 11 percent in bituminous coal and 22 percent in passenger cars. Business failures climbed by 6 percent.

Against this backdrop of economic contraction, the Dow Jones Industrial Average rose by 28.75 percent. Shares traded on the New York Stock Exchange increased by 23 percent over 1926, issuance of new securities by 33.5 percent. The seeming paradox of rising stock prices in the face of declining business activity demanded an explanation. Analysts responded by pointing to two unusual factors—Henry Ford and the weather.

In May 1927, the Ford Motor Company halted production at its mighty River Rouge plant to retool for the Model A. While Ford's manufacturing operations remained shut, a key outlet was unavailable to the company's many suppliers. U.S. economy activity, in short, was curtailed by a huge development unrelated to the general level of demand.

Although the switch-over to the Model A was inconvenient for businesses that depended on the auto industry, it was strategically vital to Ford. The utilitarian Model T was rapidly losing market share to the speedier and more colorful Chevrolet of General Motors. Notwithstanding efforts to recast it as a closed-body vehicle, the Model T had an obsolete design.

Henry Ford had been slow to acknowledge the need for a new model. After he made the fateful decision, production difficulties compelled him to postpone its introduction from September to December. The delays whipped up intense curiosity regarding the new Ford. Rumors about its design filled the newspapers. When Ford finally took the wraps off, a crowd allegedly numbering one million stormed the company's New York headquarters just to see the Model A. In the end, though, Ford failed to turn back Chevrolet's bid for supremacy in the low-price, high-volume segment of the market. General Motors president Alfred P. Sloan, Jr., later remarked that observers were surprised by Ford's "catastrophic and almost whimsical" decision to take such a long hiatus for retooling.

Freakish weather was a second drag on the 1927 economy that bore no relation to fundamental demand. Heavy rains, cold spells, and floods disrupted business, as did a jumbling of the seasons. "The summer seemed to come only in autumn, and autumn in early winter," *Barron's* reported.

Interestingly, the weather problems represented an instance of at least partially accurate forecasting. *Barron's* reported on December 6, 1926, that a number of meteorologists were predicting the worst winter in years. Storms in the Western U.S. and abnormal European weather conditions were the tip-offs. In the event, the delayed arrival of spring had an adverse effect on business.

The Luckiest Blankety-Blank

The present vantage point offers several potential explanations for 1927's exceptional returns, other than the Ford shutdown and cold weather. The upbeat political climate is an obvious possibility. "Give part of the credit to President Calvin Coolidge," wrote John R. Dorfman in the *Wall Street Journal* in a 1996 retrospective. As Dorfman noted, Silent Cal was the stock investor's ideal President. He kept government's hands off business and cut taxes incessantly.

Granting Coolidge a bit of the credit for the 1927 stock price escalation is not entirely unjustified. At least he did nothing to stand in the way of the bull market. That was consistent with his general approach to governing, which relied heavily on doing nothing about most things.

"If you see ten troubles coming down the road," Coolidge once said, "you can be sure that nine will run into the ditch before they reach you and you have to battle with only one of them." H. L. Mencken observed of Coolidge that "his ideal day is one in which nothing whatever happens." According to Walter Lippmann, "Mr. Coolidge's genius for inactivity is developed to a very high point. It is far from being an indolent inactivity. It is a grim, determined alert inactivity which keeps Mr. Coolidge occupied constantly." Will Rogers wrote that Coolidge retired a hero, "not only because he hadent [sic] done anything, but because he had done it better than anyone."

The following representative comments by biographers give the flavor of Coolidge's management of the nation's affairs:

- "Coolidge was aware that he had not been a constructive statesman, and his answer was that he was living in a period when constructive statesmanship was not demanded or required."
- "He was not a man who felt altogether well. His extraordinary amount of sleeping and napping, up to ten and eleven hours a day, suggests that."
- "Nicholas Murray Butler, the Republican party's intellectual-in-chief, said that the President 'was wholly lacking in imagination.'"
- "If the idea of a world economic conference ever entered President Coolidge's head, he probably expelled it."
- "The lesson of Calvin Coolidge is that of a man bred and trained to avoid the daring."

On the face of it, a more plausible assessment of Coolidge's role in the 1927 bull market is that he was simply in the right place at the right time. We have the testimony of Mencken, who confessed that he could "find no relation of cause and effect between the Coolidge somnolence and the Coolidge prosperity." And after all, lucky timing was the hallmark of the man who occupied the quintessentially nonessential office of Vice President when Warren Harding died.

Mencken recalled that Coolidge had not been the most obvious choice for the vice presidential nomination at the 1920 Republican convention. "Half a dozen other statesmen had to commit political suicide in order to make way for him," he wrote, "but all of them stepped up docilely and bumped themselves off." A short while later, Mencken was startled to find a Boston journalist, who had followed Coolidge from the beginning of his career, laying odds that Harding would be assassinated before completing half his term. When his fellow newspapermen cautioned that such talk was injudicious, the bookmaking reporter replied, "I am simply telling you what I know. I know Cal Coolidge inside and out. He is the luckiest goddam ——— ——— in the whole world."

In 1928, Coolidge chose not to run for reelection, apparently never dreaming that a calamitous depression would begin within months of his retirement. "There was a volcano boiling under him, but he did not know it, and was not singed," wrote Mencken. "When it burst forth at last, it was Hoover who got its blast, and was fried, boiled, roasted and fricaseed."

The True Author

Historians generally assign the greater share of the credit for the 1927 rally not to Coolidge, but to Benjamin Strong. As governor of the Federal Reserve Bank of New York, Strong engineered the expansion of credit that market analysts at the time regarded as the basis of the bull market. A number of thoughtful economists have since argued against that view, but the debate is only about causality. There's no denying that in the early stages of the rally that lasted until 1929, broker loans mushroomed.

Benjamin Strong headed the New York Federal Reserve Bank from 1914 until 1928. By the midpoint of that span, he had established himself as the preeminent central banker in the United States. Thanks in part to his great prestige, New York overshadowed Washington in Federal Reserve policy making during most of the Twenties.

With the U.S. economy in the doldrums in 1927, Strong pushed through an easy money policy. In view of their lean inventories, however, corporations were not clamoring for additional credit. Banks consequently channeled a substantial portion of their enhanced lending capacity into financing of securities purchases. In August, the discount rate was cut from 4 percent to 3½ percent. For 1927 as a whole, out-standing broker loans rose by a staggering 26 percent.

Despite the flood of credit into margin lending, Strong insisted that his policy was correct. By lowering interest rates, the Federal Reserve could potentially stem the flow of gold into the United States. That could revive sagging European economies and promote U.S. foreign trade. Critics accused Strong of excessive preoccupation with the British pound's exchange rate, while speculation went out of control. "I think the conclusion is inescapable," he countered, "that any policy directed solely to forcing liquidation in the stock loan account and concurrently in the prices of securities will be found to have a wide-spread and somewhat similar effect in other directions, mostly to the detriment of the healthy prosperity of this country."

Teach Me Tonight

In the fall of 1927, Columbia University's extension division began offering a course entitled "Security Analysis." The instructor later used the same title for an immensely popular textbook, coauthored with one of the 1927 enrollees. At the time, no similar courses were being offered by practitioners, much less the father of securities analysis, Benjamin Graham.

Registrants exceeded 150, more than the classroom could accommodate, and gate-crashers reportedly had to be barred at the door. The following year, registrations rose still higher. Graham had warned his 1927 students that any stocks he discussed were merely illustrations. Under no circumstances were they to be regarded as recommendations, he stressed. Some of the illustrations happened to skyrocket, however. Graham later reckoned that those issues moved up no more than the roaring market itself did. Nevertheless, the students perceived that their teacher was dispensing valuable tips. Not surprisingly, some of the fall 1927 enrollees thought they could benefit from taking the course again in fall 1928.

Much as Graham enjoyed teaching, by the way, he didn't give up his day job. During the first term in which he offered his course, the youthful hedge fund manager was locking horns with the management of Northern Pipeline.

The crude oil transporter's stock was then trading at 65. By scrutinizing Interstate Commerce Commission documents, Graham had discovered that the company was sitting on a bond portfolio, which had no application to its business, worth the equivalent of $90 a share. The most sensible thing in the world, he reasoned, was for Northern Pipeline to liquidate the securities and distribute the proceeds to holders.

Management didn't see it that way, however. "Running a pipeline is a complex and specialized business, about which you can know very little, but which we have done for a lifetime," the president and his brother, the general counsel, condescendingly told Graham in 1926. "You must give us credit for knowing better than you what is best for the company and its stockholders."

Graham rejected management's advice to sell his stock if he didn't like the way Northern Pipeline was being run. Instead, he launched a campaign to compel the company to disgorge its idle cash. His first attempt, at Northern Pipeline's 1927 annual meeting, failed abysmally. A year later, though, management agreed to the distribution plan.

Although Graham had rounded up enough proxies to obtain board representation, it was another factor that evidently turned the tide. Northern Pipeline was one of 31 companies that emerged from the 1911 breakup of the Standard Oil monopoly, founded by John D. Rockefeller. The Rockefeller Foundation wound up with a 23 percent stake in the pipeline. Graham appealed unsuccessfully to the institution's financial adviser to side with him in the proxy battle, but his pitch apparently didn't fall on deaf ears. When the foundation intimated that shelling out some cash might not be such a bad idea, Northern management quickly dropped its vehement opposition to Graham's proposal.

Should Credit Get the Credit?

Benjamin Strong's loose credit policy may have gotten more credit than it deserved for the 1927 bull market. As we'll see in the next chapter, easy money also got a lot of blame for the 1929 Crash. Among the finger-pointers was Herbert Hoover, the President who was "roasted and fricaseed" for a Depression that he more or less walked in on. In Hoover's estimation, the Federal Reserve Board transformed "an American wave of optimism, born of continued progress over the decade . . . into the stock-exchange Mississippi Bubble." Historian Robert Sobel, in contrast, thinks that "Strong's decision to gamble that the low rates would not seriously damage the American economic and financial structure was a reasonable one," given the precariousness of the international situation at the time.

It's impossible to sort out the question of credit's role without getting entangled in ideology. Some economists are hell-bent on demonstrating that extreme market fluctuations are exclusively monetary events. By their lights, inflating the currency raises the price of stocks in nominal dollars and that's all there is to it. Other economists are no less determined to prove that financial markets are rational. According to that school, there wasn't really any speculation in 1927–1929, so it's a meaningless exercise to figure out whether Strong caused it. More likely, they would argue, the banks merely accommodated the financially justifiable increase in demand for stocks. Under an assumption of rational capital markets, the rise in prices during 1927 was merely commensurate with earnings expectations that look excessive only in hindsight. As Sobel has emphasized, Charles Lindbergh's solo flight across the Atlantic fired the imagination of investors, who fiercely bid up the aviation stocks. Yet another group contends that the stock market is wholly irrational. In this view of the world, securities prices rise and fall largely because of fads and manias. For defenders of Strong, the implications of this view are no less favorable than the implications of a perfectly rational market. That is, if stocks fluctuate for reasons unrelated to interest rates or the money supply, the Federal Reserve can't be held accountable.

Whatever the true cause may have been, 1927 felt like a great new era for investors. At 37.48 percent, the S&P 500's total return was only the third highest since the turn of the century. But as a warmup for an even bigger gain in 1928, it was most definitely a Very Good Year.

∽ 1928 ∽

*R*ecurrent depressions are, then, temporary pauses or retrograde movements in the rising tide of prosperity, and they are of interest mainly to the speculator or trader who is concerned with the ceaseless fluctuations of the market. To the investor, who is interested in the long-term trend, their importance is much less and turns on the time at which he may best buy or sell.

—STEWART MACDONALD, *Barron's*

*A*s our imperfect financial machinery operates, it often drives security prices materially above or below the levels of their intrinsic worth.

—DWIGHT C. ROSE,
A Scientific Approach to Investment Management

*W*oman has a natural shopping instinct and, when interested in buying anything, she is willing to spend the necessary time and energy to get exactly what she wants.

—CECELIA G. WYCKOFF, *Magazine of Wall Street*

And So Say All of Us

"Unanimous agreement that business will be good this coming year" was how the *Wall Street Journal* summarized the expectations for 1928 of business leaders and bankers. "I see nothing except soundness in the general economic situation," said General Motors president Alfred P. Sloan. "Credit is abundant and rates are low; inventories are low and, taking it all in all, I am very well satisfied as to the outlook." GM's finance committee chairman, John J. Raskob, chimed in, "Everything indicates that 1928 will witness the greatest prosperity our country has ever enjoyed." He cited negligible inflation, abundant credit, and strong farm purchasing power as a consequence of good crops, as well as the spillover from Ford Motor Company's intended resumption of production after a prolonged retooling.

"I feel that the retail business of this country can look forward to continued increased business for some time to come," commented Woolworth's president, H. T. Parson. The only potential obstacle to another year-over-year improvement, according to Parson, was "some upsetting influence in the early summer of 1928 on account of politics." Another possible stumbling block mentioned by Nathan S. Jonas, president of Manufacturers Trust Company, was the foreign situation. Although there were reports of improving economic conditions in Germany and Central Europe, he said, much of the business activity in those regions was being sustained through low wages and minimal profits. Furthermore, Jonas remarked, industrial conditions in the British Empire left much to be desired, notwithstanding the pound's recent strength.

The Power of Credit

Richard Schabacker, writing in *Forbes*, perceived a possible tightening of credit as the main threat to a continuation of the 1927 bull market. "There can be little doubt," he declared, regarding the steep rise in stock prices since 1921, "that the underlying cause for such advances has been easy money." A healthy business climate and benign government policies had contributed, according to Schabacker, but only as background factors.

Aside from the questionable monetary outlook, Schabacker said, conditions were satisfactory. Corporate earnings were not likely to change sufficiently from 1927 to affect the market either way, he thought. Similarly, Schabacker contended that the upcoming U.S. presidential elections were unlikely to make much difference in the short run, whatever the outcome. Technical conditions, he judged, were less positive than they had been a year earlier, but did not signal danger. Low bond yields were driving cash out of bonds and into stocks.

Another positive factor that Schabacker mentioned was growing demand from investment trusts. The forerunners of modern mutual funds, the investment trusts enabled small investors to acquire diversified stock portfolios. During 1928, 186 investment trusts were organized, up from 140 in 1927. To put those figures in perspective, a cumulative total of just 40 were organized prior to 1921. Significantly, too, the investment trusts of the late Twenties tended to be active buyers and sellers of stocks. The earlier trusts, by contrast, were fixed pools of securities, like unit trusts of a later period. Much as the burgeoning mutual funds were credited with fueling the 1995 bull market, investment trusts were regarded as a bulwark of the 1928 rally.

Finally, among factors that Schabacker deemed important, commodity prices had bottomed out. By the beginning of 1928, they were already at their highest levels in more than a year. If the commodity price rebound were to continue, said Schabacker, the near-term effect would be a new high in the stock market. At a later point, however, monetary policy would undoubtedly tighten to head off inflation. Considering also the large outflow of gold from the United States in the final months of 1927, coincident with a rapid expansion of credit, the Federal Reserve seemed likely to begin hiking interest rates. Deflation and lower security prices would follow, by Schabacker's reckoning.

Stock prices might continue to climb during the first half of 1928, even in the face of Fed tightening. But Schabacker warned that such a rise would be "chiefly speculative." A first-half rally, he thought, would only increase the likelihood of a correction in the second half.

Public and Private Opinions

"The Trader" column of *Barron's* shared Richard Schabacker's optimism, noting that the big banking houses were universally recommending purchase of quality stocks. Considering that the powerful du Pont interests remained constructive on the market, perhaps the general bullishness was warranted. Furthermore, *Barron's* observed, short interest continued to provide strong support for many stocks. And little noticed amidst the upward march of the averages were selective corrections that indicated continued discrimination by investors.

As for monetary factors, "The Trader" gave considerable weight to Treasury Secretary Andrew Mellon's unconcern. Let others worry about gold outflows, said Mellon. They didn't fundamentally alter the U.S. money market outlook. Similarly, the $3.6 billion of outstanding stock-brokerage loans, up by 26 percent from a year earlier, was no cause for alarm. According to *Barron's*, the Treasury Department was privately expressing the view that an expansion of such debt to $5 billion would not unduly strain the country's finances.

A bit later, President Coolidge himself took the unprecedented step of *publicly* stating that he didn't believe brokerage loans were out of hand. According to his official statement, the rise in outstandings simply paralleled increases in bank deposits and the amount of securities on the market.

In reality, Coolidge was concerned about the rising tide of speculation. Privately, he told a journalist, "If I were to give my personal opinion about it, I should say that any loan made for gambling in stocks was an 'excessive loan.' "

Coolidge's concept of being a public servant, however, required him to keep his private opinions private. Despite Commerce Secretary Herbert Hoover's urgings to seek greater control over the financial markets, the President maintained a hands-off-business policy. Back in 1926, Harvard professor William Z. Ripley had pointed out to Coolidge the dangers of stock market pyramiding and price rigging. Probing into the matter, Coolidge concluded that there was no legal basis for intervention by the federal government. By all accounts, his sensation upon reaching this conclusion appeared to be immense relief.

A less reticent Chief Executive might have helped to temper the stock-buying frenzy of 1928. Instead, Coolidge was widely blamed, following the 1929 Crash, for failing to calm the raging market. It would have been quite out of character for him to have taken the bull by the horns, however. Coolidge was renowned for his afternoon naps, which reportedly lasted two to four hours. His press conferences were heavy on protests that he had too little information to warrant action.

Everybody into the Pool!

If economic and monetary obstacles didn't immediately threaten the bull market, *Barron's* nevertheless perceived one worrisome sign of speculative excesses. The danger signal was the growing activity of stock pools. These were essentially schemes to run up prices, then leave small investors holding the bag.

The pool's participants would begin by accumulating a large block of a glamorous stock with comparatively few shares outstanding. Then, with the collaboration of the specialist on the exchange floor who handled its trading, the conspirators would commence buying and selling from one another. As both the volume and the artificially manipulated price rose, tape watchers perceived a powerful upward trend. Eventually, the public buying itself began to propel the stock upward. At that point, the pool participants stepped aside. When the price got high enough, they liquidated their shares, ultimately causing the bubble to burst.

Incredibly, the victims of the pools didn't howl in protest. Instead, they attempted to get wind of the next pool that was in formation, hoping to jump in and out before the inevitable price collapse. In response, pool participants ceased trying to conceal their machinations. By letting out word that they were going after a stock, they could create the desired bandwagon effect in short order. Small investors eagerly joined the throng, even while realizing they'd lose badly if they failed to get out before the operators "pulled the plug."

Up and up, then down and down went prices, with no regard to fundamental value. Indeed, the pool organizers' peculiar code of ethics frowned upon efforts to run up a stock by spreading the idea that its earnings were about to rise. With the financial press freely reporting the creation and dissolution of stock pools, *Barron's* was justified in suspecting that unhealthy speculation was taking hold.

Durant's New Incarnation

Among the market's most spectacular speculators in 1928 was William Crapo Durant, the visionary who created General Motors in 1908. As the complexity and day-to-day administrative burdens of that organization grew, its mercurial founder became less and less the ideal person to run it. A friend once remarked that Durant was happy only when he was "hanging to a windowsill by his fingertips." By 1917, the more sober-minded du Pont interests had used their large investment in the company to obtain complete financial control.

To call Durant careless about money would be an understatement. In 1920, Pierre du Pont, then serving as GM's chairman, became worried by reports that Durant was pledging the automaker's stock to finance his speculations. John Raskob, who as GM's finance committee chairman later spoke so glowingly of the 1928 business outlook, was dispatched to determine just how overextended Durant might be. In a jocular tone, Raskob asked Durant how much he owed—was it $6 million or $26 million? "I will have to look it up," Durant answered, in dead earnest.

Horrified upon hearing Raskob's report, du Pont pressed Durant for a more precise rendering of accounts. His actual obligations to bankers and brokers, it turned out, totaled $34 million. If the financially straitened Durant were forced to sell out, the huge block of shares suddenly thrown onto the market would depress the stock's price. Raskob quickly devised a bailout plan, which left Durant solvent but shorn of the greater part of his GM stock. His role as a General Motors executive ended, leaving him free to shift his energies to speculation, for which he was temperamentally well suited. After all, as an editorialist in New York's *Evening Mail* pointed out, Durant may have come near to burying himself with GM stock, but nobody could accuse him of being afraid to invest in his own company.

A natural-born bull who supposedly never sold a share of stock short, Durant was fabulously successful in the rising market. "Durant Put at Top of Wall Street Winners," proclaimed a front-page story in the *New York Times*. Among his triumphs during the Twenties was a reported $2.5 million gain on United States Cast Iron Pipe and Foundry Company, which rose by 40 points in just two days. His estimated take on a double in Studebaker was $4 million.

Durant's dealings on the Exchange became legendary. By one account, probably only somewhat exaggerated, he personally traded a billion dollars' worth of stock during 1928. Rumors that Durant was involved in a stock sufficed to drive its price higher. As a bit of newspaper doggerel had it, prices could be jolted by a tip "from the aunt/ Of a fellow who's related to a cousin of Durant." Ever bullish, Durant's only worry was that the Federal Reserve would try to restrain the stock market's astonishing ascent. That would be a foolish move, he warned.

How the Sluggers Fared

Ty Cobb retired from baseball in 1928. A biographer ventured that his Coca-Cola investment was probably the most successful financial venture of all time by any athlete in any sport. When the Crash came, Cobb suffered no major losses, excepting a decline of about 50 percent on American Can. The astute speculator kept right on buying Anaconda Copper, Coca-Cola, and General Motors.

Cobb also built his wealth through parsimony. He used to collect pieces of soap that his teammates left in the showers, shipping them to his Georgia farm for use by the hired hands. Noticing that the Detroit fans had developed a custom of hurling their straw hats onto the field on Labor Day, Cobb had the grounds crew collect them. These, too, went to Cobb's farm, to be worn for protection from the sun by his donkeys and field hands. At the age of 73, Cobb entertained a visitor in his 11-room villa in an exclusive section of Atherton, California. The grounds were large enough to encompass a ball field, yet the mansion had no working lights, heat, or hot water at the time. Cobb was suing Pacific Gas and Electric over a supposed $16 overcharge.

Babe Ruth was not quite as careful with his money as Cobb. He reportedly lost $100,000 on horse racing bets during a single trip to Cuba. Fortunately, the Bambino received some good financial advice. A $150,000 trust fund was set up to prevent him from invading principal. The trust paid out $12,000 annually, a high current yield that suggested the funds were not deployed in speculative common stocks.

The Bull Rages On

Despite many observers' misgivings about the high level of brokers' loans, money remained easy in the early part of 1928. Under the influence of Federal Reserve Bank of New York governor Strong, the chief aim of monetary policy continued to be support for the sagging European economy.

The perception was becoming more widespread, however, that credit expansion was fueling speculation. In March 1928, as stock pools reached their apogee, a pool in Radio Corporation of America drove up the share price by 61 points in four days. Political reaction was crystallized in a resolution, introduced by Wisconsin Senator Robert La Follette, Jr., in favor of curbing broker loans. And, for the time being, the European situation appeared to be stabilizing.

At long last, Strong conceded that the focus of U.S. monetary policy needed to change. Now in failing health, the New York Fed chief recommended a boost in the discount rate from $3\frac{1}{2}$ percent to 5 percent. In February, the Federal Reserve raised this key interest rate to 4 percent and in May hiked it to $4\frac{1}{2}$ percent. Other interest rates rose in sympathy, quickly putting a crimp in small business and construction activity.

Stock prices, on the other hand, kept on rising. Radio Corporation of America jumped 18 points, to $138\frac{1}{2}$ on March 12, as New York Stock Exchange volume leaped to an unprecedented 3,875,910 shares. During the spring, the Exchange was repeatedly compelled to close on Saturday to catch up with the immense volume of paperwork generated by the frenzied trading.

Scribe Sits Out Rally

One celebrity who skipped the 1928 bull market was a rising Broadway gossip columnist named Walter Winchell. Then earning the handsome, if not quite princely, salary of $300 a week, he resolved to save at least $50 out of each paycheck. Once he had accumulated a tidy stash, Winchell took to displaying his bank passbooks to fellow night-club denizens and crowing, "Look at those numbers!" All the while, he resisted Eddie Cantor's blandishments to invest his money in stocks. The comedian boasted of making more than $100,000 in a few hours, but Winchell was unmoved.

Even though his friend Cantor lost $2 million in the 1929 Crash, Winchell's aversion to stocks eventually softened. Twenty-odd years later, he journeyed to the New York Stock Exchange, with Marlene Dietrich, Jackie Gleason, and several other entertainers in tow, on a fund-raising mission for cancer research. Pleased by the traders' generosity, Winchell announced, "I'd like to buy something around here. What are you fellows selling in this store?" He went home with $50,000 worth of AT&T, Du Pont, and General Electric shares. That purchase didn't rock the indexes, but as we shall see, in another of the stock market's greatest years, Winchell became a mighty influence indeed.

Money Thirst Unslaked

Broker loan outstandings actually increased by a greater amount in the tight-money second half of 1928 than in the entire easy-money year of 1927. Hoping to drain liquidity from the system, the Federal Reserve sold a substantial portion of the government bonds it had accumulated in the course of its earlier injection of liquidity. Like the discount rate increases, these open market operations had no lasting impact.

The central bank's powerlessness reflected no lack of cooperation by Federal Reserve member banks in New York. These traditional suppliers of credit to the brokerage firms complied with the Fed's demands to cease pumping funds into Wall Street. Almost immediately, though, private bankers and corporations filled the lending gap. Borrowing from the very same New York banks that had pulled in their horns, the "outside participants" turned around and lent the proceeds to stock speculators.

Whatever credit remained available in the financial system, despite the Fed's newly restrictive policy, gravitated toward the highest bidders. These were stock buyers, who gladly borrowed at 8 percent or 9 percent in pursuit of profits that appeared unlimited. Foreign banks and corporations seized the opportunity to lend at such exorbitant rates. Broker loans likewise sucked in cash that investors were pouring into investment trusts, the forerunners of modern-day mutual funds.

Reliance on nonbank lenders placed the long-lived rally in a precarious position. A sharp sell-off, which *Barron's* later blamed on rising money market rates, began on the West Coast on June 11. Shares of the Bank of Italy (predecessor of the Bank of America) plunged by 100 points that day. On June 12, panic gripped the New York market. Volume smashed through the five-million-share barrier and Radio Corporation of America plummeted by 23½ points.

During June, the Dow industrials fell from a high of 220.96 to as low as 201.96. Before long, however, liquidations ceased and the market bottomed out. Even the most conservative investors became convinced that prices were dirt cheap. The buying resumed.

Banking authorities warned that further speculation would strain the money markets, but to no avail. Outstanding broker loans soared to a new record in early July, prompting yet another hike in the discount rate, this time to 5 percent. Another severe drop in stock prices followed.

Shady Operators Update Their Methods

"We are living in an age of unceasing change," wrote Warren Beecher in the *Magazine of Wall Street* at the end of 1928. "Scientific progress in its steady advancement continually affords new and better ways to accomplish the everyday tasks of trade, industry and domestic living." Stock market pundits hailed such innovations as justifications for abandoning traditional valuation measures. No one took Beecher's words more to heart, however, than the Street's crooked operators.

A few years earlier, prosecutors had cracked down on bucket shops. Those tricksters charged commissions but executed no trades. Instead, they bet that the stocks their customers bought would fall in price. That way, the bucketeers could return less cash than the buyers gave them. Naturally, there was a danger that the price would go up, but it could be minimized through stock manipulation. If all else failed, a bucket shop would close its doors, then reopen under a new name. Following the 1921 crackdown, however, many of the bucketeers were behind bars.

By 1928, a prolonged bull market had rekindled the public's hopes of striking it rich. The ever resourceful swindlers took to the telephone to peddle worthless securities. Their efforts were abetted by "tipster sheets," which fabricated rationales for purchase. Sophisticated telemarketing scripts played on the potential victim's vanity and greed, all the while emphasizing the valuable inside information possessed by the caller. The new-style scam artists relied on the fact that telephone conversations were not matters of legal record and could not be used in court.

Strong's Death Fails to Weaken the Market

Despite periodic setbacks during the second half of 1928, the bull refused to die. In the fall, the *Magazine of Wall Street* reported a strong public appetite for new issues of stock. Companies were only too happy to oblige, particularly with the market for bond offerings in the doldrums. Early October brought another rally, followed by an attempt by bears to drive prices down. That effort did not succeed for long, as investors found renewed hope in bullish third-quarter earnings reports.

The rally survived beyond the death, in October, of New York Fed chief Benjamin Strong. Long afterwards, critics would blame the loose credit policies that he promoted during 1927 for speculative excesses that allegedly precipitated the 1929 Crash. Even Republican Herbert Hoover, elected President in the month after Strong died, accused him of "crimes far worse than murder."

But if Hoover was not as sanguine about stock market speculation as Coolidge had appeared to be, investors nevertheless rejoiced over his victory. In the words of the *Magazine of Wall Street*, "The election of Herbert Hoover on November 6 unleashed on November 7 the greatest concentrated public buying of stocks in the financial history of this country." The previous spring's speculation, tremendous though it was at the time, was "utterly dimmed" by the new run-up in prices. Furthermore, noted the financial periodical, the latest rally took place "in defiance of high money rates, cautioning remarks from high authorities in the financial and banking field, and the skepticism of professional traders."

From 257.58 on the day before the election, the Dow soared to a record high of 295.62 on November 28. By then, the New York Stock Exchange had traded close to seven million shares in a single day. Radio Corporation of America, which had astonished investors with a rise to 138½ in March, climbed to 400. According to Max Winkler, a financial editor who later served as economic adviser to the Senate Subcommittee on Banking and Currency, the market was discounting not only the future, but also the hereafter.

America Goes to the Polls

A spirited debate of the issues characterized the 1928 presidential election. The issues in question were not, as one might have expected, protective tariffs, the equity of the prevailing tax system, or the disposition of natural resources available for generation of electric power. Certainly, there was no controversy about the stock market's spectacular rise, which would culminate just a year later in the Great Crash. Instead, the dominant issues in the race were Democratic nominee Al Smith's Roman Catholic religion, his open defiance of Prohibition, and his identification with the big-city machine politics of Tammany Hall.

Evangelist Billy Sunday observed that Smith numbered among his supporters "the damnable whiskey politicians, the bootleggers, crooks, pimps and businessmen who deal with them." Sunday, a former major league baseball player and self-appointed "Ambassador of God," further observed that Smith's female boosters were "street-walkers."

In rebuttal, editor and social commentator H. L. Mencken commented that Hoover's backers were "sorry betrayers of intelligence who, like Hoover . . . flatter and fawn over the hookworm carriers in order to further their own fortunes." ("Hookworm carriers" was a Menckenism for rural Americans, otherwise referred to as "morons" who were "probably hopelessly uneducable.") Hoover's allies, Mencken continued, were the "degraded pimps and harlots of politics."

Men of the cloth from a variety of denominations affirmed Billy Sunday's analysis. "If you vote for Al Smith," the minister of Oklahoma City's largest Baptist church told his congregation, "you're voting against Christ and you'll all be damned." A Unitarian spokesman opposed Smith's candidacy on the grounds that the Unitarian denomination was persecuted in some Catholic countries.

One fundamentalist periodical, the *Fellowship Forum*, was the first of many to print what purported to be an oath taken by the Knights of Columbus. Members of that Catholic fraternal organization allegedly swore to "hang, waste, boil, flay, strangle, and burn alive" the "execrable race" of Protestants. Other techniques that Knights of Columbus supposedly promised to use when annihilating heretics included poisoning, strangulation, and "crushing infants' heads against the wall." The *Baptist Trumpet* (Killeen, Texas) prophesied that upon a Smith victory, "the Romish system will institute persecutions again, and put the cruel, blood-stained heel upon all who refuse her authority." According to an interesting theological argument presented in the *Baptist and Commoner*, Smith's election would lead to all married Protestants being deemed adulterers, on grounds that they hadn't been married by Catholic priests. "To vote for Al Smith," concluded the editorialist, "is to say our offspring are bastards."

Democrats responded in like spirit, circulating a faked photograph of Hoover dancing with the improbably named black Republican leader, Mary Booze. In further support of Smith, Democrats claimed that Hoover had interrupted his work as chairman of the Special Mississippi Flood Relief Commission in 1927 to engage in sexual liaisons with black women.

Seat of Power

During 1928, New York Stock Exchange turnover reached a record 917.5 million shares. The then-staggering trading volume dramatically increased the value of seats on the Exchange. From a low point during the year of $290,000, the price soared to $595,000. That level was not seen again until 1986, by which time inflation had greatly reduced the dollar's purchasing power. Adjusted for the change in the Consumer Price Index, the 1928 peak price in New York Stock Exchange seats was three-and-a-half times as great as the record of $1,150,000 set in 1987.

Year-End Wrap-Up

Stock prices took yet another tumble in December, when the corporate and private suppliers of brokerage loans temporarily reclaimed their "surplus" funds to meet year-end cash needs. In just eight days, the Dow slid by 13 percent from its November 28 record high to 257.33. Radio Corporation of America suffered a one-day loss of biblical proportions—72 points on December 7.

Interest rates for brokers reached a forbidding 12 percent, but still the speculators clamored to borrow money to plow into stocks. Despite Federal Reserve pressure throughout 1928 to limit their brokerage loans, the New York member banks quickly filled the vacuum left by the nontraditional lenders' temporary retreat. This restoration of liquidity enabled the market to regain lost ground, and then some. The Dow Jones Industrial Average finished 1928 at a record high of precisely 300.00.

Total return for the Standard & Poor's 500 measured 43.61 percent in 1928, nearly six percentage points above the preceding year's sizzling performance. The rally was unprecedented on several grounds, according to the *Magazine of Wall Street*. For one thing, it had occurred in the face of the highest money market rates in years. Second, stocks had risen in defiance of efforts by the banking authorities to talk the market down. Finally, all records had been shattered during a presidential election year. (Indeed, 1908 is the only other presidential election year among the 10 best years examined in this book.)

I Remember It Well

Bernard Baruch characterized the spectacular rise in stock prices during 1927–1928 with such terms as "madness" and "delirium." The legendary speculator contended that this sort of collective insanity was a deeply rooted human trait. "Perhaps," wrote Baruch in his autobiography, "it is the same kind of force that motivates the migrations of birds or the mass performances of whole species of ocean eels."

Following the Great Crash of 1929, Baruch popularized the mass hysteria hypothesis by bringing about the republication of a book that had first appeared in 1841. Entitled *Extraordinary Popular Delusions and the Madness of Crowds*, it described several seemingly lunatic episodes of speculation of the past. During the Dutch tulip craze of 1634–1637, according to author Charles Mackay, "the ordinary industry of the country was neglected, and the population, even to its lowest dregs, embarked in the tulip trade." A comparable national obsession arose when the South Sea Bubble engulfed England in 1720. "It seemed at that time as if the whole nation had turned stock-jobbers," wrote Mackay. "Exchange Alley was every day blocked up by crowds, and Cornhill was impassable for the number of carriages." Similarly, said Baruch some 30 years after the fact, "In our own day the stock market madness of 1927 to 1929 swept through every level of society."

Baruch had first read *Extraordinary Popular Delusions* in the early 1900s. Accordingly, the folly of 1927–1929, as he styled it, should have been apparent to him early on. Indeed, popular legend has it that Baruch deftly sidestepped the Great Crash. For his own part, he later claimed to have recognized the danger that the Federal Reserve had created by loosening credit in 1927. As his friends heard the story, Baruch cut short a Scottish vacation when he realized that stocks were vulnerable. Sailing home, he liquidated and waited for the inexorable decline. "Several times in 1928, in fact, I sold, only to have the market continue upward," he wrote in his 1957 autobiography.

By the time this account appeared, Baruch's memory may have been a bit hazy. Although the record confirms his initial warnings that the market was overvalued, he evidently didn't enjoy being a doomsayer. In 1929, Baruch succumbed to the infectious euphoria and published an article predicting still greater prosperity. For years afterward, critics of Wall Street regularly trotted out the piece as evidence of the New Era's skewed perspective.

According to James Grant's 1996 biography of Baruch, "The weight of the evidence supports the conclusion that he didn't sell out in time." The fabled adviser to Presidents failed to recognize the severity of the nation's economic problems for several months after the Crash. His fortune remained intact largely because he wasn't overextended on margin and because he didn't reflexively buy at the "cheap" prices of late 1929. (Still greater declines were yet to come.)

Baruch's reputation for foreseeing the Crash appears to derive mainly from the fact that unlike so many others, he hadn't been wiped out. Amidst the grinding poverty of the Depression, his continued high lifestyle and largess to charities reinforced the impression that he had sagely anticipated the inevitable debacle. In an early example of a "soft money" political donation, Baruch allowed his office to serve as a free research bureau for the 1932 Democratic presidential campaign. Upkeep for the facility that year ran nearly $90,000. Certainly, Baruch did nothing to discourage the inference that these outlays were possible because he had shrewdly sold out before the disaster.

Brave New World

Cecelia G. Wyckoff, writing in the *Magazine of Wall Street*, contended that the continued rise in stocks during 1928 had obsoleted many well accepted theories of stock valuation. Historical benchmarks, after all, derived from a period in which the list was dominated by remote-seeming industrial enterprises. Nowadays, Wyckoff explained, people could invest in companies that manufactured products familiar from everyday life. Investors naturally felt at home with stocks connected with radios, refrigerators, automobiles, and even breakfast food. Additionally, they now recognized that security prices reflected not only current earnings, but also future prospects.

The average man was a bull on America, according to Wyckoff, so it followed that he'd be bullish on stocks. "Most business men believe," she wrote, "that under the leadership of Herbert Hoover this country is entering the greatest commercial renaissance of all ages."

Wyckoff's comments proved too optimistic with respect to her own business fortunes. The *Magazine of Wall Street* circulation had reached 75,000 in 1927, a year after she became sole owner, but the publication went into decline during the Depression. At the time of her death in 1966, circulation had fallen to less than 10,000.

Still, Wyckoff, known to her friends as Carrie, hadn't done badly in an era in which Wall Street's doors were mostly closed to women. Financial writer and securities analyst Victor Morris recalls that even as late as the 1950s he wasn't permitted to cite a woman as a source, even if she were a company's official investor relations officer. In the face of such prejudice, Cecelia Wyckoff listed herself in the magazine's masthead as "C. G. Wyckoff." She employed the pseudonym "Charles Benedict" in writing for an audience that was largely skeptical about women's understanding of financial matters. When Morris arrived for an appointment at the offices of the *Magazine of Wall Street*, he didn't realize, until he entered Wyckoff's office, that "the publisher" with whom he was to meet was a woman.

Cecelia Wyckoff, née Shere, was born in Detroit in 1888. After moving to New York to study singing, she went to work for Ticker Publishing Company, the publisher of the *Magazine of Wall Street*. By the age of 24, Miss Shere was the company's treasurer. In 1913, she acquired a 25 percent interest in the company and married her boss, Richard Wyckoff. Shortly after the wedding, Mrs. Wyckoff obtained another 25 percent of the ownership, then became sole proprietor in 1926. The couple divorced in 1929 and Richard Wyckoff died in 1934, having unsuccessfully tried to regain control of the company in court. Victor Morris recalls Cecelia Wyckoff as a tough cookie.

Incidentally, Cecelia Wyckoff was not alone among journalists in disguising her sex for professional reasons. Financial columnist Sylvia Porter used the byline "S. K. Porter" when she began covering Wall Street for the *New York Post* in 1935. In person, however, this striking woman made no attempt to conceal her feminine charms. Once at a social gathering, attired in an extremely décolleté gown, she was greeted by New York Federal Reserve briefing chief Randolph Burgess with the words, "Why, Sylvia, I've never seen so much of you." (The spirited Burgess went on to a distinguished career as executive committee chairman of National City Bank, later Citibank, and U.S. ambassador to the North Atlantic Treaty Organization.)

A Skeptic's Retrospective

Ben Graham took a less rosy view than his friend Carrie Wyckoff did of the change in valuation standards. In his landmark 1934 text (coauthored with David Dodd), *Security Analysis*, Graham invoked the phrase that had once connoted an unending reign of prosperity. "Instead of judging the market price by established standards of value," wrote Graham, "the new era based its standards of value upon the market price."

Graham's association with Wyckoff began in 1919. He submitted an article entitled "Bargains in Bonds" to the *Magazine of Wall Street* and quickly became a regular contributor. Eventually, Graham was offered the publication's chief editorship, with a generous salary and a sizable share of the profits. After considering the offer seriously, he turned it down, perhaps influenced by the lure of a junior partnership that he received in 1920. Graham capitalized on his friendship with the Wyckoffs, however, to land his brother Victor a job in the periodical's advertising department.

Victor swiftly rose to head the department, then rode the crest of the *Magazine of Wall Street*'s soaring circulation during the Twenties. Advertising sales climbed and Victor prospered. Unfortunately, he then fell in love with a young woman, whom he married in 1928. Carrie Wyckoff was furious. According to Ben Graham, she had amorous designs on Victor, or hoped he would marry her younger sister, or both. Victor left her employ and embarked on a far less successful career in investment banking. Throughout it all, Ben remained on good terms with both Wyckoffs, even following their divorce.

Contemporary Dissent

Deviation from traditional valuation standards in 1928 was recognized as a danger by another of the *Magazine of Wall Street*'s contributors, Loring Dana, Jr. "The characteristic of the new doctrine," he wrote, "is the utter abandonment of any of the old-time conventional yardsticks to measure 'intrinsic values.'" Cast aside, claimed the author, were such touchstones as price-earnings ratios, market-to-book ratios, and even the notion that capital must earn a fair return. Fittingly, Dana incorporated the Coolidge prosperity's nickname in the title of this article: "The New Era of Fabulous Stock Prices."

In Dana's view, the decoupling of price and value ultimately reflected an excess of capital in the United States, relative to the available investment opportunities. Up until the World War, he explained, the nation had been capital-poor. But now domestic industries had all the capital they needed. Their productive capacity was sufficient to serve the domestic market, as well as all foreign markets that were open to U.S. exports. "We have passed the stage of a country 'poor' in capital and as yet are unaccustomed to the practice of lending our surplus wealth abroad," wrote Dana.

True, America had purchased billions of dollars of foreign securities since the end of the war. Even so, savings of every sort were piling up at home. According to Dana's figures, per capita savings bank deposits had risen by 113 percent in the past decade, while the amounts placed with building and loan associations had grown from $2 billion to $7 billion. Admitted assets at 41 leading life insurance companies had swollen from $7 billion to $13 billion just since 1922.

As yet another means of sopping up the nation's surplus demand for investments, Dana said, America was "manufacturing" securities. For good measure, lenders were throwing billions of dollars into the call money market to finance the purchase of the newly printed stocks. With so much money chasing so few bona fide investment opportunities, it was no wonder that traditional valuation measures were becoming difficult to apply.

The Party's Over

Loring Dana, Jr.'s fears proved well justified. Although the stock market continued to rise after the end of 1928, it famously crashed on Black Tuesday, October 29, 1929. Thanks to prescient comments such as Dana's, and despite the less prescient views during 1928 of publisher Wyckoff, the *Magazine of Wall Street* gained a reputation for having anticipated the Crash.

On volume of 16.4 million shares—a record that stood for 40 years—the Dow fell by 31 points, or 12 percent of its value. Blue chips plummeted—AT&T by 38 percent, Standard Oil by 42 percent, General Electric by 58 percent. The Dow Jones Industrial Average suffered a 41 percent peak-to-trough decline during October and did not recover its 1929 high until 25 years later. By the end of the session, $14 billion in value had gone up in smoke.

Who Knows What Tomorrow May Bring?

Bernard Baruch was not the only speculator who capitalized on the Crash by publicizing his alleged prophetic powers. Joseph Kennedy, father of a future President, likewise boasted of having foreseen the calamity. Evidently, Kennedy not only liquidated prior to Black Tuesday, but also cleared more than a million dollars by selling short. Kennedy, who later served as the first chairman of the Securities and Exchange Commission, later vacillated between denying and hinting that he had, indeed, sold short.

Joe Kennedy's version of his astute market-timing insight has been retold countless times. He claimed that he saw the day of reckoning at hand when he discovered that the man shining his shoes had accumulated a number of valuable inside tips. "When the time comes that a shoeshine boy knows as much as I do about what is going on in the stock market," Kennedy later said, "it's time for me to get out." Only a fool, he added, would hold out for top dollar.

The well informed speculator was Patrick Bologna, who operated a shoeshine stand in Manhattan's financial district. From that strategic location, he was able to gather genuinely valuable information from celebrated pool operators such as William C. Durant, founder of General Motors, and Bernard Smith, who when the Crash arrived won his greatest fame, along with the nickname "Sell-'Em Ben," by turning bear raider. According to Kennedy biographer Ronald Kessler, Kennedy's attribution of his bearish epiphany to Bologna was baloney. The realization that it was time to sell originated with Kennedy's mentor, Boston attorney Guy Currier.

The future chief securities watchdog's notion of repaying this kindness was to wait until Currier was away on vacation, then rifle his files for sensitive information. According to Kessler, Kennedy used this information in engineering a motion picture studio merger that was tremendously lucrative to himself, but left Currier feeling double-crossed. (Over the years, Currier's protégé acquired a reputation for stabbing his friends in the back. One Wall Steet wit commented, "I don't know why Joe Kennedy turned on me—I never did anything to help him.")

Tramp Saves Fortune

On the evening before the Crash, recalled film star Charlie Chaplin, he dined with Irving Berlin. As Chaplin remembered it, the songwriter was ebullient about the market's prospects. A waitress at his favorite restaurant had parlayed a modest stake into $40,000 in less than a year. Berlin himself was sitting on a profit of more than a million dollars, in a total portfolio worth, by some estimates, $5 million.

Chaplin advised Berlin to take his profits and get into cash, as he himself had done in 1928. Owning stocks was unwise, explained the Little Tramp, when unemployment stood at 14 million (as Chaplin later recalled). According to Chaplin, Berlin accused him of being unpatriotic and exclaimed, "Why, you're selling America short!" Berlin's fortune was wiped out when, in *Variety*'s immortal phrase, Wall Street laid an egg. A couple of days later, said Chaplin, Berlin came to the set of his film *City Lights*. Stunned and apologetic, he asked where the comedian had gotten his information.

The answer was the book *Social Credit*, written by a British mechanical engineer, Major C. H. Douglas. Chaplin was greatly impressed by Douglas's analysis of the economic system, as well as his conclusion that all profit came out of wages. The system's inherent flaw, according to Douglas, was that aggregate purchasing power was chronically below the level of productive capacity. To ameliorate the situation, the government should distribute "social credit," that is, dole out cash.

Suffice it to say that Douglas's theories made a less favorable impression on economists than they did on the autodidactic Chaplin. "His ideas were ridiculed by most of the economics profession," writes Leslie A. Pal of Carleton University. Maurice Pinard of McGill University says of social credit, "The doctrine rested on a basic fallacy." By the middle of World War II, according to Pal, "Major Douglas and his followers had degenerated into anti-semitism and conspiracy theories of global cabals of financiers."

Even supposing there was some validity to Douglas's ideas, Charlie Chaplin's impulse to liquidate probably didn't proceed from any keen analysis. Three-and-a-half decades after the fact, he recalled that his sell signal was a 1928 unemployment report of 14 million. To be sure, procedures for collecting economic statistics weren't as advanced in the Twenties as they are today. But if Chaplin's figure was correct, then unemployment was substantially higher in 1928 than contemporary sources were estimating several years later, amidst a full-blown Depression.

According to B. R. Mitchell's *International Historical Statistics: The Americas 1750–1988* (Stockton Press, 1993), the unemployed numbered two million in 1928. That total was higher than the preceding year's one-and-a-half million, but it was below the levels observed as recently as 1921 and 1924. The peak unemployment level (which may be what Chaplin hazily remember many years later) was 13 million in 1933.

It shouldn't be surprising that the great comedian got a few of the details wrong. After all, he referred to his economic guru as "Major H. Douglas." Other sources invariably use both initials (which stand for Clifford Hugh) or his surname alone.

It remains an open question whether Chaplin's reminiscence of Berlin eating humble pie is more or less accurate than his recollection of economic statistics. The composer's daughter, Mary Ellin Barrett, reports that Berlin took his total wipeout of 1929 with good grace. "Luckily I had a rich wife," he later joked. Indeed, Mrs. Berlin's grandfather was a prospector who had become one of the fabled "silver kings" of the great Comstock Lode in Nevada. Some reckoned him the wealthiest man west of the Hudson River. Fortunately, his granddaughter's trust fund had been invested conservatively, so she and her husband were not impoverished by the Crash. "Trouble's just a bubble," Irving Berlin lyricized, "and the clouds will soon roll by."

Although the great songwriter and his family were spared the economic hardships of the Depression, Berlin suffered a psychological depression following the Crash. During a two-year dry spell, Berlin found himself unable to produce any fresh, catchy melodies. Finally, the logjam was broken in the summer of 1931. Among the memorable songs he wrote for the musical *Face the Music*, which opened the following February, was "Let's Have Another Cup of Coffee." Berlin's gently mocking ode to optimism included the line, "Mister Herbert Hoover says that now's the time to buy." The Great Engineer's reputed market call was a bit premature, as prices didn't bottom out until July 1932. The succeeding year, however, witnessed one of the greatest bull markets of the century.

Irving Berlin lived another 60 years beyond the Crash, leaving him plenty of time to recoup his losses before dying at the age of 101. Perhaps he found inspiration in the lyrics of a hit song that Charlie Chaplin wrote with a couple of collaborators: "When there are clouds in the sky, you'll get by/ If you SMILE." At any rate, Berlin didn't appear to resent Chaplin's avoiding the 1929 debacle. The Little Tramp's seeming lack of patriotism, however, continued to rankle the composer of "God Bless America." Chaplin especially irked Berlin by declining to return to his native England during World War II to show solidarity with his countrymen. Nevertheless, the songwriter and the silent screen star remained friends. Berlin's daughter says that in her first memories of her father, he appears always in motion and a bit comical, "like Chaplin in a speeded-up silent film."

A Forgotten Prophecy

Along with Charlie Chaplin, Sinclair Lewis is a celebrity whom legend records as having foretold the 1929 Crash. Returning to New York from a European trip in August 1928, the novelist gazed out onto Madison Avenue from the offices of publisher Harcourt, Brace & Company. "Within a year this country will have a terrible panic," Lewis reportedly said. When asked why he thought so, he replied, "I don't think. I know. Can't you *see* it, *smell* it? I can *see* people jumping out of windows on this very street." It was quite a remarkable premonition, as the story has come down. Curiously, though, when Lewis was reminded of his prediction shortly after the Crash, he couldn't recall it.

The Delphic Oracle of Business

Probably the most dramatic forecast of the October 29, 1929, debacle came from Roger W. Babson. Addressing the National Business Conference on September 5, 1929, the renowned economic prognosticator warned that "sooner or later a crash is coming, and it may be terrific." The consequences would be dire, he warned. Factories would close, unemployment would rise, and a serious depression would succeed New Era prosperity. Stock prices collapsed as soon as the news hit the tape, a move that was dubbed the "Babson Break."

By Babson's own admission, he had made essentially identical forecasts in 1927 and again in 1928, without yet being vindicated. *Barron's* chimed in that Babson had been crying wolf for *four* years. Moreover, the periodical pointed out, Babson's own investment research outfit had forecast good market conditions as recently as September 3. The Wellesley, Massachusetts, firm had urged its clients to work "with the construction gang, and not the wrecking crew." According to *Barron's*, the September 5 slump was in truth the result of weak technicals, brought on by profit taking following a spectacular three-week rally. "The Babson statement," concluded the publication, "could hardly be deemed significant, and served only as a convenient explanation of the much-needed corrective of the technical situation." *Business Week* pooh-poohed "the portentous prophecies of Jeremiahs." Quoting a Wall Street wit, the magazine dismissed the September 5 sell-off as "an attack of Babsonmindedness."

Babson subsequently lent comfort to his critics by prematurely predicting an economic recovery in September 1930. A measure of irony was attached to his assorted sobriquets—"The Sage of Wellesley," "The Seer of Wellesley Hills," "The Delphic Oracle of Business," and "The Wizard of Babson Park." As for his analytical methods, a generally complimentary biographical note published by Babson College, which he founded, concludes:

> His pseudoscientific notion, that the laws of physics account for every rise and ebb in the economy, had no more validity than the ancient beliefs that the stars govern the destinies of men or that base metals could be transmuted into gold or silver.

In fairness, Babson's sophisticated notion of a four-phase business cycle remains highly regarded by some thoughtful students of the economy. Along with John Moody, he ranks as one of the originators of the systematic compilation of business statistics. Babson was also a deeply religious man, renowned for his integrity and philanthropy. At one point, he hired unemployed stonecutters to carve mottoes such as "Save" and "Be Clean" on boulders in Dogtown, a section of his hometown of Gloucester, Massachusetts.

Among Babson's other eccentricities:

- As the result of a youthful bout with tuberculosis, he required fresh air at all times. At the offices of Babson's Statistical Organization (later Business Statistics Organization), windows were kept open even during the winter. Secretaries wore woolen robes with hoods and sheepskin boots. Unable to remove their mittens because of the cold, they typed by striking the typewriter keys with a miniature rubber hammer designed by Babson.
- Babson ran for President on the Prohibition Party ticket seven years after the repeal of Prohibition. (He lost.)
- Endangering his reputation as a statistical expert, Babson estimated that the bad influence of movies accounted for 85 percent of all crimes committed in the United States.
- In a final bid for immortality, Babson decided, in 1948, to devote himself to discovering an antigravity substance. Undeterred by the lack of any theory to support his investigations, Babson proposed to test thousands of materials until he found one that worked. He recalled from his seafaring youth that it was accepted knowledge among sailors that climbing a mast was easier at high tide than at other times. "I'm no scientist," Babson declared, in a monumental understatement.

While JFK Slept

At the opposite end of the spectrum from early bird Roger Babson—in terms of stock market clairvoyance—was Joseph Kennedy's son, Jack. In the fall of 1930, the 13-year-old future President wrote to his father from the Canterbury School in New Milford, Connecticut: "Please send me the *Litary* [sic] *Digest* because I did not know about the Market Slump until a long time after, or a paper. Please send me some golf balls. . . ." Fortunately, young Kennedy later chose to establish his intellectual reputation as a historian, rather than as a forecaster.

They're Breaking Up That Old Gang of Mine

As devastating as the 1929 debacle was, still greater losses were suffered in 1930–1932. The Dow, which fell from 300 to 248 during 1929, dropped to 165 the following year and to 78 the year after that. Between September 1 and November 1, 1929, the aggregate value of securities listed on the New York Stock Exchange fell from $89.7 billion to $71.8 billion. By July 1, 1932, the figure was down to $15.6 billion. From a price of 101 at the market peak of September 3, 1929, Radio Corporation of America stock plunged to a low of $2\frac{1}{2}$ in 1932. For many investors, the worst times came well after Black Tuesday.

A case in point was speculator par excellence William C. Durant. By some accounts, he had astutely pulled out of the market in May 1929. After the Crash, the story has it, he jumped back in, aggressively margining his purchases. By the end of 1929, in any event, Durant's brokers began to call in his debt. Late in 1930, the onetime kingpin of General Motors confided to an old friend that he was wiped out, yet he maintained a public display of confidence. Responding to reports that he had been sold out after failing to meet a $5-million margin call, he declared, "I'm the richest man in America . . . in friends." In dollars and cents terms, however, he was obliged to file for bankruptcy in 1936.

His optimism unstilled, Durant blamed his insolvency on a handful of brokers who greedily tried to obtain a preferential position in the settlement of his debts. Among his subsequent ventures was an 18-lane bowling alley in Flint, Michigan. But this was to be no ordinary bowling alley. Durant saw it as "the first unit in a chain of recreational centers" that would make the blue-collar sport respectable, inviting participation by women and church groups. He also gave serious consideration to raising capital for the inventor of a remote control device for radios and the developer of a powerful new toothpaste formulated to combat "smokers' teeth."

Smart Money

High-stakes speculators were not the only ones riding high in 1928 and headed for a nasty fall. The more cerebral Benjamin Graham was successful enough by that year to agree to take a long-term lease on a duplex in the luxurious new Beresford Apartments on New York's Central Park West. Decorating it was to require a small fortune, and as a result of construction delays, the self-made near-millionaire's family wasn't able to take possession of the new residence until October 1929.

Graham later recalled that prior to the Crash, he and Bernard Baruch "agreed that the stock market had advanced to inordinate heights, that the speculators had gone crazy, that respected investment bankers were indulging in inexcusable high jinks, and that the whole thing would have to end one day in a major crash." Despite his acute perception, Graham declined to nudge his investment partnership toward a more defensive position. And much to his subsequent regret, he turned down Baruch's offer to go partners, which would have cushioned him considerably in the ensuing market downturn.

The Benjamin Graham Joint Account lost 20 percent in 1929. Early the following year, the 93-year-old scion of a uniform manufacturing fortune urged Graham to sell all his securities and return all of his partners' capital. "I'm much older than you," the man counseled him, "with lots more experience, and you'd better take my advice." Graham didn't. In 1930, his fund lost 50.5 percent.

Needing to cut back on living expenses, the Grahams sublet their Beresford digs. Graham eschewed taxis in favor of the subway. When dining out, he scanned the menu for the cheaper entrees and switched his weekly dinners with his mother to Chinese restaurants. (Mom's chauffeur got the boot, as well.)

Everybody Ought to Be Rich

So far had William Durant's fortunes fallen by 1932 that the *New York Times* ignored his involvement in its front-page account of the newly disclosed 1929 pool in RCA stock. In just one week, the operation had cleared almost $5 million on a $12.7 million investment. Aside from a table listing Durant as a 25,000-share participant in the pool, the *Times* account made no mention of him. Five years earlier, the same newspaper's headline had proclaimed, "Durant Snaps His Whip over the Ticker."

Instead of focusing on Durant, the *Times* highlighted equivalent-sized or smaller participants such as Walter P. Chrysler and Percy A. Rockefeller. Prominently featured as well was a 50,000-share player, Nicholas F. Brady, the chairman of New York Edison. (Brady died two years before the RCA pool came to light. Eulogies by Al Smith, Franklin Roosevelt, and others emphasized his religious devotion and charitable works.) The *Times* also detailed the role of the pool's manager, Michael J. Meehan. (The Senate Committee on Banking and Currency desired to question Meehan about his firm's dual role as the pool's broker and the New York Stock Exchange specialist in RCA. Members were informed, however, that "on the advice of three physicians" Meehan had sailed for Europe the preceding night.) Some later accounts characterized the whole shebang as Meehan's brainchild, but the 1932 *New York Times* story labeled it the "Raskob Radio Pool."

John J. Raskob, the General Motors finance committee chief who had heralded the rosy business outlook of 1928, remained publicly bullish until the eve of the Crash. Raskob famously expressed his views in an August 1929 interview in the *Ladies' Home Journal* entitled "Everybody Ought to Be Rich."

In the interview, Raskob pointed out that a $10,000 investment in General Motors stock 10 years earlier had grown to more than $1.5 million. "It may be said that this is a phenomenal increase and that conditions are going to be different in the next ten years," he said, on the brink of a decade-long depression. "That prophecy may be true, but it is not founded on experience," Raskob concluded.

Fortunately, the financially astute executive was personally getting out of the way of the coming debacle. He managed to reduce the modest losses he incurred on Black Tuesday through "wash sales." This technique, which was subsequently outlawed, involved trades made solely to establish tax losses.

In between prophesying continued prosperity and sidestepping the Crash, Raskob had been tapped by his friend Al Smith as chairman of the Democratic National Committee during the 1928 campaign. (It didn't seem to matter that Raskob had voted for Coolidge in 1924 and had vowed to do so again if Silent Cal agreed to seek reelection.) In his role as chief party fund-raiser, Raskob displayed the same financial acumen with which he had earlier engineered the du Pont interests' rise to power at General Motors. For only the second time in history, the Democrats had more cash to spend in a presidential race than the Republicans.

Raskob's success as a political fund-raiser depended partly on accepting contributions that some within the party considered tainted. Another of his clever ideas involved a $1.5-million loan to the Democratic National Committee by the County Trust Company. The bank was headed by Jim Riordan, a close friend of Smith's. Raskob persuaded a number of Smith's intimates to sign the note, assuring them, they later recalled, that they'd never be called upon to make good. Plenty of money would flow in, Raskob argued, once Smith was elected. It was a good thing, too, because some of the endorsers knew they'd be hard pressed if the loan were called. Raskob, although wealthy enough to guarantee the full $1.5 million personally if there had been no legal limit on individual campaign contributions, refrained from signing the note himself.

Unfortunately, County Trust became gravely imperiled by the Crash, driving Riordan to suicide. Raskob stepped in as president, with Smith as chairman, and deemed it necessary to call the Democratic National Committee's loan immediately. The resulting financial shock caused immense bitterness within Smith's inner circle. Tim Mara, an ex-bookmaker who owned the New York Giants football team, was on the hook for $50,000. He told Raskob he'd have to go to hell to collect it.

As a result of the bad feelings, several of Smith's longtime pals shifted allegiance to his former protégé and future rival, Franklin Delano Roosevelt. Raskob smoothed things over a bit by deciding to build the Empire State Building and hiring Smith as president of the venture.

∽ 1933 ∽

*T*he extraordinary recovery and reformation measures undertaken by our Government will in some ways speed our journey toward economic revival, in other ways retard it. But we are heading in the right direction.

—JOHN D.C. WELDON, *Magazine of Wall Street*

*S*peculators, not investors, make stock markets in the long run. Confidence to borrow money with which to acquire stocks and reasonable assurance of rising profits are essential to a sustained speculation for the rise.

—"THE TRADER," *Barron's*

*I*nflation is to economics what sex is to literature. No man can write of either without writing of himself.

—*Fortune*

What Slough of Despond?

Two generations removed from the Great Depression, it's hard to believe that the Dow Jones Industrial Average soared by 66.69 percent in 1933. And unlike the Very Good Years of 1927 and 1928, this wasn't a rally fueled by securities lending. Loans to brokers, as well as by brokers to customers, declined during the year. What could investors have been thinking? America's long economic ordeal was not yet half over at that point. Judging from a present-day perspective, a bet on a robust recovery must have appeared foolhardy.

Even more outlandish, from the present vantage point, was any expectation of striking it rich in the stock market. As popular history has recorded it, the New Era's successful speculators were totally discouraged by the 1929 Crash. Now they stood in breadlines by day and slept in Hoovervilles by night. To these millions of unfortunate souls, siren songs about looming capital gains ought to have represented a cruel mockery.

The common people, according to such accounts, were penniless and despairing. They had neither the requisite optimism nor the means to speculate on America's future. The single ray of hope, or so the lore has it, was Franklin Roosevelt's election as President in November 1932. In his March 1933 inaugural address, FDR reassured Americans that the only thing to fear was fear itself, a stirring phrase that according to one source may have come from a department store newspaper advertisement.

Yes, Samuel Rosenman, who edited Roosevelt's papers, speculated that the President's inspiring line was adapted from the words of Henry David Thoreau. First Lady Eleanor Roosevelt lent support to that hypothesis. But that's not how it it happened, according to Raymond Moley, a Columbia professor who served as Assistant Secretary of State under FDR. Moley told columnist William Safire in 1966 that the "fear itself" phrase appeared in a department store ad in February 1933. Another Roosevelt adviser, Louis Howe, added the now immortal words to an earlier draft of the speech that had been prepared by Moley and the President. According to Moley, Howe read nothing but detective novels and newspapers and may never have heard of Thoreau.

According to the story that's been handed down, however, there was plenty to fear for the lucky few who still possessed a bit of capital. Didn't the wealthy, after all, revile "that man in the White House" as a dangerous radical? As every schoolchild has heard, Roosevelt was denounced as a traitor to his class, bent on destroying through inflation whatever wealth he couldn't confiscate. Against that sort of a backdrop, it sounds implausible that speculators rushed back into the market in 1933. Still more paradoxically, the number of persons earning a million dollars or more increased by 130 percent over the preceding year in the nine months following FDR's inauguration. (*Barron's*, commenting at the end of 1934, attributed this statistic to rapid rises in securities and commodities prices in anticipation of currency inflation. The publication observed, however, that the sudden enrichment occurred before all of the New Deal's financial market reforms became effective.)

In reality, the mood of investors was far from universally bearish at the end of 1932. Between July 8 and September 7 of that year, the Dow industrials had nearly doubled. Rail stocks had risen almost threefold over roughly the same period. The immediate pretext for this extraordinary two-month surge in equity prices was a successful renegotiation of Germany's First World War reparations. At the same time, the stock market was living up to its reputation as a leading indicator of the economy. In the fall of 1932, U.S. business activity picked up decidedly.

About the only sour note for many investors was the realization, early in the presidential campaign, that Herbert Hoover was probably going to lose. But when that dread event came to pass, stocks actually headed higher for a few days. In the meantime, business prospects remained upbeat. "While Wall Street generally recognizes the recovery will be slow, there is no longer a panicky attitude toward the market," commented the *Wall Street Journal* on January 2, 1933.

Without denigrating the horrific suffering of millions of Americans during the Depression, we can dismiss any characterization of the 1933 rally as an outright anomaly. Hard as times were, investors did not lack hope. Franklin Roosevelt's 1932 campaign theme song, "Happy Days Are Here Again," was only a shade more optimistic than some of the most prominent market forecasters.

The Sun Will Come Up Tomorrow

B. C. Forbes fairly bubbled with glad tidings as he looked ahead to 1933. He saw an improving picture, both on Main Street and on Wall Street. Only in the political realm were investors in for periodic disappointment, as far as *Forbes's* publisher could tell.

Surveying the economy, Forbes believed that clearcut signs of recovery would appear in the spring. Joblessness would drop somewhat in the second quarter, he thought, and more decisively around year-end. As employment rose, Forbes predicted, installment buying would resume. Furthermore, cash buying must soon pick up, he reckoned. Better-off consumers who had been able to spend, but reluctant in light of economic conditions, had to deal with the accumulated wear and tear on their existing stock of goods. Prices of agricultural and other commodities, said Forbes, would rise spectacularly. And in several industries, he predicted, the leaders would cooperate in stabilizing prices, avoiding a return to levels that he deemed irrational.

The picture was, if possible, brighter on the financial side. Forbes predicted that dividend increases would be outnumbering decreases before the end of 1933. Bank reopenings would exceed bank closings, he contended, and commercial loan volume would pick up gradually. The U.S. gold hoard, Forbes said, would rise from an already "enormous" level of $4.5 billion. In the bond market, he forecast rises in both new issue volume and credit quality.

Political factors were less uniformly bullish, in Forbes's estimation. The problem, though, wasn't that FDR was going to bankrupt the country through deficit spending. Rather, Forbes worried that Roosevelt wouldn't be able to deliver on his campaign promise of *reducing* the deficit. (Forbes was particularly skeptical of ballyhooed plans to erase government debt by repealing Prohibition and then taxing beer.) Aside from the fact that FDR had wildly overstated the potential for federal spending cuts, said Forbes, economizing by the government could not, by itself, cure the deficit.

Forbes financial editor Richard W. Schabacker was likewise optimistic about stocks at the beginning of 1933. Even after a sharp rebound from the lows of 1932, he perceived no material downside in prices. On the other hand, Schabacker estimated that the Dow could triple in the next big upturn, which he thought might not begin until 1934. Schabacker was quick to point out that even a tripling would not return prices to their New Era peak of 1929. Presciently, he contended that no reprise of the 1927–1929 rally was likely for another 10 to 20 years. (In the event, it took the Dow Jones Industrial Average 21 more years, until 1954, to return to its 1929 high.)

The *Magazine of Wall Street*'s January 21, 1933, edition presented a veritable laundry list of bullish signs:

- A return of banking confidence.
- A cessation of currency hoarding.
- Plentiful credit availability.
- Good demand for bonds.
- Cost cutting by large corporations that could put some in the black by the first quarter.
- The greatest zeal for governmental budget balancing observed at the federal, state, and local levels in 10 years.
- Possible shortages of cotton, canned goods, and leather, which would boost prices.
- Economic improvement abroad, "particularly in Germany."
- Good prospects for an international agreement to stabilize exchange rates and prevent further declines in commodity prices.

From a technical standpoint, too, the market appeared to be in fairly good shape going into 1933. "The Trader" column of *Barron's* reported that there appeared to be no big sellers waiting in the wings. No huge blocks were coming out on bad news. Gone was "the insistent urge for cash at all cost," that had succored the bears in the darkest days of 1932. By the same token, the large speculators, whom *Barron's* deemed essential to a recovery, remained on the sidelines. Burned in a false recovery back in the spring of 1930, they didn't yet see the Depression in the process of solution, much less solved. Trading was thin as a consequence. The main spur to transactions was optimism on the part of investment counselors and brokerage firms. According to "The Trader," the buy recommendatons from these quarters were probably more confident and outspoken than at any time since 1929.

Contrary to what investors nowadays might suppose, the market prognosticators expressed no fear that the Depression was intractable. Nor was *Forbes*, a later generation's self-proclaimed Capitalist Tool, fretting that Franklin Roosevelt would institute socialism. To be sure, B. C. Forbes preached the Republican gospel when he called for "sorely needed" tariff protection and a balanced budget. He likewise warned that "revolutionary" schemes would be proposed to provide relief to farmers. At the beginning of 1933, however, Forbes did not regard FDR's election victory as an obstacle either to economic recovery or to stock market gains. "January, 1934," he wrote, "should find this country distinctly more favorably circumstanced than it is at the opening of 1933."

Wish I'd Said That

Franklin Roosevelt may not have been the only President to crib his inaugural address from the newspapers. In 1932, a humorous item in the *Boston Transcript* told of a man answering his child's question about the difference between a statesman and a politician: "A statesman, my son, wants to do something for his country; a politican wants his country to do something for him." Was 15-year-old John F. Kennedy taking notes?

Honeymoon Ends before Wedding Ceremony

Before we leave off debunking latter-day perceptions of the response to the 1932 election, let's consider what A. T. Miller wrote a month and a half *before* Roosevelt was inaugurated:

It is only fair to recognized that in the weeks since the election the enthusiasm with which the American people looked upon the "New Deal" has waned. If hope is to be maintained it is imperative that March 4 usher in decisive and constructive political leadership.

It was by no means a foregone conclusion that FDR would provide such leadership. H. L. Mencken rated Roosevelt the weakest of the candidates offered to the 1932 Democratic convention. No more than a third of the delegates actually favored him, in Mencken's estimation, yet he was nominated through "curiously fantastic" political maneuverings. Roosevelt had accomplished little in national affairs, Mencken pointed out, and his competence was plainly in doubt. The Baltimore curmudgeon further groused that the Democratic nominee's only valuable asset was his surname, which was associated with Republican triumphs. "To add to the unpleasantness," Mencken concluded, "there was grave uneasiness about his physical capacity for the job."

In time, Roosevelt came to be viewed as either a messiah or an autocrat. But based on postelection commentary, the force of FDR's personality was not apparent until after his inauguration. In its 1932 year-end wrap-up, the *Wall Street Journal* reported, "On November 8, Franklin D. Roosevelt, the Democratic nominee, was elected President, but this seemed to have little effect on the market." FDR's ability to move Congress to effective action was unproven. "It looks as if he doesn't have enough oxen to pull the legislative covered wagon out of the mire," commented the *Magazine of Wall Street*. On the whole, it's not surprising that after a brief postelection spurt, stock prices marked time for several weeks. Investors had no compelling reason to suppose that Roosevelt would either pull the economy out of its funk or destroy the propertied class.

Nostalgia Isn't What It Used to Be

As the baby boomers heard ad infinitum from their parents, the Depression was a soul-trying period that instilled good values. It suffices to summarize the testimony of just one randomly selected subject of Studs Terkel's 1970 oral history of the 1930s, *Hard Times*. According to a suburban car dealer named Blackie Gold, schoolchildren of the era always said "Yes, sir" and "No, sir" and never talked back to their teachers. There were no protest marches, no race riots, and no beatniks. ("We never heard of a goatee.") Gold reminisced fondly that if a recruit to the Civilian Conservation Corps smelled particularly bad, he would be overpowered by 10 or so of his comrades and forcibly bathed. Any CCC rookie who insisted on looking "like a hillbilly" would get his head shaved, willy-nilly. To the best of Gold's recollection, the worst theft that occurred during the Depression consisted of pilfering a potato. "In the Thirties," he implausibly claims, "the crimes were a hundred percent less than they are now."

For anyone who wishes to get a true sense of the Depression, financial periodicals can complement the sometimes hazy recollections of people who lived through it. From the same musty pages that document investors' expectations and subsequent market movements, it's possible to construct an insightful social history.

One clear impression is that religion was more woven into the fabric of American culture during the Depression than today. Consider a joke that ran in the *Wall Street Journal*'s "Pepper and Salt" column on the final day of 1932: A woman composes a telegram to inform a friend in a distant city of the birth of her first child. In its entirety, the message reads, "Isaiah 9:6." The new mother presumes that her friend will recognize the biblical verse ("For unto us a child is born, unto us a son is given"). Unfortunately, the recipient of the telegram is unfamiliar with Scripture. She tells her husband that their friend has had a boy weighing nine pounds, six ounces, whom she has inexplicably named "Isaiah."

A lot has changed since the 1930s, besides the downplaying of religion in public discourse. For one thing, "Pepper and Salt" emphasizes light verse these days, rather than jokes. But devotees of the column aren't likely to encounter doggerel that presumes more than a passing familiarity with the Bible. Furthermore, many contemporary readers wouldn't understand a key premise of the "Isaiah 9:6" joke: The story hinges on the fact that senders of telegrams must be terse because they're charged by the word.

Also undercutting the joke's effectiveness is its reliance on a now-repudiated stereotype of the empty-headed woman. *Fortune* perpetuated another misogynistic image by contrasting the generally continued confidence in the dollar with the "womanish terror" of active traders of foreign exchange who perceived inflationary portents in the bombast of populist Senators. Equally jarring to latter-day sensitivities is the racially oriented humor that regularly appeared in premier financial publications during the 1930s. Nowadays, the editors of *Forbes* wouldn't dream of printing the "darky" jokes for which their predecessors actually awarded prizes.

To be fair, though, such material should be evaluated (if not therefore excused) in light of the times. *Amos and Andy*, a radio program that crudely portrayed African-Americans as dishonest and lazy, was immensely popular in 1933. Consider, as well, that in the same year the *Magazine of Wall Street* saw nothing objectionable in the following line of tribute to the recently deceased President of the New Era: "Anybody who knew Calvin Coolidge knows why the Yankees are still the dominant racial element in America."

A final, dramatic illustration of social change since the Depression can be found in cigarette advertisements. Today, whatever cigarette advertising is still permitted in the United States must warn prospective buyers about the product's health hazards. By contrast, a Camel ad from 1933 emphasizes the brand's supposed health *benefits*. According to the copywriters, smokers who switch to Camels become less nervous and irritable. Celebrity endorser Mike Thompson, who is described as football's most famous referee, exults, "Camels don't upset my nerves even when I smoke constantly."

R. J. Reynolds, the manufacturer of Camels, includes in its advertisement a helpful test for readers to determine whether they are too "jumpy" as a result of smoking competing brands. The diagnostic procedure involves using a pencil to spear a finger ring that has been suspended on a string. Succeeding once in three tries represents good performance, say the admen. They then note that a champion fencer who smokes Camels accomplished the feat on his first attempt.

In the Meantime, In-Between Time

Inauguration day for U.S. Presidents was accelerated to January 20 by the Twentieth Amendment to the U.S. Constitution, which was ratified during 1933. In that year, however, Franklin Roosevelt had to wait to be sworn in until March 4. The defeated incumbent, Herbert Hoover, was eager to make arrangements for international negotiations on economic problems and World War I debts. He felt he should obtain the incoming President's approval of his plans, but Roosevelt held aloof.

Despite his subsequent reputation as an inflexible opponent of government initiatives to end the Depression, Hoover was not altogether passive. Bowing to economic realities, he had launched the Reconstruction Finance Corporation. The RFC's lending provided critical support to the banking system and eventually became an important arm of the New Deal. Hoover also advocated the same sort of monetary expansion that later produced good results for Roosevelt. Unlike FDR, however, Hoover never conceived of exerting political pressure on the Federal Reserve to achieve his policy objectives. (Roosevelt's overhaul of the banking system during 1933 made a strong impression on the Fed governors. Realizing that still more radical measures were possible, including even nationalization of the banks, they refrained from raising the discount rate or constraining monetary expansion through open market operatons. FDR later exerted more direct pressure through the Banking Act of 1935. This law centralized control over the regionally based Federal Reserve System in the hands of the Federal Reserve Board in Washington, the easier for politicians to keep an eye on things.) Acknowledging that forceful action was required, Hoover appealed to FDR to undertake joint action to restore confidence. He particularly hoped to dispel mounting fears that the incoming Administration would resort to inflationary policies in an attempt to revive the economy.

Roosevelt, however, steadfastly rejected Hoover's overtures for joint action. His motives can't be known for certain. Putting the best face on it, FDR may have felt that until March 4, he was merely a private citizen and shouldn't mix in. Perhaps Roosevelt simply wanted to avoid being associated with an unpopular Administration that the electorate had rejected decisively. In many Republicans' estimation, FDR cynically desired to claim all of the credit for measures that would have accomplished more if they hadn't been delayed until after his inauguration. Historian Michael E. Parrish reports that Roosevelt was willing to endorse Hoover's declaration of a bank holiday, but that Hoover insisted on tying that measure to several others that would have restricted Roosevelt's options down the road. For his own part, Hoover took few forceful steps during the final days of his presidency. His most notable action was signing a bankruptcy bill that provided relief to debt-laden individuals, farmers, and railroads.

With immense uncertainty prevailing about the direction of government policy, a long-simmering bank panic began to heat up. The Depression had created massive loan-quality problems. Up until early 1933, the Federal Reserve and the Reconstruction Finance Corporation had managed to stave off disaster. Now the situation worsened, with Hoover unable to enlist Roosevelt's cooperation and unwilling to act decisively on his own.

At this point, the states took the lead. On February 14, Michigan's governor headed off massive withdrawals from troubled Detroit-area banks by declaring a bank holiday through February 21. Maryland, which was already experiencing bank runs, followed with a three-day moratorium. Indiana restricted withdrawals of deposits. Despite Hoover's pleas, Roosevelt refused to endorse a federal bank holiday proclamation that was almost identical to the one he himself promulgated just a few days later. The banking troubles demoralized the bond market and stocks soon caught the malaise. On February 26, the Dow slid to its 1933 nadir of 50.16, leaving it 37 percent below the peak of September 1932.

Bank holidays or withdrawal restrictions spread to several Ohio banks, then to Alabama, Arkansas, California, Kentucky, Louisiana, Oklahoma, Pennsylvania and Tennessee, as well as selected cities in other states. On March 2, eight additional states suspended banking operations and some savings banks experienced runs. Money market rates rose sharply. Finally, on March 4, shortly before Franklin Roosevelt was inaugurated, New York and Illinois closed their banks. Securities and commodity exchanges in those states suspended trading for the duration. For the Chicago Board of Trade, the shutdown was the first since 1848. As fears intensified, Americans hoarded currency and foreigners withdrew gold from U.S. banks.

Set 'Em Up, Joe

The only bright note during February were votes by both the Senate and the House of Representatives to repeal Prohibition. Ratification by the states was still required before liquor once again could flow legally. Still, the prospective restoration of booze was viewed by many economic observers as a salutory stimulant.

An End to Inaction

Roosevelt had maintained a low profile during the long delay between election and inauguration. Once esconced in the White House, however, he quickly proved himself an activist. The new Chief Executive began by summoning Congress to a fateful special session. On March 6, he closed all remaining banks for four days, banned the export of gold and halted all foreign exchange transactions. Three days later, FDR signed the Emergency Banking Act, a scant eight hours after Congress first got a look at the bill. The bank holiday was extended indefinitely.

How's that again? The President closed the nation's financial institutions, preventing people even from obtaining cash for their household transactions, and the stock market went on to have one of the greatest years in history? This is not a surprising outcome only from a distant vantage point. Many business people had feared that shutting down the banks would throw society into disarray. Instead, Americans breathed a sigh of relief.

About three years after the event, W. K. Kelsey described the bank holiday in Detroit in *Barron's*:

When the two largest banks of the fourth largest city of the United States closed their doors in the last week of February 1933, tying up half a billion dollars of depositors' money, there seemed to be only one thing for the people of Detroit to do, and they did it. They laughed.

After three years of hoping to see the Depression hit bottom, residents of the Motor City saw the bottom drop out. Suddenly, wrote Kelsey, millionaires and beggars were on equal footing. No one had any money beyond the change in their pockets. There was no cash for meeting payrolls and no credit that could be relied upon. Cooperation was more sensible than crying over spilt milk:

That penniless springtime of 1933 revealed the people of Detroit to one another. It broke down the barriers of class. It ended whatever talk there might have been of Communism, Fascism, or social conflict. Folk realized that ahead of them was a long, hard pull, and quietly they made up their minds to pull together.

Kelsey's 1936 judgment that social harmony had been achieved was a bit premature. Still ahead for Michigan lay much bitter labor strife, including the sit-down strikes of 1937. Even so, Frederick Lewis Allen confirms the impression that the bank holiday massively released tension throughout the country.

In a nationwide radio broadcast on March 12, Roosevelt appealed for cooperation in restoring public confidence. It worked. The next day, banks in the Federal Reserve cities reopened. Clearinghouse banks followed suit on the 14th and before long, all safe banks were operating once again. Back into the banking system flowed currency that the previously fearful customers had hoarded. By March 15, deposits had overtaken withdrawals. When the New York Stock Exchange resumed trading on that day, the Dow soared to 62.10, up a whopping 15 percent from the previous (March 3) session's close of 53.84. Never before had the stock market risen so dramatically in a single day.

Between February and July, the index climbed by more than 100 percent—from 50.16 to 108.67—the only time that feat has ever been accomplished within the space of a single year. In yet another sign of reversal of investor sentiment, broker loans outstanding bottomed out for the year on March 16. Call money rates fell from 5 percent to 4 percent and then to 3½ percent on St. Patrick's Day. Commodity trading recommenced with the end of the bank holiday and cotton prices rose steeply.

The Depression, as it turned out, was many years from conclusion. But for a brief, shining moment in 1933, investors believed they were in the money. Monthly volume on the New York Stock Exchange during both June and July were higher than in any previous month except October 1929, which included the Great Crash. For 1933 as a whole, trading volume didn't match 1929's record, yet it reached a level that was not surpassed until 1955.

Do Something—Anything!

Contemporary investors can be forgiven a bit of confusion regarding the stock market's response to the New Deal. FDR's programs aren't explainable by any consistent theory of political economy. Both his detractors and his admirers tend to agree that Roosevelt lacked the intellectual depth to articulate such a theory. For ideas, he relied on extremely bright advisers, who were split into two camps. One group put the highest priority on immediate economic recovery, while the other regarded the Depression as an opportunity to bring about a permanent reform of the U.S. economy. FDR came down on neither side, instead giving both factions the impression that their notions would carry the day. On the whole, Roosevelt's personal genius lay more in the direction of orchestrating political deals than in formulating a coherent program. Contradictions in policy inevitably emerged.

Then, too, there was the small matter of getting elected in the first place. Candidate Roosevelt insisted on the importance of balancing the budget. In later decades, he was demonized as the instigator of the infernal doctrine of deficit spending. But in 1932, Republican Herbert Hoover was not the only one preaching that a balanced budget was instrumental to a sustained recovery. The Democratic leadership overwhelmingly agreed with him. During the debate on the Revenue Act of 1932, Speaker of the House John Nance Garner emotionally called on members to stand up and be counted for fiscal responsibility and a balanced budget. Not a single Representative remained seated. Later that year, Garner was FDR's running mate.

In light of his later actions, was Roosevelt insincere and opportunistic in vowing to make the government's revenues equal its expenditures? If so, he went rather far in maintaining the charade. Legislation enacted during the dramatic administration-launching Hundred Days, including the National Industrial Recovery Act and the Agricultural Adjustment Act, contained self-funding provisions. Roosevelt repeatedly sought to balance the budget by raising taxes. (In fact, his vigorous pursuit of this policy helped to set off a recession in 1937. Only then did he begin to shift toward an explicitly Keynesian program of stepping up government spending in order to increase the nation's purchasing power.) Within a month of taking office, FDR signed the Economy Act, which, in the *Wall Street Journal*'s words, granted "dictatorial powers to the President in effecting economies, in reducing pensions, veterans' compensation and federal salaries." Roosevelt promptly exercised this new authority with an executive order chopping $400 million from veterans' pensions.

If politics had been the sole consideration, Roosevelt probably would have focused his budget cutting elsewhere. His predecessor had treated veterans' benefits as a sacred cow until after he'd been defeated for reelection. What's more, in 1932 almost 20,000 World War I veterans had assembled in Washington to demand early payment of a previously awarded bonus. Federal troops under the command of General Douglas MacArthur were dispatched to maintain order. Exceeding the orders of Commander in Chief Herbert Hoover, they descended on the Bonus Army, with bayonets fixed and backed by tanks that were armed with machine guns. An infant was killed in the ensuing tear-gas attack.

Public opinion split between sympathy for the Bonus Expeditionary Force (as the marchers were officially known) and a condemnation of the lot as pawns of communist rabble-rousers. But it's safe to assume neither the Bonus Army nor its sympathizers were great fans of Hoover. Yet here was Franklin Roosevelt slashing the benefits of many likely supporters, all for the sake of economically dubious fiscal restraint in the depths of a depression.

In hewing to the need for balanced budgets, FDR wasn't opposing direct assistance to the needy on moral grounds, as Hoover had. Two years earlier, as governor of New York, he had forthrightly defended government aid to the unemployed, "not as a matter of charity, but as a matter of social duty." Muddying the waters even further, Congress during 1934–1935 raised government salaries and voted veterans a bonus, thereby undoing the economies achieved through the Economy Act. How can we gauge the market impact of the New Deal's fiscal effects when it's impossible to pin down what those effects were?

It's a riddle, indeed, whether Roosevelt's economic policy (if he had one) was good for the economy. What's clear is that the stock market liked what FDR was doing. At least, equity prices soared during the early months of his first term. Exactly what it was that the market liked is not self-evident. At the time, political commentators cheered the very fact that he was doing *something*.

The most plausible source of the stock market's initial enthusiasm appears to be the monetary impact of Roosevelt's emergency measures. Even before taking office, Roosevelt had told the press that his administration might be "forced to an inflation of our currency." His advisers persuaded him that an expansive monetary policy would stimulate demand for goods and services by raising prices. This bullish view of inflation was shared by most economists of the time. Moreover, the remedy of increasing the money supply enjoyed political support from groups as diverse as Eastern bankers and rural populists. Much more swiftly than he was able to address deep-rooted social problems, FDR managed to increase the availability of credit, reduce the dollar's gold value, and muzzle any Federal Reserve opposition to his machinations.

Good Neighbors

Among Franklin Roosevelt's first foreign policy initiatives was the dispatching of Ambassador Sumner Welles to Cuba to restore order and protect U.S. business interests. Political upheaval had engulfed the Caribbean island in the wake of economic woes brought on by the Depression.

The Cuban people's response to Welles's mediation efforts was a general strike, which led to the ouster of President Gerardo Machado. All members of his government who didn't flee immediately were thrown into prison.

One such unfortunate, a congressman and former mayor of Santiago, was released after six months on a writ of habeas corpus. As a potential assassination target of Cuba's Communist Party, he was perhaps fortunate in being ordered to leave the country by the new strongman, Fulgencio Batista. The now nearly penniless aristocrat made his way to Miami. Among the family members he rejoined there was his son and namesake, who in 1958 triggered one of the year's most successful initial public offerings. The boy, Desiderio Alberto Arnaz y de Acha III, became known the world over as Desi.

Does Inflation Help Stocks?

April Fool's Day marked 1933's low point for aggregate market value of stocks and bonds listed on the New York Stock Exchange. During the ensuing month, in the *Wall Street Journal*'s words, "inflation fever" gripped the stock market. The United States was jettisoning its hard-money policy and investors loved it. Already, the Emergency Banking Act had effectively taken the United States off the gold standard, by terminating redemptions of dollars for the yellow metal. Official abandonment of the gold standard occurred on April 19, whereupon the Dow rose 9 percent, then another 6 percent on the following day.

The market appeared to be correctly anticipating the favorable impact of monetary expansion on economic activity. In May, Congress empowered the President to reduce the dollar's gold content by as much as 50 percent. The same legislation authorized an expansion of the money supply through issuance of $3 billion in paper money. Later in the year and into early 1934, Roosevelt pegged the dollar price of gold above the world market level. In response to that incentive, gold production and gold imports to the United States rose dramatically. The Federal Reserve bought this gold at $35 an ounce (up from the previous price of $21). Sellers of the gold deposited the proceeds in their banks, thereby increasing the reserves within the banking system. The money stock consequently grew at a robust rate of almost 11 percent annually between April 1933 and March 1937. Checked by political pressure from FDR, the Federal Reserve didn't rein in monetary expansion, as it had during Hoover's presidency. In the judgment of W. Elliot Brownlee, "it is this monetary expansion that seems to have been the fundamental factor in the nation's economic recovery." People now found that they had sufficient cash on hand. Perceiving that prices for goods were going to go up, they began to spend. Previously idled plants resumed production and hired workers, who likewise started to spend their new wages.

Note, however, that the stock market's "inflationary fever," as reported by the *Wall Street Journal*, was not followed by ruinous hyperinflation. *Fortune* noted at the end of 1933 that while the dollar had declined by about one-third in the foreign exchange market, its purchasing power within the United States hadn't fallen much. The National Industrial Conference Board's cost-of-living index was up by only 9 percent. (Wholesale prices had risen by a heftier 17 percent, which the stock market cheered as a harbinger of increased revenues for business.) Inflation hadn't gone out of sight, in *Fortune*'s view, because the public hadn't lost confidence in the dollar. Roosevelt, according to the editorialist, had provided reassurance that a broad recovery would commence before the government's mounting debt burden got out of hand.

The 1933 stock market rally, in *Fortune*'s estimation, hadn't reflected an expectation of accelerating inflation. Rather, buying common stocks was the orthodox response to a currency being detached from gold or falling on the foreign exchange markets. The two largest upturns of 1933 coincided perfectly with the dollar's two biggest drops against other major currencies. If investors were truly expecting an upsurge in inflation, *Fortune* argued in December, they would be buying stocks as a hedge, according to established practice. Stocks would then be rising violently, which at the moment they were not.

Still, *Fortune* had to concede, rising inflationary concerns could perhaps be divined in the weakness of high-grade bonds and the contrasting strength in foreign bonds convertible to gold. In particular, domestic bonds were set back in November when an executive assistant to the Secretary of the Treasury resigned in protest of FDR's currency experimentation.

The *Wall Street Journal*, moreover, linked the stock market's movements with inflation throughout 1933. May's advance, on the biggest monthly volume since April 1930, was attributed to inflation talk and evidence of a pickup in business activity. When the World Monetary and Economic Conference convened in London in June, the dollar fell sharply against foreign currencies and the Dow hit a new high. In July, President Roosevelt sent a message to the conferees in London, declaring that the United States was unable for the time being to discuss monetary stabilization. Copper prices hit a 1933 peak of nine cents a pound, while the stock market marched straight up, reaching 105.15 on July 8.

The upward march of prices was accompanied by improving conditions in the real economy. Steel production unseasonally rose in the spring. Carloadings and consumption of electricity moved above their 1932 levels.

Meanwhile, the Special Session of the 73rd Congress adjourned on June 16 with a final whirlwind of activity. The Glass-Steagall Act overhauled the U.S. banking system. At the insistence of Republican Senator Arthur Vandenberg of Michigan, the Act instituted national bank deposit insurance, a measure that FDR had opposed. (According to presidential adviser Raymond Moley, conservatives Vandenberg, Vice President Garner, and RFC chief Jesse Jones "rammed [deposit insurance] down Roosevelt's throat, and he took credit for it ever after.") Even commentators who had reservations about the scheme credited it with reviving public confidence in the banks. The National Industrial Recovery Act (more about which in a moment) was approved on the same day. Meanwhile, Roosevelt signed a bill cutting veterans' compensation and okayed the centralization of farm credit agencies. Investors cheered the federal government's increased activism.

Interestingly, in light of the very different experience of 1927–1928, the spring-to-early-summer rally of 1933 occurred while loans on securities were declining steadily. This trend continued through year-end, with reductions in loans both by banks to dealers and by dealers to customers.

Reserving Judgment

Americans lacked purchasing power in 1933, but they were rich in proposals for licking the Depression. Formally trained economists were not the only ones to push forward grand solutions. Among the more dubious was the social credit scheme of mechanical engineer Major C. H. Douglas, which beguiled Charlie Chaplin. Then there was the Townsend Plan, the brainchild of a California doctor. Francis Everett Townsend advocated the distribution of $200 monthly to every citizen aged 60 years or older, on condition that the money be spent in the United States within one month of receipt.

Meanwhile, Louisiana Senator Huey Long, a onetime traveling salesman turned populist politician, was readying his Share Our Wealth program for introduction in 1934. A tax-the-rich scheme called End Poverty in California (EPIC) was led by muckraking novelist Upton Sinclair. After Sinclair captured the 1934 Democratic gubernatorial nomination, the major motion picture studios were galvanized by the fact that they were prime targets for tax hikes. They helped to ensure Sinclair's defeat in the general election by "documenting" on film an imaginary invasion of the state by criminals and communists lured by EPIC's utopian visions.

For a few months in late 1932, Technocracy was all the rage. Dubbed "Technocrazy" by Forbes, the movement was conceived by engineer Howard Scott. Technology, said the consultant to the radical Industrial Workers of the World, could produce extraordinary riches if unfettered by the existing system of credit and prices. The improbable solution proposed by Scott was to put the economy under the control of engineers. Among their key tasks would be replacing gold with some sort of energy money. Implementing this radical program was no obstacle: "Technocracy is not interested in political methods," Scott loftily announced.

Mainstream economists devised no miraculous cures for the Depression. To their credit, however, they never embraced extraordinary popular delusions such as the Townsend Plan and Technocracy.

One anti-Depression idea that won respect from economists, despite originating outside their professional ranks, was the Commodity Reserve Currency Plan. The concept was to maintain aggregate purchasing power by making a designated "market basket" of basic raw materials exchangeable for a fixed number of dollars. The plan's originator was none other than the father of security analysis, Benjamin Graham. (Earlier, Thomas Edison had advanced a more rudimentary version of the idea.)

Graham's formal study of economics was limited to four weeks at Columbia in 1912. Part way through the semester, he had taken a leave from college to head the U.S. Express Company project that tipped him off to the bright prospects of IBM. Although Graham never resumed the economics course he had dropped, he reported that he educated himself on the subject "by reading, meditation and practical experience." Evidently, Graham was a good teacher, as his commodity reserve idea drew praise from the eminent Princeton economist Frank D. Graham (no relation), as well as the notice of John Maynard Keynes.

Others regarded Ben Graham's commodity reserve proposal seriously, as well. William McChesney Martin, later the head of the Federal Reserve System, published the plan in a journal that he coedited. Secretary of Agriculture Henry Wallace also appears to have explored the concept. Graham further learned that a friend, who happened also to be a classmate of Franklin Roosevelt, had interested the newly elected President in the idea.

The biggest break of all came when Bernard Baruch, the intimate of Presidents, offered to talk up the idea with FDR. Wanting to associate himself with a proposal that he believed had merit, Baruch discussed it with Roosevelt. Apparently, though, the President thought that having already introduced so many economic innovations, it wouldn't be politically wise to implement another. Baruch dropped the idea like a hot potato, a response that Graham deemed typical of the notoriously self-centered financier.

Kicking the Clouds Away

Seasoned investors have frequently heard about the motion picture industry's imperviousness to recessions. Validating this core concept of cyclical stock rotation is the well known popularity of frothy movie musicals during the Depression. Finding it difficult to cope with harsh reality, the public turned to escapist fantasy. So, while the rest of the U.S. economy languished, Hollywood posted boffo revenues. This is a story worthy of Tinseltown's greatest screenwriters, but it's a very loose adaptation of the facts. The movie industry's supposed imperviousness to the business cycle is, as the lyric puts it, part of a "Barnum and Bailey world, just as phony as it can be."

To be sure, the 1929 Crash caused no immediate hemorrhaging among the studios or theater operators (exhibitors). That was largely thanks to the recent debut of talking pictures, however. As Robert Sklar recounts in *Movie-Made America* (1994), movie attendance and exhibitors' profits actually rose in 1930. In 1931, both the theaters and the studios remained profitable, but earnings declined sharply from the preceding year. "By 1932," writes Sklar, "no one claimed that the movie industry was 'depressionproof.'" In aggregate, the studios and theater operators lost more than $85 million in that year.

The studios' losses steepened in 1933. By the end of that year, almost one-third of all movie theaters had closed their doors. Thanks to a cut in average ticket prices from 30 cents to 20 cents, attendance was down by "only" 25 percent from its 1930 high. Paramount, the leading studio of the silent era, was in bankruptcy, while RKO and Universal were in receivership.

Incredibly, the Depression is routinely cited as the era that confirmed Hollywood's insulation from fluctuations in the general economy. The truth is that the studios were in deep trouble. But it didn't take them long to hit upon a solution: More sex. Relying on risqué language and glimpses of nudity was the perfect way to stimulate ticket sales.

In response to this provocative behavior, the U.S. Roman Catholic bishops launched the Legion of Decency. The organization set out in 1933 to boycott films that the Church found objectionable. Various Protestant and Jewish organizations threw their support behind the effort.

The motion picture industry quickly bowed to economic pressure. With movie audiences already dwindling, they could not afford a boycott. Accordingly, the studios agreed to begin actually abiding by their

IT WAS A VERY GOOD YEAR

own Production Code of 1930. In Sklar's words, the Code "went about as far as it could toward expressing the Catholic bishops' viewpoint without converting the movies from entertainment to popular theology."

Under the modus vivendi arranged by the industry and the Legion of Decency, sex and crime continued to be depicted in films. Both sides recognized that if they excised these essential elements, film attendance would approach oblivion. Any film character who engaged in bad behavior, however, had to be punished or reformed by the last reel. This restriction constrained the creativity of screenwriters considerably. It seems unlikely that the studios would have accepted it if the threat of a boycott hadn't caught them in a weakened position. On the face of it, the movie industry's immunity to recessions is no less a fantasy than the vision of life portrayed in the film musicals of the Depression years.

Wishes for a Speedy Recovery

In the sober judgment of many analysts both in 1933 and subsequently, the early New Deal influenced the economy and the stock market primarily through monetary expansion. Franklin Roosevelt's conservative critics have long contended that the United States ultimately pulled out of the Depression only because of the stimulative effects of World War II. Be that as it may, industrial policy drew a great deal of comment during the earlier of the two Very Good Years of the Thirties.

The focal point of the discussion was the National Industrial Recovery Act, enacted by Congress on June 2, 1933. Briefly, the legislation sought to revive the economy through cooperation among business, labor, and the government. Under the Act's auspices, the National Recovery Administration (NRA) oversaw the creation of more than 700 industry codes of "fair competition." After 40 years, the federal government's fight against collusion by businesses was effectively suspended.

In the beginning, a key objective of the NRA was to raise prices. The thinking was that once people concluded that deflation had ended, they would begin to spend and business would step up production, in order to beat further price increases. Within a year of its creation, however, the NRA was recognized, in the *Wall Street Journal*'s words, as "a long-range medium to control and influence the economic life of the nation."

Roosevelt, for his part, regarded the NRA as "a permanent feature of [America's] modernized industrial structure," rather than a mere emergency measure for combatting the Depression. "Those who now doubt its permanence," wrote the *Wall Street Journal* at the end of 1933, "are an almost negligible handful." Two years later, the U.S. Supreme Court put the NRA out of business by ruling the National Industrial Recovery Act unconstitutional. By then, the scheme had begun to fall apart under the weight of its internal contradictions. The conflicting interests of large corporations, small businesses, and labor proved irreconcilable in the end.

In the judgment of W. Elliot Brownlee, Roosevelt's use of essentially compulsory government-sponsored coordination of industry was the least effective of his intended economic remedies. Looking back, the legislation was unrealistic in seeking simultaneously to increase wages and employment, boost production and consumption, stabilize prices, and improve corporate profits. Broadus Mitchell concludes that the National Industrial Recovery Act exemplified "the confusion explicit in the New Deal."

Confused though its mission may have been, however, the NRA pursued objectives that had long enjoyed enthusiastic support within big business. Following World War I, various industries had drawn up their own codes of "fair competition," with the blessing of the Federal Trade Commission. Participation wasn't mandatory under the law. But companies that signed on, then failed to abide by the codes, were turned over to the Justice Department for prosecution. During Herbert Hoover's presidency, the cotton, textile, sugar, copper, and rubber industries' institutes advocated liberalization of the antitrust laws and industry agreements to control production. Gerard Swope, president of both General Electric and the U.S. Chamber of Commerce, called for work sharing and wage adjustments to reduce the gap between productive capacity and aggregate purchasing power. Under Swope's proposal, production and consumption were to be coordinated by trade associations with mandatory membership. All in all, the plan differed in none of its essentials from the National Industrial Recovery Act.

Indeed, some business leaders were prepared to go well beyond NRA-sponsored coordination within industries. John C. Cresswill reported in the January 20, 1934, issue of the *Magazine of Wall Street* that the "more democratic-minded" heads of major corporations had reconciled themselves to the end of the 1920s-style ascendancy of business over government. The wisest course for business, they felt, was to accept industry's inevitable socialization, while steering it away from pernicious Marxian or other doctrinaire varieties.

Next on the agenda was a grander coordination of the hundreds of industry associations through as few as 24 "associational groups," bound by common interests such as raw materials or markets. "All of which," wrote Cresswill, "gets pretty close to the Guild idea of the Middle Ages." Besides reviving medieval forms of industrial organization, progress demanded national economic planning, in Cresswill's opinion. To skeptics who objected that nobody knew enough to perform such a complex task, he replied that no one ever would know enough until planning was instituted.

Second-Half Letdown

The Dow reached its 1933 peak of 108.67 on July 18. Over the remainder of the month, the index slid to 88.42. American Commercial Alcohol plunged from 89⅞ to 29⅛ in just four days. Investors were discouraged by cost increases for industry that the NRA was instituting under a Blanket Code. Also taken as a bearish sign was the failure of the World Monetary and Economic Conference to achieve any results. Gradually, too, the realization set in that the recent burst of industrial activity was unsustainable. In part, the pickup had simply reflected purchases made to beat the price increases that the NRA was preparing. Recovery slowed down in the face of unabsorbed production and uncertainty about monetary policy.

August's action was dominated by the NRA's introduction of industry codes. The iron and steel pact mandated a 40-hour workweek and a minimum hourly wage of 40 cents. It was an eventful month for the New York Stock Exchange, which tightened its restrictions on margin trading. Two days later, no doubt coincidentally, a gas bomb exploded at the exchange and forced a noon shutdown. (Nor, evidently, was there any direct connection between the bomb and the NYSE's September 1933 murmurings about moving to New Jersey to escape the imposition of new taxes by New York City. The idea was dropped after the city backed down.) On August 29, President Roosevelt lifted the gold embargo and allowed newly mined gold to be sold at world market prices. Gold stocks rallied sharply, and the following day call money dropped to ¾ percent, the lowest rate posted since 1908.

As measured by the market value of all New York Stock Exchange listed stocks and bonds, September 1 marked the 1933 market peak.

Roosevelt signed NRA codes for additional industries, including oil and bituminous coal. Business indicators were turning downward and labor strikes were proliferating. During October, steel capacity utilization slid from 37.5 percent to 29 percent.

Opposition to the NRA was mounting, particularly in farm regions. At midmonth, wheat and cotton prices plummeted, followed shortly by a drop in stock prices. In short order, the President cooked up the Commodity Credit Corporation to make crop loans, based on acreage reduction. Roosevelt also promised to lift commodity prices to substantially higher levels before attempting to stabilize the dollar. Stocks rallied when he established a government market in gold, which was viewed as a step toward a managed currency. But when the Reconstruction Finance Corporation's gold purchase plan failed to bolster commodities prices, the market traded back down.

Stocks were volatile for the remainder of the year. Intermittent strength was attributed in part to the inevitability, then the actuality, of repeal of Prohibition. Also helping were a government agreement to purchase silver and convert half of it to coin. Business indicators such as building construction and steel production turned up in December, while a wave of dividend resumptions and increases further bolstered optimism. Also in that month, however, a pool in Atlas Tack collapsed, taking a good portion of the market down with it.

A Scorecard for 1933

Despite a lot of ups and downs, total return for the S&P 500 was a sizzling 53.97 percent in 1933. It was the Very Best Year of the twentieth century. The Dow Jones Industrial Average, which had bottomed out at 41.22 on July 8, 1932, finished the year 1933 at 99.90.

At the end of 1933, opinion remained divided about Franklin Delano Roosevelt and his brain trust of academic aides. John Cresswill complained in the *Magazine of Wall Street* that "under our noses, day by day, a large-scale redistribution of wealth and confiscation of large incomes is now going on." "Smart aleck professors and dollar-a-year people" in New Deal agencies raised the ire of another columnist for that periodical.

No one could deny, however, that FDR was a doer. Nowadays, it's true, what he was doing wouldn't win much applause. Politically, his policies of promoting inflation, limiting competition, and expanding the role of government are nonstarters. And it's by no means clear that stocks would rally in response to such a program. High rates of inflation didn't seem to help stock prices much in the late 1970s, while the great rally of 1995 took place in the context of largely tamed inflation.

Depression times were different, though. Slim Collier, a bartender interviewed in Studs Terkel's *Hard Times*, recalled that cash was rare. One time, when he found a dollar, his father gravely took charge of it and doled it out to him a dime at a time. With no television and with many people lacking radios, said Collier, even a neighboring farmer's foreclosure had to serve as entertainment.

Businesspeople, no less than workers, were weary of economic stagnation by 1933. Frederick Lewis Allen wrote that the daily newpapers praised the NRA for introducing "a new era of co-operaton between industry and government." (Allen's applying of the Coolidge-years "new era" phrase to the New Deal was probably an unintentional irony.) Inflation was taken as bullish news, even though it had been considered bearish in 1932.

In any event, investors found much to like in the early days of Franklin Roosevelt's record-long presidency. Still to come was bitterness over the New Deal's tightening of securities market regulation. NRA-induced amity didn't last very long. As labor discord mounted, new economic strains emerged and the stock market reacted to them.

The decade of the 1930s proved to be the most volatile ever for the Dow Jones Industrial Average. Volatility, however, meant that the period included big upswings, as well as large downturns. Two of the market's Very Good Years occurred during the Thirties, versus none in the Forties, Sixties, or Eighties. Clearly, economic prosperity is not a necessary precondition for extraordinary returns in common stocks.

HARPER'S WEEKLY

JOURNAL OF CIVILIZATION

VOL. XLII.—No. 2179.
Copyright, 1898, by Harper & Brothers.
All Rights Reserved.

NEW YORK, SATURDAY, SEPTEMBER 24, 1898.

TEN CENTS A COPY.
FOUR DOLLARS A YEAR.

COLONEL THEODORE ROOSEVELT, U.S.V.

Some traders blamed Theodore Roosevelt's antibusiness rhetoric for the Panic of 1907, but it didn't seem to impede the rally of 1908. Roosevelt is pictured here on the cover of *Harper's Weekly*, September 24, 1898. (Photo courtesy of *Corbis-Bettmann*.)

In 1915, familiarity with Hollerith tabulating machines like these gave pioneer securities analyst Benjamin Graham the inside track on one of the century's greatest investments. A stock market veteran talked him out of the idea. (Photo courtesy of *Corbis-Bettmann*.)

The New Era promised limitless prosperity and ever-rising stock prices. During 1927–1928, "Silent Cal" Coolidge characteristically refrained from public statements of concern about speculation. President Coolidge is pictured here in headdress and robes after joining Sioux Indians as Chief Leading Eagle. (Photo courtesy of *UPI/Corbis-Bettmann*.)

Crackpot economic theories persuaded Charlie Chaplin to liquidate his stocks in 1928. The comedian was thereby saved from the 1929 Crash, unlike the title character of his 1947 film, *Monsieur Verdoux.* (Photo courtesy of *Springer/Corbis-Bettmann.*)

Joseph Kennedy was tapped to head the Securities and Exchange Commission on the theory that it takes a thief to catch a thief. The notorious stock manipulator proved an effective watchdog of Wall Street. When he stepped down in 1935, the market slumped briefly. (Photo courtesy of *UPI/Corbis-Bettmann.*)

Franklin Roosevelt rallied the market from the depths of the Depression by projecting confidence, instituting economic reforms—and inflating the currency. (Photo courtesy of *UPI/Corbis-Bettmann*.)

In 1954, stock tips broadcast on Walter Winchell's Sunday evening radio program generated massive trading volume on Monday morning. Here the ex-vaudevillian demonstrates his hoofing prowess. (Photo courtesy of *UPI/Corbis-Bettmann*.)

En route to winning the 1908 batting championship, Ty Cobb (*center*) was photographed with a carton of Coca-Cola. The Georgia Peach later made a killing in the stock, which he recommended to his friend, Tris Speaker (*left*). Duffy Lewis is the third player shown at a 1950 old-timers' game. (Photo courtesy of *UPI/Corbis-Bettmann*.)

Waning public confidence in the banking system helped persuade Federal Reserve chairman Arthur Burns to ease back in the fight against inflation. As interest rates came down during 1975, stock prices soared. (Photo courtesy of *UPI/Corbis-Bettmann*.)

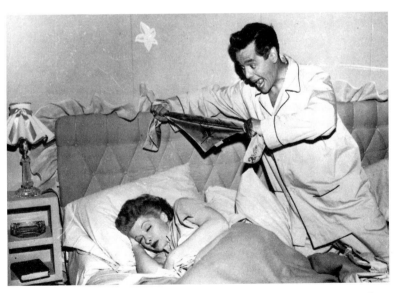

The top executives of Desilu Productions discuss corporate strategy. President Desi Arnaz and vice president Lucille Ball masterminded one of the most successful initial public offerings of 1958. (Photo courtesy of *UPI/Corbis-Bettmann*.)

Among key economic policy makers, Bill Clinton was only the second-best saxophone player. But when he orchestrated a bailout of Mexico in 1995, first chair Alan Greenspan played a superb obbligato. (Photo courtesy of *Reuters/Corbis-Bettmann*.)

❦ 1935 ❦

The rush of gold to this country this autumn, which further added to banking reserves, was a vital influence in sending stocks to a new high since 1931.

—Business Week

The stronger the business world becomes the more lustily it denounces the New Deal and all its works. The break between business and government is final and bitter.

—"An Open Break," Magazine of Wall Street

In this country the incumbent political party always gets credit for satisfactory economic conditions and blame for unsatisfactory conditions, regardless of whether its policies actually had anything to do with either condition.

—LAURENCE STERN, "Managed Recovery vs. Depression," Magazine of Wall Street

You've Lost That Loving Feeling

In 1935, as in the Very Good Year of 1933, the stock market enjoyed excellent returns despite the continuing Depression. Equally paradoxical, according to later impressions of the period, Franklin Roosevelt occupied the White House during both rallies. If FDR was truly a traitor to the monied classes who promoted antibusiness policies at every turn, why were investors so bullish?

The 1933 upturn, at least, is understandable in light of the early New Deal cooperation between business and the Roosevelt Administration. The National Industrial Recovery Act implemented ideas that had been floating around for some time within the business community. Coordination in production and pricing spelled profits. Restored profitability promised to put people back to work, which in turn meant more money in people's pockets and rising demand for goods and services.

By 1935, however, the honeymoon was over. Reviewing the situation at year-end, the *Magazine of Wall Street* predicted that Roosevelt would veer leftward in his 1936 reelection bid. Regrettably, the campaign rhetoric would probably "crystallize the New Deal conception of Government and business as eternal foes." While FDR deserved credit for containing the crisis in the spring of 1933, he was guilty of multiple sins in the intervening year:

- Vacillating and uncertain monetary policies.
- Intrusion of government into every aspect of business.
- Maintenance of a "motley crew of amateur advisers and consultants."
- Persecution of utilities and the financial markets.
- Hasty adoption of a "stupendous" social security program sure to promote insecurity.
- Unceasing derogation of businessmen.

The *Magazine of Wall Street* sadly concluded that industry, which had tried to go along with Roosevelt, now perceived that "the advance toward socialism by indirection had to be stopped."

At least as late as 1935, then, business was willing to concede that FDR's early programs may have had a positive impact on the economy. With the 1936 election approaching, however, Republicans were reluctant to give too much credit to the role of government policy, as opposed to individual initiative. Between politically minded spin control and honest inability to sort out the various economic influences, investors were not sure how to respond to developments on the Washington scene.

It's not surprising, therefore, that confusion initially greeted the Supreme Court's May 27 finding that the National Industrial Recovery Act was unconstitutional. Momentous though the decision seemed, the market's response was muted. Seven months after the fact, the *Wall Street Journal* provided a rather implausibly convoluted analysis. Enactment of the legislation in 1933 was good news, the publication claimed, because it reduced the crisis-bound demand for radical government intervention. Invalidation of the NIRA in 1935 was also good news, according to the *Journal*. Besides showing that the Constitution wasn't being torn to shreds, the high court relieved business of the burden of trying to guess the unguessable intentions of regulators.

Complicating the interpretation was the decreased effectiveness of the National Recovery Administration by the time of its abolition. The authorizing legislation had been due to expire in June. It was widely assumed that if Congress was to renew the NRA's mandate, it would have to revise the price-fixing provisions. These had proven nearly impossible to enforce and in one industry, lumber, had already collapsed. As early as February 2, the *Magazine of Wall Street*'s "E.K.T." saw a 50/50 chance that the Supreme Court would kill the NRA.

According to *Barron's*, the NRA was effective only as long as industrial prices were falling. Business welcomed FDR's invitation to discipline "scalawags" who undersold the competition. Acceptance of collective bargaining with labor was viewed as a reasonable quid pro quo for the long-dreamed-of opportunity to fix prices without fear of prosecution. Once Roosevelt's inflationary policies kicked in, however, price cutters became less of a threat. Business support for the NRA quickly dissipated. After a failed attempt to cut hours and boost wages during 1934, the NRA had "lapsed into frenzied inactivity," in the words of the *Wall Street Journal*'s Bernard Kilgore.

Perhaps the truth is that political developments, including the NRA's demise, made little difference to the value of common stocks. One thing that's clear from reading the financial press is that editorialists love to pontificate about government policy. Opining on such matters no doubt flatters their sense of self-importance. It's not self-evident, however, that a market timer can succeed by understanding events on Capitol Hill better than the next fellow. As suggested by the NIRA's brief history, the connection between legislation and the Dow is frequently obscure.

Just Around the Corner

Unlike the editorial writers, investors appeared little concerned about the mounting antagonism between government and business during 1935. Instead, they took heart from strong indications of an economic rebound. According to the *Wall Street Journal*, sober citizens had made up their minds that a normal and natural recovery would occur, "with the New Deal or against the New Deal or without the New Deal."

Experts endorsed the public's decision to have another cup of coffee and another piece of pie, as Irving Berlin's lyric went, while the Depression took care of itself. The *Wall Street Journal*'s year-end wrap-up carried the optimistic headline, "Trends of 1935 Bear Earmarks of a Final Chapter in History of Depression." By the author's count, though, the upturn that began in June was the seventh since the 1929 Crash. Still to come was the 1937 recession, precipitated in part by President Roosevelt's reawakened impulse to balance the federal budget.

With the benefit of hindsight, the stock market's 1935 optimism may seem extraordinarily myopic. But the upturn then underway was the lengthiest observed since the beginning of the Depression. It had also lasted longer, according to the *Journal,* than the majority of false starts toward recovery from previous economic slumps. Production indexes had surpassed the highs of the unsustainable boom of 1933, although construction and capital goods still languished. By year-end, even those laggard sectors showed signs of reviving. Based on information available at the time, then, the rally of 1935 was not as incongruous as it might now appear.

FDR Struggles to Get America off the Dime

Stocks may have had favorable prospects at the beginning of 1935, but they certainly didn't have momentum. Both the economy and the market had been marking time since the euphoria of 1933. Measured against the 1923–1925 average, the Federal Reserve Board's adjusted index of industrial output averaged above 80 percent in the first half of 1934, then slipped to below 75 percent in the second half. For the year, the Dow Jones Industrial Average advanced by a mere 3.7 percent. The average public utility share fell by nearly half during 1934, as investors reacted to the regulatory winds that culminated in enactment of the Public Utilities Holding Company Act of 1935.

As far as the limited statistics then available indicated, unemployment was no lower at the end of 1934 than at the beginning of 1933. And this was true despite the stimulus of the largest peacetime government expeditures in history. Bank deposits grew sharply during 1934, thanks to a credit expansion staged to finance the deficit, but private industry displayed little appetite for commercial loans. Public securities issuance was likewise moribund. Lack of predictability in monetary policy was cited as a cause of the business paralysis. As the *Magazine of Wall Street* saw it, "The more the government runs into debt, the less willing is private capital to enter normal long-term employment."

Gold Bugs the Market

Compounding the uncertainty about money was the unsettled status of gold. The Roosevelt Administration had progressed from manipulating the gold price during 1933 to pursuing a "streamlined" gold standard. A brief foray into bimetallism, in the form of the Silver Purchase Act of 1934, further confused the issue.

Meanwhile, the Supreme Court was being asked to rule on the government's right to abrogate clauses in public and private contracts that required payment in gold. The question, deemed by *Business Week* the most momentous monetary decision to come before the justices since the Civil War, arose from a joint resolution of the 73rd Congress. Considering that the government had taken gold out of circulation under the Anti-Hoarding Act, there was none to be paid. Congress meanwhile had made all other money equal in power for paying debt. It therefore concluded that anyone who insisted on being paid in gold was obstructing the power of Congress to say what money is. Prominent among the plaintiffs opposing this reasoning was one Norman C. Norman, holder of one $1000 bond of the Baltimore & Ohio Railroad.

If upheld, the gold clause abrogation was expected to benefit many railroads and public utilities, as well as some industrials. These were companies that could not afford to satisfy their payable-in-gold obligations as a result of Roosevelt's 40 percent hike in the dollar price of the yellow metal. A rejection of the abrogation would cause many of the debtor companies to fail, setting back the national recovery. That would be bad news for stocks. Such a deflationary outcome was so unpalatable, however, that the prospect might scare the government into new efforts to inflate the currency. That would probably be *good* for stocks.

Slow Starter

During January 1935, the Dow opened at 104.51 and closed at 101.69. Would-be bulls were reluctant to commit themselves while the gold clause issue was pending before the Supreme Court. One Senator, renowned as a constitutional expert, was reportedly predicting a "split decision." He thought the Court would compel the government to honor its obligations in gold, but repudiate gold clauses in private contracts. The Massachusetts Federal District Court added to the market's monetary uncertainties. On January 4, it held unconstitutional a provision of the gold-hoarding law that compelled citizens to yield their privately owned gold coin to the government. Other worries included President Roosevelt's proposal of an unbalanced budget and his push for a social security plan requiring large payments by industry.

The gold issue continued to cast a pall until February 18, when the high court justices voted five-to-four to uphold the government's abrogation of gold clause contracts. Prices rose on the 17th, but the rally soon quieted down. Hesitancy was blamed on new proposals being vetted in Congress. They included regulations on the public utility industry and a measure that would make bank credit an adjunct of the Treasury.

Get It in Writing, Then Pray

Prior to the Supreme Court's ruling on the gold payment clauses, *Business Week* canvassed lawyers who had read the principal briefs presented in the cases. Most felt that the plaintiffs' briefs made a good case. After all, the contracts in question stated plainly that payment in gold was required. There was no suggestion that the obligors had been coerced or misled. The precedents for upholding the government's position were dubious. Later on, when the decision came down, Justice James McReynolds wrote on behalf of the four dissenting jurists that upholding abrogation would "bring about the confiscation of property rights and repudiation of national obligations." Nevertheless, 19 of *Business Week*'s 20 lawyer-handicappers predicted that the justices would permit the gold clauses to be invalidated.

Investors should remember *Business Week*'s survey whenever they bank on the sanctity of contracts. A good illustration involves the collapse of energy prices in the early 1980s. To the lay investor, the situation seemed black and white. Natural gas pipeline companies were obligated by the terms of their procurement contracts to pay for gas at previously contracted, but now above-market prices. The pipeline operators' declarations of force majeure seemed to nonlawyers an outrageous attempt to renege on clear-cut, enforceable obligations. In the end, though, the companies successfully renegotiated the terms. Gas producers settled for half a loaf.

Whenever the legal system threatens to overthrow the principle that a deal is a deal, Cassandras warn that routine commercial relations will founder. Yet somehow the system survives. How good, then, is a contract that's as good as gold? No better than it was in 1935, evidently.

Quiet Time

March's New York Stock Exchange volume was the smallest in more than a decade. The Dow retreated from 103.37 to 100.81, dipping to 96.71 in the interim. Investors fretted about FDR's message to Congress, in which he called for the abolition of public utility holding companies. Congress, for its own part, demanded an investigation of AT&T. Strikes were threatened in the automobile, rubber, and bituminous coal industries. On top of all the domestic troubles, the foreign scene was darkening. Germany announced a new conscript army, while in Belgium a cabinet crisis precipitated a currency devaluation.

Several announcements of dividend increases interrupted the generally bearish string of events. *Barron's* characterized the credit markets as extremely easy. Additionally, the British pound fell to its lowest price ever in terms of gold, creating inflationary pressure in the United States that was likely to help equities. Stocks failed to take their cue from these factors, however.

The Bull Begins to Stir

The 1935 bull market finally got into gear when President Roosevelt issued two proclamations that boosted the price of newly mined silver from 71 to 77.57 cents a pound. Speculation in silver mining shares, which had led every major stock market advance during the New Deal, dramatically boosted stock trading volume. *Barron's* reported that investors, as opposed to speculators, accounted for the market's subsequent advance. Corporations and investment trusts were buying stocks with previously idle cash, as well as new funds received from such sources as bond redemptions. By the end of April, the Dow stood at 109.48, up by 8.6 percent for the month.

During the first half of May, prices rose in response to the inflationary implications of a veterans' bonus bill then before Congress. Various financing schemes were advanced for the proposed measure, which passed both houses but was ultimately vetoed by FDR. One idea was to use the remainder of the profit realized by the federal government through devaluation of the dollar. A more inflationary alternative, proposed by Congressman Wright Patman of Texas, was for the bonus to be paid with $2 billion of newly issued currency. Stocks slumped on May 23, when the Senate sustained President Roosevelt's veto of the Patman bill. Then, on the 27th, the Supreme Court ruled the National Industrial Recovery Act unconstitutional, the first such invalidation of major New Deal legislation. May concluded on a note of uncertainty, with the Dow at 110.64, down from an intramonth peak of 116.58.

In June, stocks resumed their climb in the face of several bills under consideration by Congress that were deemed unfavorable to business. Adding to the bad news was the entry into reorganization proceedings by two railroads, the Chicago & North Western and the Chicago, Milwaukee, St. Paul & Pacific. Late in the month, Roosevelt's special message to Congress advocated "soak the rich" taxes on large incomes, corporations, gifts, and inheritances. Despite all, the Dow Jones Industrial Average advanced from 109.74 to 118.21.

Not from Central Casting

The Roosevelt Administration was not a strong proponent of separation of powers, insofar as the principle got in the way of its policies. Bending the independent and uncentralized Federal Reserve System to its will was no simple matter, though. It was a stroke of good fortune, then, that when the senior position on the Federal Reserve Board (then called "governor") became vacant, a candidate was at hand whose views were highly compatible with the White House's. Utah banker Marriner Stoddard Eccles hadn't gone to college and he wasn't a Democrat (although he'd voted for FDR). But he had become convinced that easy money was essential to pulling the country out of the Depression.

In an even more radical stance for a banker, Eccles advocated deficit spending as a means of reviving aggregate demand. Roosevelt was still apologizing for running an unbalanced budget in 1935, but when the recovery faltered in 1937, he came around to Eccles's view. It was an analysis, incidentally, conceived independently of the like-minded John Maynard Keynes.

Eccles accepted FDR's appointment as governor on condition the President promise to back his plan for overhauling the Federal Reserve System's structure. Although Eccles's proposals were controversial, most of them were enacted through the Banking Act of 1935. Most important, the new structure substantially centralized the power of the Federal Reserve's Open Market Committee. That change irked Carter

Glass, who'd insisted on a decentralized regional set-up when he coauthored the Federal Reserve Act of 1913.

Now, Eccles had to avoid further irritating the Virginia Senator. As
chairman of the key subcommittee of the Senate Committee on Banking and Currency, Glass represented an obstacle to Eccles's confirma-
tion to the newly created post of chairman of the Board of Governors
of the Federal Reserve. Accordingly, while he privately continued to
press the White House for increased public works, Eccles turned down
speaking engagements for fear of antagonizing Glass. "He is refusing
all kinds of invitations, some of which would do us a world of good,"
complained Presidential press secretary Stephen Early. "We are under
attack with our best gun silenced."

Road Rally

Beginning in June, American industry enjoyed its most sustained recovery up to that point of the Great Depression. For the year, the
gross national product increased by 16.5 percent. Production indexes
surpassed the levels attained during the furious boom of 1933.

Driving the 1935 economic recovery was a 52 percent year-over-
year rise in auto sales. General Motors boosted its dividend by 51 percent and its share price rose by 65 percent. Timken Roller Bearing
more than doubled its earnings per share as its stock soared by 157
percent. Chrysler tripled between its low and its high of the year. "Today, no one in Detroit mentions depression," wrote W. K. Kelsey in
Barron's at year-end, "because it is over."

The turnaround was remarkable. In June 1933, bank deposits in
Detroit were down by 75 percent from the comparable month of
1929. Building construction had fallen by 96 percent over the four-
year period. According to Kelsey, one could have shot a machine-gun
down the aisles of the leading department stores without hitting a customer. Now the local employment rate was back to about 80 percent
of its 1929 level, up from just over 40 percent at the nadir in 1933.
(Employment had jumped 62 percent between November 15 and December 15, 1934, alone.) Car sales received a special boost in November when the New York Automobile Show was held two months
earlier than in previous years, permitting carmakers to introduce their
new models two months ahead of the usual schedule.

Despite all the signs of renewed prosperity, however, unemployment stood at 10 million, while national income remained $20 billion
to $30 billion below peak years of the Twenties. As the *Magazine of*

Wall Street saw it, the much-ballyhooed recovery was partly a statistical illusion. Yes, measures of business activity had rebounded to within 3 percent or 4 percent of their average 1923–1925 levels. But no one seemed to be taking into account the growth in population during the interim. Secretary of Agriculture Henry Wallace provided some per capita figures that painted a less rosy picture than conventional economic indicators. By Wallace's reckoning, physical volume of consumption goods, including automobiles, had recovered only about half their Depression declines. Capital goods, on a per capita basis, were just one-third of the way up from the bottom.

Summer Rally

The market climbed on increased volume during July, taking heart from stepped-up steel production, electric power output, and residential construction. On the political front, the House rejected the Administration's public utility holding company bill and Congress appeared lukewarm to other FDR proposals. Meanwhile, the Federal Court of Appeals in Boston declared Agricultural Adjustment Administration processing taxes unconstitutional, further bolstering hopes for a judicial dismantling of the New Deal.

Volume and prices continued to rise in August. Business was brisk in a wide range of industries. Steel production, electric power output, residential construction, retail trade, and automobile production all flashed favorable signs. Additionally, the threatened war between Italy and Ethiopia helped drive chemical, steel, and copper shares to new highs. Congress adjourned and a Republican triumph in a special Congressional election in Rhode Island suggested that public opinion was turning against Roosevelt.

More good news came in the form of a series of favorable dividend announcements and encouraging trade developments. Another upbeat development was the publication of correspondence between FDR and Roy W. Howard, chairman of Scripps-Howard Newspapers. Roosevelt promised to give business a "breathing spell" from new regulatory constraints.

Howard, by the way, had a long and distinguished career in journalism. At 29 he became the first president of the United Press. Under his leadership, the Scripps-Howard chain grew from 8 to 29 newspapers. He was equally well known as the reporter who, in November 1918, broke the news that Germany and the Allies had signed an armistice. Delirium greeted Howard's report that World War I was over. Dancing broke out in the streets of Britain, France, and the United States. Unfortunately, Howard's scoop turned out to be premature by four days.

War, rather than peace, was in the rumor mill in 1935. Despite the summer's encouraging economic and political developments, a European war scare depressed stocks in the third week of September. During the subsequent market recovery, gains were confined to shares of companies likely to benefit from war. Rails were weakened by a disclosure that the management of New York Central had been criticized by the Reconstruction Finance Corporation, as well as rumors of difficulties at other lines.

It Takes a Thief

Stocks dipped briefly on September 12 on the announcement that Joseph Kennedy was resigning as chairman of the Securities and Exchange Commission. The press applauded his performance as first head of the regulatory body. Kennedy had aided the economic recovery, the editorialists claimed, through his extraordinary energy and ability to recruit outstanding individuals to the SEC. These included a future SEC chief and later Justice of the Supreme Court, William O. Douglas.

Kennedy's widely praised record as the securities industry's chief overseer confounded many New Dealers who had opposed his selection in 1934. Columnist John T. Flynn of the *New Republic* wrote that the outgoing chairman had been the SEC's most useful member. A year earlier, in response to Kennedy's being named to the post, the very same Flynn had sputtered, "I say it isn't true. It is impossible. It could not happen." FDR had gone "to the bottom to the heap" to find Kennedy, he editorialized. "Setting a wolf to guard the sheep," was how Agricultural Adjustment Administration general counsel Jerome Frank characterized the President's decision.

The consternation that greeted Kennedy's anointment as SEC chief was understandable. As a young Wall Street operator, he had specialized in insider trading, a practice that while not yet illegal, was already considered unsavory. From advance knowledge of the acquisition of Pond Coal Company alone, Kennedy personally cleared $675,000 on an investment of $24,000. "It's so easy to make money in the market," he told a Harvard classmate, "we'd better get in before they pass a law against it."

Inside information was a cornerstone of Kennedy's success. Operating in league with famed bear raider Bernard ("Sell-'Em Ben") Smith, he began by gaining access to confidential loan data. Upon identifying a heavily margined investor, the two confederates staged a bear raid on the stocks in his portfolio. Then, when the bank demanded collateral from the overextended borrower, Kennedy and Smith would show up, offering to take the stock at a fire-sale price.

Less than a year before FDR tapped him as the securities industry's top cop, Kennedy participated in a pool that artificially ran up the price of Libbey-Owens-Ford from $20 to $37. Before the operators "pulled the plug," in the parlance of the day, Kennedy had pocketed over $60,000. The manipulations were brazen enough to come under scrutiny during the Senate Banking and Currency Committee's so-called Pecora Hearings into stock market abuses. Small wonder that the *New Republic* called Kennedy a "grotesque" choice for the SEC chairmanship.

To Franklin Roosevelt, though, Joe Kennedy was a logical candidate. It takes a thief to catch a thief, he told his adviser, James Farley. It also helped that Kennedy had contributed (by his own account, which may have been significantly understated) $50,000 to FDR's campaign. He raised at least another $150,000 from others, partly—according to one source—by acting as a conduit for contributors who wished to conceal their identities. Finally, Kennedy had played a pivotal role at the 1932 Democratic convention by swinging to FDR the support of his friend, press magnate William Randolph Hearst, who had originally backed House Speaker John Garner.

The grateful President tapped Kennedy as head of the newly formed Securities and Exchange Commission in June 1934. Technically, the President was empowered merely to appoint the body's five commissioners, who in turn chose one of their own number as chairman. In typical fashion, however, Roosevelt ensured Kennedy's selection by informing the other commissioners of his preferred candidate for the chairman's slot. FDR's eagerness to secure the prestigious post for Kennedy partly reflected a determination not to award him the post he really wanted, Secretary of the Treasury.

Roosevelt's instincts were excellent regarding Kennedy's enforcement talents. According to one senior SEC official, Kennedy could detect the operation of a pool merely by examining a stock's action on the ticker tape. During his brief stay at the SEC, Kennedy made considerable progress in suppressing the activities that had made him rich. His former collaborator, "Sell-'Em Ben" Smith, abandoned his bear raiding forever when the New Deal began to clean up Wall Street.

Some market pundits credited him with helping to get the 1935 rally started by breaking a logjam in new-issue financing created by the SEC's various regulations.

Kennedy's press notices weren't 100 percent favorable, however. At the end of the great 1935 rally, *Barron's* griped that shortsighted SEC regulations had "ejected big operators and annihilated the confidence of floor traders and specialists." The result, claimed "The Trader," was an unprecedentedly thin, and consequently volatile, market. Furthermore, with their personal trades now being revealed publicly on a monthly basis, corporate directors had ceased taking large risks on the future. As a consequence, *Barron's* lamented, the market was no longer discounting developments in advance, instead moving after the news was out.

Year-End Action

October's brisk trading and rising prices were supported by foreign buying. The Italian military campaign in Ethiopia initially depressed the market. Stocks soon rebounded, however, aided by favorable domestic trade news, improved corporate earnings, and a series of dividend hikes.

Stocks rose for the eighth consecutive month during November. On the 19th, the Dow reached 148.44, its highest level since July 1931. The average finished the month at 142.35. Trading volume was the heaviest since July 1933. Favorable trade reports supported the rally, along with accelerated inflow of European gold for investment in U.S. securities. Utility stocks benefited from a court ruling that held the Public Utility Holding Company Act unconstitutional. For most of December, stocks moved irregularly lower as the U.S. government curtailed its purchases of silver on the London market. Silver prices declined sharply and unsettled the stock market.

War Isn't All Hell

Although investors were troubled initially by the gathering storm in Ethiopia, they soon spied the silver lining. Military buildups abroad and at home boosted orders for warplanes, prompting 50 percent rises in aircraft stocks.

In December 1935, the *Magazine of Wall Street* presciently discussed the dilemma that the United States would face if it attempted to remain neutral in a war between, for example, Great Britain and

Germany. The same publication warned of the constitutional difficulties presented by a strong chief executive in the event of foreign conflict:

> Only Congress can declare war, but if the executive to whom neutrality decisions are delegated in these days of personal government should by any chance involve us in inescapable international difficulties the war declaration would have to follow as a matter of course.

Isolationists would later accuse Franklin Roosevelt of overreaching to drag America into World War II. Judging by the scenarios painted as early as 1935, however, FDR's maneuvers shouldn't have taken anyone by surprise.

What's New?

Two key economic trends noted during recent years are securitization and technologically driven reductions in required inventories. Commercial banks, note keen observers of the business scene, are losing their loan business to the stock and bond markets. Sophisticated data processing techniques and the introduction of just-in-time systems, meanwhile, have enabled manufacturers to save on inventory-related carrying costs.

It's trite to mention that there's nothing new under the sun. Still, like many other "innovations" of recent decades, securitization and inventory rationalization represent evolutionary, rather than revolutionary, changes. As the Very Good Year 1935 ended, the *Wall Street Journal* noted that the Depression had forced banks to shift their focus. Two underlying causes were summarized thus:

> Corporate financing, on a larger scale, is being done in the capital markets rather than through bank borrowings.

and

> New and improved methods of production [make] unnecessary the building up of large inventories.

It's convenient for journalists and quotable experts alike that there's so rarely a need to get up to speed on a new subject.

Extra Credit

Major C. H. Douglas's book, *Social Credit*, which Charlie Chaplin credited for his astute liquidation of stocks in 1928, was not forgotten. In Alberta, Canada, Douglas disciples had formed a political party. By 1935, Social Credit had come to power, promising everybody a $25 monthly stipend. How to pay for it? The obvious solution was to cut other provincial government expenditures, a large portion of which consisted of bond interest and relief. Bondholders, reckoned Premier William "Bible Bill" Aberhart, should be happy to accept a cut in their coupon from 5 percent to 2½ percent, while the Dominion of Canada should gladly take over the province's relief. "We want to make Alberta's ordinary credit gilt-edged," explained the radio-preacher-turned-politician, "before we use it as a foundation for Social Credit." In other words, the *Magazine of Wall Street* elaborated, the income redistribution scheme was to be funded by bondholders and the other Canadian provinces' taxpayers.

Bankrolling the Rally

In 1935, the American people didn't universally perceive a skyrocketing stock market as good news. The Great Crash remained a vivid memory and it was common to blame speculative excesses of the 1920s. For decades afterwards, the fear of rampant bulls persisted. For instance, Congress felt impelled to hold hearings when a dangerous-looking rally of 1954 vaulted stock prices all the way back to where they'd been 25 years earlier.

During November, Federal Reserve chairman Marriner Eccles tried to assuage the public's concerns about the 1935 bull market by pointing out that it had been paid for with cash. Broker loans weren't fueling the price rise, in contrast to the conditions of 1927–1928. Accordingly, said Eccles, there was no immediate need to raise margin requirements. Stocks rallied further in response to his statement.

The Fed chairman's observation was correct, as far as it went. New York Stock Exchange member borrowings represented less than 2 percent of the aggregate value of Big Board stocks as of December 1, 1935. The comparable figure shortly before Black Tuesday in 1929 was nearly 10 percent. Odd-lotters, who accounted for about one-third of trading volume, were buying for cash to a far greater extent than in the past.

But even though margin lending was subdued, there was nevertheless a credit-induced aspect to the 1935 rally. J. S. Williams, writing in the *Magazine of Wall Street*, argued that the observed cash buying was in reality financed by the federal government's deficit. Excess bank reserves reached a record $3 billion by year-end, aided by an influx of gold into the United States during the fall. Even the Banking Act of 1935, which liberalized national banks' authority to lend on real estate, failed to provide sufficient outlets for the idle cash. Commercial bankers considered entering new lines of business, such as personal loans and installment financing. The surfeit of lendable funds kept bond yields at their lowest level since the beginning of the century. As a consequence, investors shifted assets from bonds to stocks and then, inevitably, to lesser-quality stocks.

To be sure, the auto-led economic recovery garnered much of the credit for 1935's rising stock market. Also contributing was renewed confidence in the banking system. Bank suspensions totaled a mere 34, down from 4000 in 1933. Widespread dividend increases were yet another fundamental factor supporting the advance in stock prices. But notwithstanding the Fed chairman's disclaimer, the rally was at least partly nurtured by a favorable monetary climate. The upturn in inflationary expectations, which market pundits likewise pointed to in explaining the rally, was not unconnected with the easy money environment.

Tallying the Rally

Wall Street was in its glory once again in 1935. Between February and November, trading volume tripled. From the year's low of 96.71 of March 14, the Dow Jones Industrial Average soared as high as 148.44 on November 19. The aggregate market value of all stocks listed on the New York Stock Exchange rose by 46 percent between April 1 and December 1.

This move represented the largest and most sustained rally since 1929, a fact that wasn't universally regarded as cause for rejoicing. *Business Week* reminded its readers how "the 1929 will-o'-the-wisp faded out and left the stock industry up to its knees in the unlighted swamp." It was time for a letup, in that periodical's view, and the market obliged. The rally halted and volume fell off.

For the year as a whole, the Dow rose by 38.5 percent. The S&P 500 posted a whopping 47.66 percent total return. Bellwether issue General Motors was up by 153 percent for the year. RCA doubled, AT&T tripled, and U.S. Steel quintupled.

Grading the Forecasters

Loyalty to the chief perhaps accounted for Roosevelt Administration officials' increased confidence in an industrial revival as 1935 began. But Calvin Coolidge's Vice President, Charles G. Dawes, was similarly sanguine. He thought a pickup in durable goods would occur around midyear, simply because of the need to fill unmet demand of the preceding five years. The upturn would come, said Dawes, despite the New Deal rather than because of it. (Dawes also served as Comptroller of the Currency, ambassador to Great Britain, president of the Reconstruction Finance Corporation, and America's first Director of the Budget. In addition, he composed a work that was frequently performed by violinist Fritz Kreisler and he was cowinner of the 1925 Nobel Peace Prize. Alluding to Dawes's extraordinarily passionate oratorical style, Warren Harding called him "the only man I've ever seen who could go on talking with both feet in the air." Dawes was renowned as well for popularizing the use of expletives in public discourse.)

One of the few pessimists in public life was Roosevelt's former Director of the Budget, Lewis O. Douglas, who warned of the dangers of deficit spending. The *Magazine of Wall Street*'s A. T. Miller shared Douglas's fundamental concern about unbalanced budgets. Destructive inflation was the inevitable consequence, he thought. Yes, in the short run, farmers' purchasing power was up and consumer spending was recovering. But consumers were not buying houses, owing to residential construction costs that remained out of line. Sustained recovery and stock price improvement, said Miller, depended on a willingness of businesses to resume investing in plant and equipment. He insisted that they would do so only if Roosevelt relieved fears about his fiscal policies, ceased kowtowing to the American Federation of Labor, and steered Congress away from radical legislation.

While A. T. Miller's fundamental outlook seemed bleak, his technical assessment was fairly rosy. Stocks had made a classic double-bottom in July and September of 1934, he believed. Toward year-end, two weeks of horizontal drift had been followed by a one-day drop that initially looked worrisome. There was no follow-through, however, and volume declined in conjunction with the sell-off. Furthermore, Miller argued, sentiment had improved on perceptions of a profound shift in the Roosevelt Administration's attitudes and policies. "It is quite obvious that the Administration for many weeks has been striving to bring about a restoration of confidence on the part of private capital and private initiative," he declared.

Miller the technician called events better than Miller the fundamentalist. At the end of 1935, the *Magazine of Wall Street* was still fulminating about Roosevelt's extremism, but stocks were up sharply.

Laurence Stern, also writing in the *Magazine of Wall Street*, agreed with the market's perception that FDR was moderating his antibusiness stance by the end of 1934. He thought it undeniable that the peak in governmental experimentation had passed. Stern argued that while a balanced budget was not feasible in the near term, a start along the road to balance would give business the courage to resume investing. By shifting its focus from expensive public works programs to make-work projects, he contended, "it is practically and politically possible for the Administration to cut the deficit for the present fiscal year without withholding adequate relief for any needy person in the country."

Business Week, which shared Stern's cheerful outlook, handicapped the 1935 economy fairly accurately. The periodical was on target in foreseeing an upbeat year for auto sales. Another good call was its prediction of a new attempt to regulate the public utilities holding companies. On the money, too, was the publication's reckoning that a Supreme Court setback to the government's gold clause abrogation was "almost impossible." There was, however, no inkling in *Business Week*'s preview that the Supreme Court would soon undertake to dismantle the New Deal's industrial policies. Any revamping or elimination of the price-fixing provisions of the NIRA, thought the magazine's prognosticators, would be dictated by the White House.

The *Wall Street Journal*'s Bernard Kilgore was another prognosticator who had a pretty good handle on the positive developments of 1935. "Business probably will be better; quite a bit better, as measured by the commonly accepted indices," he wrote. Because of the unconventional state of money and banking, however, Kilgore thought the foundation had been laid only for a temporary boom, rather than lasting prosperity. Still, the system was not in as dire straits as some of FDR's opponents contended. "Through a series of *financial engineering* feats such as have never been performed before," Kilgore suggested, "I can see how a better foundation could be substituted later for the one that now exists." (Italics added for those who persist in believing that they saw something new in the Eighties and Nineties.)

News Travels Fast

Bernard "Barney" Kilgore, who called the events of 1935 so accurately, became chief of the *Wall Street Journal*'s Washington bureau that year at the age of 26. By then he had already gained a measure of fame as a result of the President's 1934 decision to take America off the gold standard. At a press conference, reporters pressed Roosevelt for technical details beyond the extent of his expertise in monetary matters. Finally, in exasperation, FDR told one of his questioners, "Read Kilgore in this morning's *Wall Street Journal* and you will get the answer."

Kilgore proceeded to launch the *Journal*'s weekly front-page feature, "Washington Wire," which was still going strong 60 years later. Returning to New York in 1941, he was named managing editor. In that post, he quickly ended the paper's traditional practice of closing its Monday edition on Saturday. The first time the *Journal* printed on Sunday, it carried a rather important story that it would have missed with the old practice—the bombing of Pearl Harbor. (This wasn't Kilgore's first demonstration of impeccable timing. He began his career at the *Journal* on the very day in September 1929 that the market hit an all-time high.)

Assuming the presidency of Dow Jones & Company in 1945, Kilgore brought the *Wall Street Journal* back from its low point following the Crash. Circulation had fallen from 50,000 in 1929 to a nadir of 28,000 in 1936. By the time he retired in 1966, it had passed one million, ranking the *Journal* second only to the *New York News* among American dailies.

Kilgore made no claims to being an expert on the stock market, but he saw very clearly the potential for a nationwide business newspaper. In pursuit of his vision, he fostered development of the technology that made it possible. The patented Electro-Typesetter made it possible for the first time to produce identical copy at widely dispersed points around the country.

It's Not Unusual

The 1935 bull market represented the fourth time in nine years that stocks had returned 35 percent or more. Within the 1927–1935 span came the century's only two back-to-back years of performance in that range. It was a concentration of exceptional years achieved neither before nor since.

During the middle portion of the period came not only the Great Crash of 1929, but also a more severe decline that bottomed out in 1932. Investors, having grown accustomed to roller-coaster performance, would have been skeptical if anyone had predicted that nearly two decades would pass before they'd enjoy another Very Good Year. But that gloomy forecast would have proven correct. The thrill didn't return until 1954.

In the interim, the U.S. economic recovery was cut short by the 1937 recession. Then, World War II caused immense dislocations and held back the development of new industries. Contrary to the fears of many economists, though, wartime prosperity did not set the stage for a new depression. Diversion of productive capacity had made consumer goods scarce. People were willing to spend to make up for lost time. Meanwhile, reunited couples touched off a baby boom that created massive new demand. The Korean conflict delayed the inevitable, but in 1954 the Dow Jones Industrial Average finally recovered to its 1929 peak.

∾ 1954 ∾

The backbone of America is business. Scuttle it, and America would be scuttled. Unlike Leftist revolutionaries, President Eisenhower recognizes this.

—B. C. FORBES, *Forbes*

The improvement in the standard of living here in the United States is readily recognizable but is less evident in some of the more backward countries abroad. American tourists, for instance, evince no surprise that natives in tropical countries are wearing shoes every day, whereas, before the war, these same natives—if they owned shoes at all—wore them only on Sundays and festive occasions.

—"E.K.A.," *Magazine of Wall Street*

The market is no longer a very reliable barometer of business prospects, or even a reliable barometer of business conditions. Before World War II, what happened to stock prices and the volume of stock transactions was a reasonably good omen of future business trends; turns in stocks prices anticipated turns in business 80 per cent of the time before 1939. Since then, however, the market has been a voice in the wilderness of lower Manhattan, unheeded and often off key.

—*Fortune*

At the Opening Bell

When 1954 began, stock prices had already been on a general rise for about three and a half months. Mounting enthusiasm during 1953 had enabled a new-issue boom to spill over from Canada, where it had been underway since the late 1940s. A major uranium discovery in Saskatchewan fanned the flames. Then came news that U.S. steelmakers were investing heavily in Canadian mines.

Heinz Biel was three years into writing a *Forbes* column that would run for a total of 33 years. He kicked off 1954 with pointed criticism of the recent craze for initial public offerings (IPOs). Biel took a particularly dim view of the notion that a low share price was evidence of good value:

> Canadian stock promoters have taken advantage of the American stock buyers' preferences and sold millions of low-priced but greatly overvalued shares to a gullible public. Similarly, financial pages are now full of advertisements of American investment firms offering penny shares to a naive public which is attracted by the "speculative opportunities" implied by the addition of descriptive adjectives like nuclear, oil, atomic, electronic, etc., to the corporate name, but few people ever seem to take the trouble of simply multiplying the price with the number of shares. If they did, they would realize that they might get a much better bargain by buying du Pont at twice its present price.

IPO promoters of later years likewise capitalized on the allure of hot industries, from alternative energy to biotechnology to the Internet. The low-priced stock illusion persisted, as well.

Slow Dancing

In contrast to the stock market's surge during late 1953, the U.S. economy was looking tired. Rated capacity utilization in the steel industry, which measured well above 100 percent earlier that year, had fallen below 90 percent. A major factor underlying that drop was a slowdown in auto production from a 7.5-million annual rate in July to under 6 million. Additionally, consumers were balking at new purchases of major appliances and businesses were turning conservative in their capital spending plans. Housing starts were down, to boot.

Despite the hints of oncoming recession, the 1954 outlook was not entirely bleak. *Iron Age* reported that although steel industry operating rates were down, the order outlook was improving. Furthermore, there was a chance that a monetary and fiscal stimulus would revive economic growth. *Barron's* columnist H. J. Nelson predicted that easier money would be the first line of attack. Tax relief was another possible tool, to be supplemented, in the event of a bona fide economic emergency, by public works spending.

The Boy Wonder

Nelson's prediction of an easier money policy required a bit of courage, considering the difficulty of pinning down the prevailing philosophy of the Federal Reserve. The central bank was now headed by William McChesney Martin, who, two decades earlier, had published Ben Graham's proposal for a commodity reserve. An FDR supporter nominated for the Fed chairmanship by fellow Missourian Harry Truman, Martin was twice reappointed by Republican Dwight Eisenhower, and once each by Democrats John Kennedy and Lyndon Johnson. He enunciated no guiding principles for Fed policy other than to say, "Our purpose is to lean against the winds of deflation or inflation, whichever way they are blowing."

Such apt metaphors were more to be expected of Martin than dogma. He famously remarked that the Fed's job was "to be the chaperon at the party who must take away the punch bowl just as the party gets going." Skeptical of both the quality of available statistics and the ability of economists to interpret them, Martin commented, "I rely on my staff the way a drunk relies on a lamppost; for support, not for illumination."

His own lights largely involved long experience in reading the tone of the financial markets. Son of a president of the St. Louis Fed, Martin made partner at the then small brokerage firm of A. G. Edwards at 24. Four years later, he was named a governor of the New York Stock Exchange, earning the nickname "Boy Wonder of Wall Street." Martin was just 31 in 1938 when the Big Board chose him as its first full-time paid president. The previous system, in which a member headed the Exchange, broke down when president Richard Whitney was caught embezzling. To Martin fell the task of cleaning up the mess.

Having observed the markets closely over several decades, Martin didn't share the view that public enthusiasm for stocks represented a public vote of confidence in America. When ordinary people began participating in the stock market, he worried that the boom-and-bust cycle of the 1920s would repeat itself. Martin issued such a warning during a 1965 bull episode, winning a new nickname—"William Mc-Chicken Little Martin." Wright Patman, the Congressman who'd advocated an inflationary solution to the veterans' bonus issue 30 years earlier, suggested that Martin had outlived his usefulness as custodian of monetary policy. (This attack was mild in comparison with a later 47-page Patman diatribe. The Texas populist charged that Martin's "money dictatorship" had cost taxpayers $200 billion of unnecessary interest, an "all-time record for waste." Patman also blasted the Fed Open Market Committee's measures to ensure confidentiality as gestapolike.)

A few hysterical criticisms aside, William McChesney Martin won wide respect during his nearly 19-year tenure. Richard Nixon contended that no one since Alexander Hamilton had exercised as much influence over economic policy for as long a period as Martin. This was a gracious remark from a politician who blamed his defeat in the 1960 presidential election in large measure on the Fed chairman's unwillingness to ease credit. Although Martin encouraged debate and strove for consensus, he dominated the central bank through his stature and strength of personality. A standing witticism during his chairmanship, as in that of Marriner Eccles, held that the Federal Reserve's Board of Governors consisted of a chairman and six random nonentities.

Who Will Buy?

Wall Street had a blue Christmas in 1953, despite the autumn/winter rally. Many brokerage firms lost money that year and were forced to shut down or merge. "Amidst the greatest prosperity in U.S. history," wrote Robert M. Bleiberg in *Barron's*, "Wall Street has become a depressed industry."

The problem was that although stock prices were on the rise, trading volume was stagnant. Americans had never shed the aversion to owning equities that arose from the 1929 crash. To the detriment of commission-dependent brokers, the financial institutions to which people entrusted their savings were not active transactors. Fewer shares were traded on the New York Stock Exchange in 1953 than in 1925, notwithstanding a sixfold expansion in the number of shares listed. As a result of the drastic decline in turnover, seats on the Exchange sold for little more than they had in 1899. Operating costs, meanwhile, were up sharply as a function of high post–World War II inflation. Despite a late-1953 hike in NYSE member firm commission rates, Wall Street's profit outlook was not encouraging.

How the Forecasters Handicapped 1954

B. C. Forbes adopted a "cautious, but not calamitous" stance on the economy. Even before the end of 1953, employment was down from a record level and production cutbacks were beginning to hit the auto business. The boom in steel and homebuilding also appeared to be over. On the bright side, Forbes observed in his eponymous magazine, the Eisenhower Administration was putting an end to "twenty years of extravagant, reckless, demagogic, devastating spending" by the Democrats. "No longer is the taxpayers' money being shovelled out thoughtlessly to countless countries throughout the world," the unabashedly partisan publisher rhapsodized. Curtailed, too, by the GOP was the "shameful coddling of labor leaders to attract votes." Forbes concluded that although short sellers might prosper for a while, the longer-term stock market trend was favorable.

Moody's Investors Service, early in 1954, advised investors to keep a quarter to a third of their portfolios in cash. Short-run speculators should be even less fully invested in stocks, Moody's reckoned, because the market did not look very bullish in the near term. The rival analysts at Standard & Poor's considered "a sustained general movement in either direction . . . unlikely over the medium term." There was no indication from these quarters that 1954 would go down as one of the greatest years in stock market history.

Joining Moody's and S&P in the cautious camp was A. T. Miller of the *Magazine of Wall Street*. The consensus economic forecast, he noted, called for a moderate recession, defined as a 5 percent to 8 percent decline in industrial production. With the experts accordingly predicting a 10 percent to 15 percent drop in corporate earnings, Miller thought it likely that the stock averages would remain close to their 1953 range. Over the near to intermediate term, though, he saw more downside than upside in prices.

On the positive side, Miller observed, the bond market was rallying. The Treasury and Federal Reserve had shifted from fighting inflation with hard money to battling deflation with easy money. Meanwhile, demand for credit was down. As bond yields fell, investors were increasingly inclined to switch to stocks, at least the higher-quality variety. The blue chips were further benefiting from an aversion to speculation that reflected the deteriorating outlook for business activity and corporate profits.

Somewhat reassuring, in Miller's view, were the reasonable valuations of stocks, notwithstanding the late-1953 run-up in prices. Industrials were trading, on average, at less than 10 times 1953 earnings. Dividend yields in excess of 6 percent made stocks appealing in light of prevailing yields of just over 3 percent on high-grade corporate bonds.

According to the *Wall Street Journal*'s "Abreast of the Market" column, stockbrokers generally agreed with A. T. Miller's assessment that there were no speculative excesses. They perceived that the holdings of pension funds and profit-sharing plans would stay put. Furthermore, many major institutions were less heavily invested in stocks than they had been a few years earlier. They were likely to buy on weakness, said Street experts. Finally, traders argued that dividends were conservative, in comparison with earnings, and therefore would be maintained if earnings trailed off modestly.

Lucien O. Hooper, whose career as a newsletter writer ultimately spanned 63 years, was fairly sanguine about the prospects for 1954. With nearly two of every five listed stocks yielding $6\frac{1}{2}$ percent or more, he reckoned that the downside in the economy was already well reflected in stock prices. Hooper, who had earlier served as president of the Financial Analysts Federation and as mayor of Westwood, New Jersey, estimated that, on average, professional economists expected business revenues to fall by 5 percent to 8 percent. The percentage decline in pretax profits would be somewhat greater, under those conditions.

Hooper predicted, however, that *net* income would hold up fairly well. The reason was that on December 31, 1953, the federal tax on excess profits arising from the Korean War had expired. Congress had levied the tax at the beginning of 1951, retroactive to January 1, 1950. (In classic Washington fashion, the measure sprang from the Revenue Act of 1950, originally introduced as a bill to *reduce* taxes.) Once a truce was declared in July 1953, the move was underway to end the excess profits tax.

Even more bullish than the end of the excess profits tax, in Hooper's view, was a recent decline in gold prices. This showed, he said, that fears of war were receding. Hooper reasoned that a resumption of trade with Eastern Europe and the China sphere could be a boon.

Smoke Gets in Your Eyes

One group of stocks that Lucien Hooper was not optimistic about in the short run was the cigarette companies. The problem, as he saw it, was not all the lung cancer talk. More harm had been done, Hooper contended, by the "cigarettes-are-bad-for-you-but-our-brand-is-not-as-bad-as-the-others" style of advertising. He regretted that many smokers had been scared by all this negativism. Nevertheless, Hooper saw some hope for the longer run. Producers would soon change the emphasis of their ads, he predicted. And after all, people would continue to smoke.

The chatter about lung cancer that Hooper downplayed had been growing steadily louder over the previous few years. Then, late in 1953, Dr. Ernst Wynder of the Sloan-Kettering Institute presented startling new evidence of a link between tobacco and cancer. Wynder found that laboratory rats showed a significant tendency to develop malignant tumors when their backs were shaven and then painted with liquefied cigarette tar.

Smokers might have found the experimental results more persuasive if the critters had inhaled the material. Unfortunately for health crusaders, Wynder had determined that it wasn't feasible to set up the experiment that way. Like most small animals, rats breathe exclusively through their noses, which have extremely effective filtering systems. In order to infuse enough potential carcinogens into rat lungs to make the test fair, the researchers would have had to pump in massive amounts of smoke. So much, in fact, that the test animals would have asphyxiated on carbon monoxide.

Don't Rain on My Parade

Dissenting from the upbeat stock market scenarios painted by B. C. Forbes and Lucien Hooper, some pundits were bearish at the beginning of 1954. *Business Week* reported that many Wall Streeters regarded the late-1953 upturn as a false rally.

What worried these pessimists was the prospect of intensifying business competition. A narrowing of profit margins, they feared, would offset the benefit of the disappearance of the excess profits tax. Already, aggregate production was down, demand for money was slack, and business failures were at their highest postwar level. As a matter of fact, said *Business Week*, business conditions would be worse if Uncle Sam hadn't bolstered the economy through deficit spending.

I Can't Give You Anything but Love, Baby

While Lucien Hooper waited for a bounce-back in cigarette stocks, his fellow *Forbes* columnist Michael Kourday urged investors to play the baby boom. Kourday didn't use that phrase, but he spotted the trend.

In the post–World War II era, Kourday noted, the population of junior consumers had swollen through both a rise in fertility rates and a decline in infant mortality. Accordingly, he recommended stocks in such areas as infant formula, baby food, and milk. (It wasn't surprising that Kourday, just three years out of college, was attuned to the youth market. He later worked in the brokerage industry and, during the early 1970s, managed the Dresser Industries pension fund.)

Also promising, thought Kourday, was Lionel Trains, Inc., a manufacturer of model electric trains. Fathers were just as enthusiastic about trains as the little ones, he pointed out, and therefore willing to shell out. To top it off, Lionel had just launched a three-dimensional camera. The toy company was thus entering "the rapidly growing stereoptic photography field."

In 1954, 3-D was the hottest segment of the photography market. The craze had taken off after World War II with the introduction of the Stereo Realist model, manufactured by the David White Company of Milwaukee. Fueling demand for the Stereo Realist were endorsements by Hollywood luminaries such as John Wayne, Bob Hope, and Jane Wyman (Academy Award-winning actress and ex-wife of actor Ronald Reagan). The biggest boost, however, came in early 1952, when *Life* magazine ran a picture of Dwight Eisenhower on a 3-D photo spree in Istanbul. By the middle of that year, the camera was selling at a 40,000-a-year rate and competing models were beginning to appear. Now-forgotten entries in the field included the Sputnik, the Owla, and the Belplasca. By the fall of 1952, the David White Company could boast that 40 percent of U.S. casket manufacturers employed its Realist 3-D photo viewer in their sales efforts.

Within a few years, however, the public lost interest in 3-D photography. The Stereo Realist was the only model produced throughout the 1960s, racking up cumulative sales of 130,000 units before being discontinued in 1971.

From an investment standpoint, the 3-D boom did not turn to total bust. Lionel, it is true, abandoned the field and commenced a long decline that ended in bankruptcy court in February 1982. Lionel shares, which Michael Kourday had recommended at 21, traded as low as $1\frac{3}{4}$ in the month of the Chapter 11 filing. But in that same year, it was reported that 35-millimeter stereo cameras in good condition sold for more on the secondhand market than when they were new. The product, in short, proved a better investment than the stock. Perhaps, to bend an old saw, every investor ought to have a hobby.

How It Went for Business

Consumers began to feel more secure in their jobs during 1954. Textile producers reported increased consumer interest in apparel and home furnishings. Aiding the rebound in that sector was a belated working off of excess inventories accumulated back in 1951. Manufacturers of railroad equipment suffered a far worse recession than business at large. Orders fell off by more than 30 percent from 1953, owing to the expiration of an accelerated-depreciation tax provision. Late in the year, though, the railroads' results began to improve and equipment orders picked up. Homebuilding, which got off to a slow start, also started to accelerate by midyear. Oil companies were up, then down, but ended the year strongly.

And the Market Boomed

Stocks began to rise early in 1954. A speculative tinge was evident from the outset, with the most active list increasingly featuring the sort of low-dollar-price stocks that *Forbes* columnist Heinz Biel had derided. By early March, the Dow was up by about 7 percent from 1953's close, climbing above the 300 mark. That level had not been seen since shortly before the Great Crash of 1929.

They Liked Ike

In the fall, attention turned to the 1954 congressional elections. Despite Eisenhower's 1952 triumph, the Republicans held only slim majorities in the Senate and House of Representatives. History showed that it was typical for the minority party to gain seats in midterm elections and it would require less than an average pickup for the Democrats to gain control of the House. Internal bickering within the GOP raised fears of a large Democratic majority there and in the Senate, as well. Investors worried that Eisenhower's middle-of-the-road policies would be replaced by antibusiness legislation.

Late in the campaign, however, the immensely popular President threw his energy into the fight. His involvement was reassuring to voters gravely concerned about the threat of atomic war with the Soviet Union. After all, this ex-general was thought of as the man who had brought the Korean War to an end. He personified the hopeful message of peace without appeasement.

Vice President Richard Nixon did not share Eisenhower's sunny manner, but he was indefatigable in his efforts on behalf of Republican candidates. In the space of 48 days, Nixon traveled to 95 cities in 30 states, made 204 speeches, and shook hands at a rate of 532 a day. In response to charges that Eisenhower frittered away too much time playing golf, Nixon claimed that Harry Truman had spent even more time playing poker. Particularly toward the end of the race, Nixon railed against communism. Political handicappers reckoned that if Eisenhower were not to seek reelection in 1956, Nixon would be the leading candidate for the Republican nomination.

When the votes were tallied, the Democrats squeaked through with only small majorities in the House and Senate. Businessmen heaved a sigh of relief, knowing that the result could have been far more unfavorable. A coalition of moderate Republicans and Democrats continued to dominate the legislative agenda.

On the day after the election, the Dow posted its largest one-day rise since September 5, 1939. The following session ended with the index at a 25-year high of 366.95. Perceived good news on the political front was reinforced by reports of vigorous corporate sales and earnings. Even stronger results were expected in the fourth quarter.

Hear Me Roar

In 1954 a young woman applied for a job at Merrill Lynch. A native of Cleveland, she had dropped out of Western Reserve University before finishing her undergraduate studies. After being turned down by the Thundering Herd for lacking a degree, she resolved to take the bull by the horns. In her application to Bache & Company, she lied, claiming to have completed college.

Muriel Siebert landed a position as a securities analyst and never looked back. In 1967 she became the first woman to buy a seat on the New York Stock Exchange. Siebert was also the first woman to own and operate her own brokerage house. From 1977 to 1982 she served as New York State Superintendent of Banking. Defeated in a race for the New York Republican nomination for Senate, she returned to the brokerage industry. The *New York Times* called her "probably the best-known woman on Wall Street."

Siebert had no difficulty competing with men, whether in finance, in politics, or what have you. "Part of the business still involves sitting down and drinking with people and God help you if you can't drink," she told an interviewer in 1986. At a recent lunch with someone who liked a drink, she reported, "I matched him Scotch for Scotch. There's no double standard here."

Although Muriel Siebert took advantage of a subsequent deemphasis of liquor in the securities industry, she didn't lose her taste for an investment bargain. In 1994, the brokerage house chief became one of 15 investors in Schmoozie's, a newly launched delicatessen in toney Bridgehampton, Long Island. Shareholders (at $35,000 a head) receive not only a cut of the profits, but also free Sunday morning home delivery of bagels, lox, and newspapers.

A Merry Little Christmas

On the whole, the tone of business entering 1955 seemed to vindicate the stock market's yearlong ebullience. The day after Thanksgiving, Chicago's Loop was so crowded with Christmas shoppers that the already doubled police contingent had to call for reinforcements. Consumers were opening their pocketbooks, encouraged by rising payrolls and falling unemployment. Also contributing to healthy retail sales were eased down payment and credit terms. Businesses deemed such concessions necessary in view of the cautiousness of customers who had taken on a bit too much personal debt during the 1952–1953 boom.

With Benefit of Hindsight

Securities analyst Lucien Hooper proved to have been on the mark in assessing the likely impact of the elimination of the excess profits tax. Pretax earnings per share for the S&P 400 industrials fell from $5.52 in 1953 to $4.98 in 1954. Net of taxes, however, EPS rose by nearly 5 percent, from $2.57 to $2.69.

Ford Motor Company posted its highest volume of car sales since 1925. Earnings remained a secret, because the company was not yet publicly traded. With all of the stock in the hands of the Ford family and the Ford Foundation, the automaker was under no obligation to publish financial statements. Company president Henry Ford II was willing to disclose, however, that after-tax income was up strongly over 1953. Ford's net rose despite a drop in pretax profit, in line with Lucien Hooper's start-of-the-year observation about the expiration of the excess profits tax. Notwithstanding Ford's bottom line improvement, executive bonuses were cut.

Cigarette consumption in the United States declined by an estimated 4 percent. The Agriculture Department cited publicity linking cigarettes to health problems, as well as a drop in the number of youngsters reaching smoking age. Additionally, the rapidly growing popularity of king-sized brands reduced the number of cigarettes smoked.

At the airlines, passenger miles rose in 1954, but the growth was concentrated in low-fare coach flights. The carriers added capacity aggressively and their costs rose more steeply than revenues. Airline stocks participated in the 1954 rally, but mostly remained below highs made way back in 1946.

With the Radio On

Around the time the Dow hit 300, radio commentator Walter Winchell began recommending stocks on his Sunday night broadcast. Always on the lookout for new audience attractions, Winchell had begun by giving horse-racing tips over the air. Stocks were a natural extension, for the market was in his blood. His uncle, George Winchel, had been a director of the New York Curb Exchange, forerunner of the American Stock Exchange.

Walter Winchell offered no incisive financial analysis, but listeners had learned to take his predictions seriously. Back in 1932, Winchell had reported in his newspaper column the arrival of gunmen from Chicago to stifle a New York gangster by the name of Vincent "Mad Dog" Coll. That very night, Coll was lured into a phone booth, where his body was riddled with more than 60 bullets. (Later, when called before a grand jury and asked for the source of his tip, Winchell responded resolutely, "I don't remember.")

Walter Winchell's huge following enabled him to work wonders for thinly traded stocks that he touted. Since the late Twenties, the onetime song-and-dance man had been recognized as the most influential force on Broadway, ranking among the world's highest-paid journalists. Mention in Walter Winchell's column carried the clout to vault obscure entertainers to stardom.

From show business, Winchell moved on to politics and world affairs. So immense did his prestige become over the years that during World War II, President Roosevelt personally intervened when the military tried to pressure the network to make him tone down his comments. Once, New York mayor Fiorello La Guardia scheduled a blackout for Winchell's regular broadcast time. "If you proceed with your plan to have a blackout Sunday," the miffed gossip reporter told the mayor, "I will announce that the only lights on in New York City are those at City Hall, where a poker game is in progress." Hizzoner promptly rescheduled the blackout. Beginning in 1948, Winchell vigorously boosted Eisenhower for the White House. On the way to the inauguration in 1953, a friend jokingly asked how it felt to elect a President. "You know, it's really quite something," Winchell replied, in dead earnest.

Typically, Winchell's stock picks skyrocketed on massive volume on the morning following his broadcast, only to come back down to earth a short while later. Financial columnist Sylvia Porter sniffed that although many of his recommendations were moneymakers, investors could have done just as well in any of hundreds of stocks levitated by the 1954 rally. Winchell retaliated by reporting in his newspaper column that an unnamed "female financial genius" had dropped a bundle on a silver stock. (In fact, Porter rode out the stock's decline and eventually made a tidy profit.)

Advance to "Go"

Walter Winchell's 1954 stock picks were as volatile as his own personality, which embroiled him in a number of legendary feuds. The averages moved up steadily, however. After flirting with its 1929 all-time high of 381.37, the Dow dropped only momentarily on August's news that the Russians had the H-bomb. The market resumed its escalation in September. On November 17, the Dow regained its previous peak for the first time in 25 years.

It had taken the Dow nearly a quarter of a century, from October 26, 1929, to March 5, 1954, to claw its way back to the 300 mark. Less than 10 months later, prices smashed through the 400 barrier. At year-end, the market stood at 404.39, up 44 percent for the year. Total return on the S&P was a sizzling 52.62 percent, the highest since 1933.

Why Did the Market Run?

In seeking to identify the causes of the 1954 bull market, we're probably safe in ruling out one hypothesis advanced by the Senate Banking and Currency Committee one year later. The Senators decided that the rise in stock prices required investigating, contrasting as it did with the general economy's listlessness. On the first day of hearings, reported the *New York Times*, "Walter Winchell's stock market tips dominated."

The Power of Negative Thinking

Instrumental in the remarkable rally of 1954 were investors' low expectations at the outset. As the year began, the most ballyhooed recession in U.S. history, in *Business Week*'s estimation, was already underway. Industrial production was falling. Some economists warned that conditions would deteriorate into a full-fledged depression. The Great Depression of the Thirties was a recent enough memory to render consumers and investors exceedingly cautious.

In the end, the worst did not come to pass. No mass unemployment developed. By June, responding to the pleas of business, the Treasury and Federal Reserve Board retreated from their hard money policy. (*Forbes* columnist H. J. Nelson's prediction on monetary affairs was thus vindicated.) At year-end, industrial production was on the rise. A feeling set in that thanks to wise monetary and fiscal policies, periodic depressions were no longer inevitable.

Lucien Hooper reported that the public had grown more willing to own stocks during the course of 1954. "The long period of chronic undervaluation of common stocks is coming to an end," he proclaimed. Moreover, in his view, the optimism was justified, even though he saw some risk of the market overheating. Companies had raised their dividends, in aggregate, during the year. The baby boomers were emerging from infancy, which meant that their consumption would increase. Accelerating technological development led to rapid obsolescence. Also, public companies continued to sell for less than their replacement value, despite the big price advances of 1954. "Add to all this," Hooper concluded, "a new generation of investors (or speculators) who knew not 1929!"

Bullishness was further reinforced by an apparent simmering down of the Cold War. The downside was a cutback in defense spending, but that contractionary effect was offset by a rebound in consumer spending and a boom in construction. The Republicans' comparatively small losses in the congressional elections further heartened businesspeople. Throughout 1954 and beyond, stocks benefited from a pervasive optimism that Americans of subsequent decades would recall fondly. After a brief jolt to this upbeat mentality, the market would enjoy another Very Good Year just four years later.

∾ 1958 ∾

*V*erging into 1958, investment-speculative sentiment remains more cautious and apprehensive than at any time in recent years—and with good reason. It has been chilled by the hard fact of important market decline: the widest decline since that of 1946–1947. And it has been chilled by the visible development of business recession, plus marked recent acceleration thereof.

—A. T. MILLER, *Magazine of Wall Street*

*Y*ou can count on our continued efforts to foster credit conditions that will contribute to high levels of business and employment. . . . But you cannot count on us to do the whole job by ourselves: business and employment do not live by credit alone.

—WILLIAM MCCHESNEY MARTIN,
Chairman of the Federal Reserve Board

*T*he institutional investors are largely responsible for promoting the new prestige of common stocks. Every institution now considers equities an essential part of an investment portfolio, and in most cases, it is a growing part.

—*Business Week*

Let Me Play among the Stars

The 1958 rally was set up by a sharp decline during the preceding fall. On October 4, 1957, the Soviet Union launched Sputnik I, the first man-made satellite. Suddenly, the United States appeared to have lost its technological edge. "Proof of Russia's superiority in certain scientific developments, with possibly serious military implications, came as a wholly unexpected shock," wrote Heinz Biel in *Forbes*.

To make matters worse, America's political leadership didn't appear to be responding to the challenge. President Eisenhower told the press that Sputnik didn't raise his apprehensions one iota. Secretary of Defense Charles Wilson, the former head of General Motors, dismissed the Russian achievement as "a nice technical trick." To Clarence Randall, the White House adviser for foreign economic policy, Sputnik I was "a silly bauble." The Pentagon compounded the blow to American prestige by announcing a cut in aircraft procurement.

Democratic Senate Majority Leader Lyndon Johnson later recalled that even after Sputnik II soared into orbit, complacency reigned in Washington:

> I said we better get going, we better step up our effort. My opponent said, and this is approximately what he said, about what he said, "I am not worried about somebody putting a basketball in the air that says, 'Beep, beep, beep.' I would rather lob one into the men's room in the Kremlin."

Stuck on the Ground

By October 21, 1957, the Dow Jones Industrial Average was down by 10 percent from its pre-Sputnik I, October 3 level. A turnaround began on October 23, following hints that the Federal Reserve System was beginning to loosen credit conditions. At least in part, the easing was necessitated by "the chaos into which defense production and financing were being plunged," according to H. J. Nelson, in *Barron's*. President Eisenhower also stoked the rally on October 23 by undertaking a tour of the country to explain his economic and defense policies.

The improved tone continued for six weeks. Aiding the market during this span was a definitive easing of monetary policy. On November 14, four Federal Reserve banks, including New York, chopped the discount rate from $3\frac{1}{2}$ percent to 3 percent. This welcome news caught most investors off guard. As recently as October 16, New York Fed president Alfred Hayes had said in a key policy speech, "I hope you agree that it would be a great mistake to relax credit constraint just as we see some hope of achieving the price stability that we have all sought so ardently." And just one week before the discount rate cut, Federal Reserve Board chairman William McChesney Martin was still arguing that the main policy focus ought to be inflation, rather than recession.

The stock market remained healthy until the news arrived that President Eisenhower had suffered a chill. On November 26, the Dow fell nine points on the revelation that the chill, in truth, was a mild stroke. It was Ike's third serious illness in just over two years and some pundits thought that health problems might force him to resign. (Fortunately, commented A. T. Miller in the *Magazine of Wall Street*, "Vice President Nixon has become increasingly equipped, regardless of differences of opinion about his stature, to assume major responsibilities, if necessary, and has gained considerably in public respect.")

On December 6, the United States made a dramatic effort to get back into the space race. Using a Vanguard rocket, the Navy attempted to launch the first American satellite. As Tom Wolfe described the scene in his account of the space program, *The Right Stuff*, the first nationally televised countdown culminated in "a mighty surge of noise and flames." Then the rocket lifted off—by approximately six inches. The first stage exploded, while the remainder of the rocket sank "very slowly, like a fat old man collapsing into a Barcalounger." "KAPUTNIK!" screamed the headlines following the fiasco. The demoralized stock market suffered another relapse.

How High the Moon?

Throughout 1957, investors fretted about inflation. With the help of collective bargaining, workers were obtaining repeated wage hikes. "Investors were justifiably worried about irresponsible labor union demands for wage increases going far beyond their legitimate claims to participate in the benefits from rising productivity," wrote *Forbes*'s Heinz Biel. Industry, unfettered by much foreign competition, had little difficulty passing along labor cost increases to consumers. The resulting rise in price levels triggered further pay raises for the approximately one million workers covered by contracts containing automatic cost-of-living adjustment clauses. Thanks to this cycle, the Consumer Price Index had been rising almost uninterruptedly since February 1956.

Lord, Mister Ford, Look What You've Done

Ford Motor Company began 1958 with its own hole to dig out from. It was called the Edsel. The costly disaster became synonymous with mismanagement and bad luck in new product launches.

For starters, the concept may have been too ambitious. Ford had just two medium-priced-to-luxury divisions (Lincoln and Mercury) to compete with General Motors's four (Cadillac, Buick, Oldsmobile, and Pontiac). The carmaker's notion wasn't simply to introduce a new model, but to launch a new division in competition with makes that dated to the beginnings of GM, 50 years earlier.

The new car's original design, by some reports, was superb. Soon, however, the accountants descended on the project and demanded cost-saving design changes. The vehicle wound up with a prow variously likened to a horse collar and a toilet seat. Ford's advertising agency, Foote, Cone, and Belding, came up with 18,000 possible names for the new car. These were winnowed to 16. Not included among the finalists were the following suggestions by poet Marianne Moore:

- Anticipator
- Hurricane Hirundo
- Mongoose Civique
- Pastelogram
- Pluma Piluma
- Utopian Turtle Top

The top two selections, Citation and Corsair, along with runners-up Pacer and Ranger, survived as the names of the new car's four varieties. For the make itself, Ford rejected all 18,000 candidates in favor of the given name of its president's father. The name had "personal dignity and meaning" to the automaker's executives, reflecting the great respect that Edsel Ford enjoyed in Detroit. Elsewhere, "Edsel" sounded funny.

When the 1957 recession began, the medium-priced segment's share of total sales started to decline. Finally, the Edsel's scheduled launch date, August 27, arrived. The Soviet Union chose that very day to announce that it possessed a missile capable of dropping a bomb anywhere in the United States.

Optimists might have reasoned that American defense spending would pick up in reaction. Such a development would likely give the economy and the stock market a welcome boost. Be that as it may, the Soviet Union's announcement didn't put people in a car-buying mood. All automakers were finding demand disappointing, especially in light of new model introductions and easier credit conditions. Consumers were constrained by price increases on new models, which coincided with a drop in the trade-in value of used cars.

Ford faced the further handicap of a botched new product. By the beginning of 1958, New York City's largest Edsel dealer had turned in its franchise. The slumping automobile sector seemed a bad omen for the stock market. "For as autos go," observed George W. Mathis in the *Magazine of Wall Street*, "so go steels, primary metals, machine tool companies, industrial machinery makers, and to a lesser extent, the rubber companies, industrial chemicals, and of course, the hundreds of smaller entities turning out component parts for the auto makers."

What a Tangled Web

"The Web Begins to Grow," proclaimed a *Business Week* headline on January 11, 1958. Was it the scoop of the century on the earliest work on the Information Superhighway? No, just an interim report on construction of the U.S. interstate highway system.

Called the biggest public works project of all time, the interstate system was to consist of 41,000 miles of highways, along with a network of auxiliary roads. For investors, the most salient point was the $2 billion that would be shelled out in 1958 for such products as paving materials, dynamite, and bridge steel.

Not surprisingly, *Business Week* also reported that the originally estimated 13-year construction period was being stretched out. The initial $27 billion cost estimate was getting upped to around $37 billion. Still, one aspect of the budget was showing a favorable variance. To pay for construction of the interstate system, special taxes had been levied on gasoline, tires, and other motor products. The government, in short, was extracting more revenue from taxpayers than originally projected.

Smoke, Smoke, Smoke That Cigarette

"Many a smoker, with a mouthpiece of cellulose acetate between him and the tobacco, is inhaling joyously without worrying about supposedly injurious tars and resins." Filter tips were in and the cigarette manufacturers' blues were out, as George J.W. Goodman told the story in *Barron's*.

Those worries about possible links with cancer, which cast a pall over the tobacco industry in 1954, had created a new opportunity. "In cigarettes, as in any mass consumer product," said P. Lorillard's president, Lewis Gruber, "there is only one overall sales problem: to find out what the consumer wants and give it to him." Nearly half of them, it appeared, wanted filters.

According to Goodman, only one of the filters on the market actually appeared to filter out harmful ingredients. Cigarette makers were happy, all the same. Filter-tip cigarettes sold at a premium to the traditional variety, yet cost no more to produce. (Lower tobacco content offset the added costs of producing and installing the filter.) Profits, as a consequence, were up throughout the industry.

In short, said Goodman, the cigarette industry had recovered from the cancer scare and resumed its healthy (no irony intended) growth. Naturally, new and damaging evidence could cause an industry relapse at any time. But the scaredy-cat smokers had already been frightened off, or so the manufacturers claimed. Furthermore, wrote Goodman, the companies argued that "should worse come to worst, and definite evidence link cancer to smoking, they might be able to isolate and remove any disease-producing element."

Up, Up, and Away

The stock market's lackluster 1957 performance persisted into early 1958. Only a modest advance greeted a drop in the discount rate from 3 percent to 2¾ percent, led by the Philadelphia Federal Reserve Bank. On January 31, stocks responded indifferently to the successful launch of Explorer I, America's answer to Sputnik I.

Auto sales remained slow, with manufacturers projecting first-quarter output of well under 1.5 million passenger cars. That was down from an estimate just a few weeks earlier of about 1.7 million and contrasted with year-earlier assemblies of almost 1.8 million. Sagging auto production in turn restrained demand for steel. Copper and aluminum were notably weak, as well.

February, however, proved to be the market's 1958 low point. The upturn from that point was consistent with the earlier view of some analysts that the impact of the Federal Reserve's November 1957 discount rate cut would begin to be felt around then. By March, the Dow began to pick up momentum.

A Multiple Fallacy

At the moment a great rally was beginning, corporate profits were dismal. Earnings for the Dow Jones industrials were down by 38 percent, year over year, in 1958's first quarter. For rails, the decline measured a staggering 85 percent. Based on these figures, prevailing price-earnings ratios were the highest since 1946, calculated Heinz Biel in *Forbes*.

Taken at face value, P/E ratios left no room for optimism. There was a fallacy in the argument, however. "Abnormally low profits are no more indicative of future earnings power than are the peak profits in a boom year," wrote Biel. "To use them as a yardstick for measuring the long-range investment values of common stocks is bound to lead to a wrong conclusion." Confident that the low point of the recession was already past, Biel urged investors not to wait too long before getting into the market. Conventional valuation measures gave the opposite—and wrong—advice.

It's Too Darn Hot

Between April and June, stock prices climbed with the help of accelerating mutual fund inflows. Pension funds also fueled the flames. Lucien Hooper of *Forbes* deemed the continued rally illogical. He insisted that valuations were rising only because of the press of dollars seeking investments. Attempts by investors to estimate future corporate earnings or time the business recovery had no role in the price surge. (Shades of 1908 and 1915!) Hooper's fellow *Forbes* columnist, Heinz Biel, confirmed the growing influence of pension funds:

> With a host of institutional stock buyers combing the list of eligible stocks with thorough due diligence, it is becoming increasingly difficult to detect outstanding values among investment-grade equities, stocks that combine quality and opportunity.

Overvaluation was becoming a favorite theme of financial columnists. A. T. Miller of the *Magazine of Wall Street* perceived that cyclicals and growth stocks were being priced on the basis of past rather than future earnings. *Forbes's* Biel decried the speculative atmosphere that allowed a comparatively staid stock such as U.S. Tobacco to rise by 33 percent within one week, solely on rumors. The basic trend remained upward, said Biel, but the second quarter's rise had been too much too soon.

As in the 1954 rally, Miller warned, the market was getting ahead of improvement in business activity. The difference was that the 1953–1954 recession had been milder than the 1957–1958 downturn. Thanks to the expiration of the Korean War–related excess profits tax, earnings rose in 1954, on a year-over-year basis. In contrast, 1957's downturn in earnings of recession-sensitive industries was the sharpest, in percentage terms, since 1938.

At midyear, the *Magazine of Wall Street*'s A. T. Miller reckoned that earnings for the Dow Jones industrials would do well to recover to around 70 percent of their 1957 level. H. J. Nelson, writing in *Barron's*, was likewise guarded about the strength of the economy. He noted that unfilled orders for all manufacturing concerns had been declining steadily since the end of 1956.

Certain indicators, it was true, suggested that the recession was bottoming out. Miller, however, judged that the coming economic recovery was already reflected in stock prices. "Yet," asked Lucien Hooper of *Forbes*, "what difference does all logic make if investors keep on buying quality blue chips just because they have money and want to put it in the stock market?" He noted that investment counselors were reluctant to advise clients to hold out for better values. There was simply too much money around and too few investors willing to supply shares.

What's in a Name?

With cigarette sales back on track, the five leading competitors were fighting fiercely for market share. One key battleground as 1958 began was the new mentholated filter tip category. R. J. Reynolds had introduced the concept with Salem, which proved an immediate success. Philip Morris quickly met the competition with Spud, a brand inherited a few years earlier in the liquidation of the Axton-Fisher Tobacco Company. "Spud, for some reason, never has caught on," *Barron's* noted. Perhaps Philip Morris could have solved the mystery by analyzing the Edsel's problems.

Follow the Money

If the prospects for economic growth didn't justify the magnitude of the 1958 rally, perhaps monetary conditions did. During the great bull markets of 1933 and 1935, inflation had been regarded as the equity investor's friend. By the 1970s, inflation was commonly viewed as the enemy of all financial assets. At roughly the midpoint of that interval, in the 1950s, many investors still may have regarded its unambiguously injurious effect on bonds as a signal that capital would migrate to stocks.

As of mid-1958, equity buyers who considered inflation bullish had plenty of reason to feel encouraged. For starters, President Eisenhower now conceded that the 1959 budget, rather than being in balance, could produce a deficit as great as $10 billion. By the summer, Treasury Secretary Robert Anderson projected a $12-billion shortfall. In lieu of the federal spending rollback that Ike's budget proposal had assumed, Anderson spoke of a new plateau for outlays. Furthermore, investors perceived that the Federal Reserve Board was merely paying lip service to fighting inflation. That, at least, was the judgment of H. J. Nelson of *Barron's*. Certainly, the monetary authorities were under pressure to pump up the still-sluggish economy. One indication of the clamoring for countercyclical measures was an April 17 disclaimer by Federal Reserve vice chairman C. Canby Balderston:

> Federal Reserve policy alone is not adequate to curb the excesses of boom periods or to turn recession into recovery. Neither monetary policy nor fiscal policy can maintain economic stability if psychology runs rampant.

Unspoken was the reality that if the Fed could be induced to open the money spigot a bit more, the psychology would surely take on a more positive cast.

The Years Have Changed You Somehow

In June 1958 Benjamin Graham reviewed the progress of the calculating machine company he'd been warned to avoid, four decades earlier, by a wise veteran. IBM's history since being listed in 1915 illustrated, in Graham's view, a fundamental shift in the stock market's orientation. Investors no longer focused on a company's intrinsic characteristics, but instead on future expectations.

By 1926, the former Computing-Tabulating-Recording Company had boosted its net profit from $691,000 to $3.7 million. No longer did its common stock represent almost exclusively intangible assets, as it had when Graham's mentor had dismissed the shares as "water." The New Era was in full swing, with the market on the verge of two back-to-back Very Good Years. Yet IBM's 1926 average price of 45 put it at the same price-earnings multiple (seven) and dividend yield (6.7 percent) that it had carried in 1915. As a matter of fact, the year's low quotation of 31 was barely above tangible book value. In that sense, the market was valuing IBM far more conservatively than it had 11 years earlier, despite the company's greatly improved balance sheet.

After the great bull market of the Twenties, however, the old approach to pricing stocks disappeared. By 1936, IBM's P/E multiple averaged $17\frac{1}{2}$ for the year. Twenty years later, the average multiple was $32\frac{1}{2}$ and in 1957 it soared to 42. IBM, which traded at seven times earnings when Ben Graham entered the investment business, was now valued at seven times *book value*.

As Graham saw it, reforms in accounting and corporate management had squeezed most of the water out of balance sheets at major companies such as IBM. But investors and speculators had put a different kind of water right back into stock prices, he argued. The greater the emphasis on future earning power, the more uncertain becomes the enterprise's true value, and therefore the more inherently speculative is the common stock. To Graham's way of thinking, the changes in the market since 1915 were not entirely to the good.

In Every Clime and Place

Notwithstanding suggestions that investors' hopes for economic recovery were exaggerated, the rally continued. In July, President Eisenhower sent the U.S. Marines into Lebanon. That country's pro-Western president, Camille Chamoun, had requested aid in quelling a rebellion against his pro-Western policies. In the United States a stock buying panic resulted. "On balance," ventured Walter Morgan, president of the Wellington Fund, "the economic effect of the Mideast development is expansionary." He credited the crisis with shifting attention from the recession, at a time when business recovery was already underway. Imrie deVegh of the deVegh Mutual Fund added that the Lebanese affair might result in increased defense spending, which would stimulate the economy. At the same time, deVegh pointed out, increased government spending could lead to higher taxes, which would adversely affect stock prices.

Near the end of July, Armco Steel led a 3 percent industry price increase on sheet and strip steel. Investors cheered this sign that industry would offset its labor cost increases, come what may. The aluminum industry followed with a price increase of its own, despite the fact that one-third of its capacity lay idle. Just one week earlier, aluminum producers had asked the government to help relieve their plight.

In mid-August, the Federal Reserve reversed the trend toward easing of credit inaugurated in November 1957. A hike in the discount rate from $1\frac{3}{4}$ percent to 2 percent signaled that the battle against inflation wasn't over. Stocks beat a hasty retreat.

America Picks Itself Up and Gets Back in the Race

Lyndon Johnson dissented from Washington's initially complacent reaction to Sputnik I. Any American who could read and write was frightened, he claimed. Russia appeared to be gaining the upper hand, militarily.

The politically adroit Senate majority leader spied a chance to make a deal. Congressional Democrats had been resisting President Eisenhower's proposals to develop long-range nuclear missiles. The fears aroused by Sputnik I, however, provided the impetus to support missile development in pursuit of space exploration. In the process, LBJ angled to create jobs in his home state of Texas.

Johnson obtained Republican backing to convene hearings on the competition to conquer space, which dramatized how badly the United States had fallen behind. From this glare of publicity came the creation of a Senate space committee, with Johnson as chairman. In addition, the Space Act of 1958 established the National Aeronautics and Space Administration (NASA), headquartered in Houston. Investors now had tangible evidence that the United States was getting back into the space race to win.

Johnson skillfully cast the issue in terms of national security. Later on, he used his typically homespun humor to explain why it was so important to match Soviet expenditures on missiles. It seems that a Texan enlisted to fight with the Confederacy in 1861, vowing he'd be back soon. "We can lick those damyankees with broomsticks," he boasted. Two years later, the man returned, minus a leg. His neighbors asked the bedraggled, wounded veteran what had gone wrong. Hadn't he claimed it would be easy to lick the North, fighting with broomsticks? Replied the rebel, "The trouble was the damyankees wouldn't fight with broomsticks."

A Bountiful Harvest

In the autumn, the U.S. economic recovery began to look more substantive. Inventory rebuilding by steel customers started to accelerate. Steelmakers' operating rates, which had fallen to 54 percent during the first half of 1958, were expected to reach 80 percent in the comparable 1959 period. Auto companies were sounding more optimistic as well, despite huge third-quarter losses at Chrysler and Edsel-burdened Ford.

Against the backdrop of weak corporate profits, Federal Reserve

Board governor J. L. Robertson said on October 21, the stock market's enthusiasm wasn't entirely reassuring. Perhaps, he suggested, the surge in equity prices reflected in part a "growing acceptance of the doctrine of the inevitability of inflation." If so, the Fed had a duty to head off "potentially destructive forces" by preserving the integrity of the dollar.

Two days later, the monetary authority boosted the discount rate from 2 percent to 2½ percent. The action was described as a technical adjustment, designed to discourage commercial banks from borrowing from the Fed in order to buy Treasury bills. Nevertheless, stocks suffered their first full-week decline since mid-August, when the central bank had first shifted course from easing to tightening.

Along with the Fed's rumblings about inflation, the market was hampered by a lack of depth. This characteristic rendered prices vulnerable to occasional abrupt corrections. A gross decline of 20 points hit the Dow industrials during October 14–16, followed by a 34-point gross drop during November 17–25.

The main tendency, however, remained bullish. For all the talk of institutional buying, argued H. J. Nelson of *Barron's*, small investors were providing the real impetus. "There can be little question," he wrote, "that speculative fever is at the highest point since the excited days of 1928 and 1929." In fact, Nelson calculated, expected earnings were being assigned a higher multiple (close to 20) than in that pre-Crash period.

Balancing Act

As year-end approached, the White House cheered the market by disclosing that it would submit a balanced budget. This feat was to be achieved despite record peacetime defense expenditures and without raising taxes. Instead, the Eisenhower Administration proposed to reduce spending by terminating temporary programs in agriculture, housing, and unemployment insurance.

Analysts didn't simply assume, however, that fiscal restraint would be accepted uncritically by Congress. For one thing, the housing industry wasn't expected to take the new austerity measures lying down. In addition, the defense budget was still up for grabs. The Pentagon hadn't yet given up entirely on its efforts to economize, despite the Sputnik shock. Chance Vought Aircraft, based in Dallas, had been hit especially hard by the sudden cancellation of the Regulus II missile. Fortunately, the company was able to call on strong political allies.

House Speaker Sam Rayburn, Senate majority leader Lyndon Johnson, and head of the House subcommittee on defense appropriations George Herman Mahon were all Texans.

What a Peculiar Way to Run a Railroad Line!

Rail stocks, which hit a 55-year low in December 1957, rose by a record 61 percent in 1958. According to A. T. Miller of the *Magazine of Wall Street*, the group's surge reflected an earnings rise that was partly an illusion. Railroads were holding back on both capital improvements and routine maintenance in order to rebuild their depleted cash positions. Furthermore, said Miller, if any permanent cost savings were achieved, the railworkers' unions would capture the benefits sooner or later.

Whatever Goes Up

The *Kiplinger Magazine* of December 1958 made the following rather startling claim: "Many, many U.S. companies are now deep in production of things for the conquest of gravity." Was Roger Babson (see "1928" chapter) not getting dotty, after all, when he launched his search for an antigravity substance?

Actually, the subject of the article was the booming aerospace industry. Rockets and missiles, according to the periodical, were just the beginning. "To come (and very probably within your lifetime)," predicted the author, "will be rocket mail ships, rocket airliners, rocket freighters. . . . Plans for these projects are already on the design boards." There they remained, but the space race became a hot investment concept after Sputnik went into orbit.

The space race launched a great many jokes, as well. "Take me to your leader" swiftly progressed from punch line to catchphrase. In a variation on the theme, an extremely short alien approached an earthling, saying, "Never mind your leader. Take me to your ladder." Soviet rocket scientists, it was rumored in another story, planned to send several cows into orbit. They could then claim credit for the herd shot round the world. Meanwhile, astronauts from (allegedly lamebrained nation of the joke teller's choice) announced their intention to travel to the sun. "Fools!" cried an American. "Your spacecraft will be incinerated by the sun's intense heat." "Imbecile!" replied the intellectually impaired space travelers. "We're going at night."

Upbeat to the End

Stocks finished 1958 on a high note. For the year, the Dow Jones Industrial Average rose by 34 percent. Total return for the Standard & Poor's 500 measured 43.37 percent.

As it turned out, A. T. Miller's expectation of at best a 70 percent earnings rebound proved too pessimistic. The Dow industrials' profits reached 77 percent of their 1957 level. Still, no 1958 quarter was up over the corresponding 1957 period. Nor can it be said that the 1958 stock rally was an anticipation of a big profit gain in the succeeding year. Full-year 1959 earnings fell short of the 1957 mark. All in all, it's difficult to ascribe the extraordinary stock market performance of 1958 to investors' anticipation of extraordinary corporate profits.

Telephone's Hour

Contributing to the market's year-end optimism was American Telephone & Telegraph's precedent-shattering decision to split its stock three-for-one. The company further stunned the market by announcing that the three shares would receive annual dividends of $9.90, a 10 percent increase from the previous $9-a-share rate. Only a month earlier, AT&T's directors had reaffirmed the old payout. The $2.25 quarterly rate had remained unchanged for so long that, in the words of Business Week, it "had the appearance of immortality."

According to the periodical, an AT&T stock split had been one of the oldest rumors on Wall Street. Not long before the speculation was finally vindicated, AT&T's shares had climbed to over $200, only to relapse to $194 when the board made no announcement. Then, with the stock trading at $202, the split and dividend hike were disclosed. Buy orders poured in so fast that trading was temporarily suspended. Upon resumption of trading, the first block changed hands at $225. Overnight, brokers said, the quintessential "widows and orphans" stock had been transformed into a genuine growth stock.

Speculators Love Lucy

Toward the end of 1958, Business Week spotted a danger signal in the market. Initial public offerings were jumping to large premiums following distribution. Market pros attributed the trend to indiscriminate buying. Comparably unbridled enthusiasm for IPOs hadn't been seen since 1946, according to some observers.

Among the most dramatic gainers was Desilu Productions, which quickly soared 32 percent after the subscription books closed. From an initial offering price of 10, the shares climbed as high as 29. At that level, the half-interest retained by founders Desi Arnaz and Lucille Ball was worth nearly $15 million. Just a short while earlier, they had turned down an offer of that amount for the entire company from oilman Clint Murchison.

Such success was customary for the company's founders. Their comedy series, *I Love Lucy*, had become the top-rated program in America within six months of its premiere. Two-thirds of all television households tuned in regularly. When Ball coordinated a real-life cesarean delivery to facilitate the addition of a baby son to the cast, 44 million viewed the blessed event. President Dwight Eisenhower's swearing-in ceremony, scheduled in an opposing slot, drew only 29 million. "This was a banner week," reported Walter Winchell in his trademark staccato. "The nation got a man and Lucy got a boy."

By 1958, Arnaz and Ball had given up the grind of a weekly series. A successor program, *The Lucy and Desi Comedy Hour*, ended when Ford Motor Company was forced to abandon its sponsorship in the wake of the Edsel's flop. But Desilu churned out one hit show after another, including *December Bride* (which became the second-highest-rated comedy series), *Our Miss Brooks*, and Danny Thomas's *Make Room for Daddy*.

Along the way, Desilu made a shrewd acquisition of the RKO film studios. General Tire & Rubber had run into a tax crisis and needed a quick capital loss to offset some profits. Arnaz was offered the chance to buy RKO if he could make up his mind within 24 hours. He sought the advice of Howard Hughes, who'd sold the studios to General Tire just two years earlier. "Grab it!" the billionaire replied immediately. "Even if you tear the studios down and turn them into parking lots, you've gotta make money." (In fact, one potential buyer of the real estate was a cemetery adjacent to RKO's Gower City lot that was running out of burial space.)

With the acquisition, Desilu Productions became the largest motion picture and television facility in the world. Seemingly unlimited in their talent for making a buck, Lucy and Desi struck oil on the RKO Culver City lot. Acting on a tip from a studio watchman, they developed a well that produced 120 barrels a day.

The television stars' capitalist exploits carried a certain irony. Five years prior to the Desilu IPO, the phenomenal popularity of *I Love Lucy* was threatened by the revelation that in 1936, Lucille Ball had registered to vote as a Communist. Arnaz quickly sprang to her defense, proclaiming that there was nothing red about Lucy except her hair—and even that was dyed. Desi reassured Americans that he, along with his wife, despised the Communists. After all, it was they who had forced his family to flee Cuba a quarter of a century earlier. Persuaded by this logic, the public accepted Ball's explanation that she had joined the Communist Party only to appease her socialist grandfather.

Good-natured and business-minded Arnaz was willing to let bygones be bygones. A few years later, he needed a narrator for a new series. The program was based on the memoirs of Prohibition-era gangbuster Eliot Ness, the man credited with putting Al Capone behind bars. In a move that proved instrumental in making *The Untouchables* yet another Desilu hit, Arnaz hired the inimitable voice of Walter Winchell at $25,000 an episode. Desilu vice president Ball, who hadn't been consulted, hit the ceiling. Winchell was the broadcaster who'd broken the story that nearly destroyed her career. The incident contributed to the breakup of the Arnaz-Ball marriage a short while later. (More significant factors included Desi's compulsive drinking, gambling, and philandering.)

The Untouchables brought Arnaz further heartache. For one thing, a childhood chum from Miami, Sonny Capone, sued Desilu (unsuccessfully) over the unsympathetic portrayal of his father. In addition, claimed mob hit man Aladena ("Jimmy the Weasel") Fratianno, crime boss Sam Giancana objected so strenuously to the ethnic overtones of *The Untouchables* that he put out a contract on Arnaz. Luckily for Desilu and its shareholders, Giancana was overruled in the matter by the less impulsive Paul ("The Waiter") Ricca and Tony ("Big Tuna") Accardo.

Why Stocks Took Off

At year-end, Robert C. Ringstad observed in the *Magazine of Wall Street*, "In the mad dash to board the equity bandwagon, the prices of leading shares have been bid to levels considered rather unrealistic by seasoned market observers." Underlying the rally, he said, was the economy's unexpected swift recovery from recession. In addition, the bond market took a heavy hit in the summer, reinforcing investors' preference for stocks. Ringstad listed several causes for especially sharp rises in certain stocks:

- Inflation psychology.
- Hopes of big returns from new products.

- Heightened earnings expectations as a result of cost-cutting undertaken during the recession.
- Market popularity for a particular kind of industry or stock.

Lucien Hooper of *Forbes* attributed the market's strength to the classic phenomenon of more buyers than sellers. The purchasers, he maintained, had discovered during the past few years that owning stocks was "one of the most profitable ways in the world to employ funds." Individuals who already owned stocks were dissuaded from selling by the prospect of capital gains taxes, as well as by optimism engendered by past profits. "At present," wrote Hooper, "the investing public, rightly or wrongly, is 'sold' on the idea that the growth of this country is perpetual, and that the experience they have had in stocks the past ten years will be duplicated in the next ten." Finally, prices of better-quality companies were buttressed by the growing influence of institutional investors. Not only were they allocating more of their assets to stocks and less to bonds, but they bought to hold, rather than to sell.

Business Week, in explaining the 1958 bull market, likewise emphasized the enlarged role of institutional investors. Most major pension funds had already abandoned their old, conservative aversion to equities. The last major holdout, the American Telephone & Telegraph pension fund, announced during the summer that it was buying stocks. Late in the year, a number of bank trust departments boosted their equity allocations.

According to *Business Week*, the institutions transmitted their enthusiasm for stocks to the public. Individual investors bought equity-oriented mutual funds in increasing numbers, while also increasing their direct purchases of shares. New York Stock Exchange volume reached its highest level since 1933. Blue chips went to premium valuations, indicating in *Business Week*'s judgment that demand far exceeded supply.

Even though top-quality stocks were in short supply, corporations made little effort to exploit the situation. For most of 1958, corporations launched few new offerings of shares. Underwriting volume finally showed a large year-over-year increase in December, but the activity was dominated by small companies.

Blue chips not only refrained from raising new equity capital, but they moved toward paying out more in dividends. By the end of the year, a number of companies had reversed dividend cuts implemented during the recession. Widespread dividend increases were expected in

1959. Investors took the rising dividend trend as a sign that earnings were rising as well.

A New New Era

To A. T. Miller of the *Magazine of Wall Street*, the stock market appeared to have gotten ahead of itself by the end of 1958. But fundamental values were not about to deter the bulls, he observed: "On the part of those with vested interest in a strong and active market, especially the brokers, 'inevitable' inflation is still being touted as ample justification for a 'new era' in stock prices."

It wasn't by chance that Miller invoked the informal title of the Coolidge Administration. As *Business Week* noted, "To some Wall Street veterans, the cult of equities has some ugly parallels to the New Era of the late 1920s." In particular, the periodical mentioned the abandonment of historical price-earnings ratios. In *Barron's*, H. J. Nelson noted the same impediment to further appreciation. Commented Miller, "We have seen excess before and the familiar rationalization of it." Investors who lived long enough would see it many times more.

On February 9, 1997, with stocks again making record highs, Thomas L. Friedman hailed the bulls' case in the *New York Times*. Prices were justified, he argued, by America's unique adaptability to a global economy. True, the country was plagued by weak public schools, crumbling inner cities, a widening income gap, and a low savings rate. "But it still seems to me," wrote Friedman, "that something more is going on with America than just another uptick in the business cycle. It is a structural change that makes America a very good fit with the brave new world." (Shades of a half-century earlier!)

Two days later, on February 11, 1997, *Times* reporter Jonathan Fuerbringer invoked the spirit of Calvin Coolidge more directly in an article entitled, "New Era for Taking Market's Pulse: Analysts Debating Valuation of Stocks." Wall Streeters embraced the 1920s phrase for limitless prosperity. They cited increased saving by baby boomers among other rationales for junking traditional valuation standards. "New Era analysts argue that measures that worked well in the past must be updated now that the investment climate has changed," wrote Fuerbringer.

Exactly 70 years earlier, not long before the Great Depression began, William R. Biggs similarly justified the market's divergence from historical valuation benchmarks. Not only were small investors becoming more sophisticated, but the Federal Reserve System had at long last tamed the business cycle. Old, discredited ideas about the stock market never die. They don't even fade away.

New Era (Partially) Vindicated

Peak-level P/E ratios were not the only sign of excessive speculation perceived by historically oriented analysts in 1958. *Business Week* also cited an unprecedentedly small premium on stock dividend yields over interest rates on top-quality corporate bonds.

"In the past," wrote H. J. Nelson of *Barron's*, "rapid lowering of the bond-stock yield spread has eventually spelled trouble for stock speculation attempting to 'discount' the future." A. T. Miller of the *Magazine of Wall Street* chimed in, "It would be unprecedented for an important cyclical market adjustment to terminate without industrial stock yield considerably above the present level and without the spread over bond yield considerably wider than it is at present." This time around, however, the narrow spread grew even narrower. Finally, in 1959, dividend yields fell below bond rates for the first time.

For as long as anyone could remember, common stocks had yielded more than bonds, in recognition of their greater risk. Surely, thought investors who paid heed to historical series, stocks were overpriced if the relationship had flip-flopped. Whenever, in the past, the yield on stocks declined to the vicinity of bond yields, stock prices fell, thereby bringing conditions back to normal.

Veteran market observer Peter Bernstein recalls the reaction of his senior associates when the impossible happened. They solemnly assured him that it was time to reduce equity holdings in favor of bonds. This time around, however, the expected return to normalcy never happened. Dividend yields remained below bond yields and stocks didn't sell off.

In Bernstein's view, the onetime, permanent shift in the stock-bond yield relationship resulted from a secular rise in inflation. Instead of experiencing intermittent instability in the price level, the United States had entered a seemingly inescapable wage-price spiral. Switching back and forth between equities and fixed-income investments was no antidote to chronic erosion of the dollar's real value.

For starters, investors now had to demand increased inflation premiums on bonds. That is, interest rates had to provide savers more than just the customary return (say 3 percent) that represented their reward for deferring gratification. Bonds would henceforth be required to generate additional basis points of interest to offset the declining purchasing power of the holders' principal.

Meanwhile, corporations thrived and began to raise their dividends steadily. Investors became increasingly willing to buy equities in anticipation of future higher dividends. In deciding how high they were willing to go in price, investors were not deterred by dividend yields that were low by historical standards. Commented *Forbes*'s Heinz Biel at the end of 1958, "The stock market today, in contrast to a year ago, obviously offers no attraction to the income-seeking investor." Investing for appreciation, he added, was "essential for the preservation of capital because of the eroding effect of inflation." The growth stock era was at hand.

Perhaps also contributing to the deemphasis of dividends was a factor not mentioned by Peter Bernstein. The expanding influence of institutional investors—that is, of pension funds—meant corporations were marketing their stocks to a new kind of consumer. With their workforces growing, the corporate employers' big liabilities lay in the future, rather than the present. "They are not fussy about obtaining a high yield," Lucien Hooper of *Forbes* wrote of the institutional investors in 1958, "provided they visualize long-range appreciation— and long-range appreciation with them is years rather than months."

In any event, the lesson that Peter Bernstein drew was that it paid to be skeptical about extrapolations from the past. And indeed, when stock yields slipped below bond yields and stayed there, the heralds of another New Era scored a victory. Just as they claimed (although not necessarily for the reasons they offered), historical analysis proved unreliable at that juncture. A fundamental change in the U.S. economy was occurring. Contrary to what historically minded investors thought, an unprecedented yield differential did not truly indicate that stocks were overpriced.

The challenge for investors is to determine how much weight to assign to this case. How should they respond when, in the future, price-earnings multiples or market-to-book ratios reach record highs? Inevitably, the newest New Era school will have a ready explanation. The latest rationale will probably involve structural changes that supposedly render the "old-fashioned" benchmark irrelevant.

Once in a while, ignoring the lessons of the past proves profitable. Certainly, relying on precedent is not an infallible approach to securities analysis. But then, neither is any other method. Taking the long view, it appears unwise to be either too willing or too unwilling to ignore history.

Prophets without Honor

Going into the extraordinary rally of 1958, A. T. Miller of the *Magazine of Wall Street* characterized conditions as "not inviting for expansion of commitments in common stocks." Investors, he acknowledged, were likely to be encouraged by the Federal Reserve's recent shift to a looser money policy. On the other hand, the Fed probably would be cautious about easing credit further, remembering that its 1953–1954 activities had contributed to subsequent inflation. Also on the positive side, investors' concerns about a protracted recession had been relieved by the pickup in defense spending. Much of the credit for that went to the Sputnik I shock. What's more, a case could be made for a rebound on technical grounds alone. Even so, said Miller, "the obstacles to anything like a broad and sustained market advance, as distinct from an interim recovery, are obvious and, in our opinion, decisive." These impediments included:

- Previous overbuilding of production facilities, which precluded a rebound in capital goods expenditures.
- Continued restraint on business inventories, reflecting weak consumer spending.
- A questionable outlook for 1958 automobile production.

According to Miller, professionals thought the Dow industrials would bottom out as low as 350 sometime between February and May. Late in the year, the experts said, a high of 500 might be seen. As it turned out, the 1958 low of 436.89 occurred on February 25. The year ended on its highest tick, 583.65 on December 31. Investors were not deterred by Miller's repeated start-of-the-year warnings about sluggish capital goods spending.

Lucien Hooper of *Forbes* thought the Dow would bottom out at around 390, more than 10 percent below the actual nadir. He was less specific about the probable high for 1958, but saw a near-term limit of 450 to 460. That forecast understated the year's peak by more than 20 percent.

H. J. Nelson of *Barron's* was no more successful in his year-ahead prognostications. Attempting to cool off the bulls, he threw cold water on the notion that increased defense spending would stimulate corporate profits in the near term. New orders for aircraft carriers, he calculated, would not produce material manufacturing activity or earnings until 1959 and 1960. Missiles, Nelson acknowledged, were on a fast track in the congressional appropriations process. The Pentagon, however, had always emphasized that long lead times caused the associated spending to enter the economic stream slowly. Around the time that Nelson was making these points, Douglas Aircraft furnished a case in point. Despite receiving a $40-million contract for transport planes, the company announced that it would lay off 200 workers.

As for market sentiment, Nelson reported that institutional interest in stocks was light. Individuals, meanwhile, remained concerned about the sustainability of dividends. From a vantage point on the brink of one of the century's outstanding years, the *Barron's* columnist saw no evidence of rising optimism.

Michael Stephen, writing in the *Magazine of Wall Street*, was even more glum going into 1958. Investors, he believed, were wrongly assuming that the November 15, 1957, discount rate cut had cured all that was wrong with the economy. Considering how abruptly the Fed had shifted from inflation-fighting to recession-busting, argued Stephen, it might be that business conditions were worse than generally thought. And despite the easing of monetary policy, U.S. banks remained in a tighter position than at any time since 1930, excluding late 1956 to early 1957.

The consumer, who had bailed out the economy in 1954, could not necessarily be counted on this time around, in Stephen's view. Not only did consumer sentiment surveys reveal pessimism, but weak stock prices generally chilled their willingness to buy. "In some ways," Stephen went so far as to say, "the current situation resembles that of 1929." The signs that a great post–World War II capital spending and construction boom had crested were sufficient, in his view, "to counsel caution to all but the boldest."

Business Week also came down on the side of caution. "Those who claim that 1958 can be profitable for the investor," the magazine reported on January 11, "are not counting on a new bull market. They think that such a development is as unlikely as an all-out bear market." Investment counselor Anthony Gaubis foresaw no major rally, although he thought prices would bottom out in February, based on past responses to changes in Federal Reserve policy. Although his market outlook proved too gloomy, Gaubis was correct in foreseeing a decline in corporate earnings.

The experts who thought stock investors could make money during 1958, said *Business Week*, believed the key was to pick stocks destined to perform well during a recession. In this vein, Thurston P. Blodgett, vice president of mutual fund manager Tri-Continental Corporation, was unenthusiastic on growth stocks and capital goods producers. He instead favored consumer stocks, including food retailers and drug manufactures, based on an expectation that consumer spending would hold up well.

Outright bullish sentiment was in short supply and heavily hedged. Heinz Biel of *Forbes* saw good value in depressed cyclicals such as U.S. Steel and Ford ("even if the Edsel should be a flop"). He thought the economic downturn would be mild and comparatively short-lived. As for the all-important confidence factor, the *Forbes* columnist reckoned the bottom had already been reached. Biel's views qualified him as an optimist, under the circumstances, yet even he warned that the possibility of a genuine depression couldn't be ruled out.

On the whole, the 1958 bull market came as a surprise to the experts. As the year began, there were abundant reasons to be cautious or even pessimistic. Investors failed to follow the script, however. The rally that actually occurred represents a sobering experience for would-be forecasters.

∾ 1975 ∾

We now find solid grounds for believing that the long winter of stagflation may soon yield to a sunnier type of economic weather.
—PETER L. BERNSTEIN, Peter L. Bernstein, Inc.

The forecasting record of professional economists, in and out of government, has been so very poor in recent years that their credibility is at a deplorable low.
—HEINZ BIEL, *Forbes*

Society's misery is the economists' good fortune.
—LEONARD SILK, *New York Times*

Setting up the Rebound

After breaking through 1000 for the first time in 1972, the Dow Jones Industrial Average peaked at 1051.70 on January 11, 1973. A decline then set in, brought on by a steady stream of economic and political shocks.

From the outset of 1973, the market was plagued by the interrelated trends of rising oil prices, escalating inflation, and a weakening dollar. Hoping to rein in these forces, President Richard Nixon slapped price controls on oil in March 1973. On October 6, the perennially volatile Middle East erupted once again as a coalition of Arab states suddenly attacked Israel. In an effort to weaken American support for Israel, the Organization of Petroleum Exporting Countries (OPEC) imposed an embargo on the United States. Oil prices, which had already risen sharply, doubled between October 1973 and January 1974.

All the while, the burgeoning Watergate scandal threatened to drive Nixon from the White House. Finally, on August 9, 1974, the besieged President resigned. The following month, Nixon's successor,

Gerald Ford, assembled leaders of business, labor, finance, and the economics profession for a summit conference on inflation. Federal Reserve chairman Arthur Burns declared his determination to persevere in limiting the growth of monetary aggregates, even though the economy was rapidly contracting.

Up until August, Burns hadn't been sure the United States was in a recession. Contrary to all precedent, U.S. real gross national product declined in four successive quarters in 1974, despite double-digit growth in the GNP price deflator. Galloping inflation obscured the signs of economic downturn and the Fed kept money tight.

To make matters worse, inventories were extraordinarily high going into the recession. Rapid inflation had encouraged a buildup of stocks to avoid further price increases. As consumer buying weakened and the inflation beast started to come under control, a massive inventory liquidation began. Demand for newly manufactured goods evaporated, precipitating a 15 percent decline in industrial production for the 1973–1975 recession as a whole. Unemployment nearly doubled to 9 percent.

Taking one consideration for another, it was a dismal time to own financial assets. By the Treasury's measure, the U.S. price level rose by 8.7 percent in 1973 and 12.3 percent in 1974. Long-term bonds performed abysmally in the face of inflation, returning –1.1 percent and 1.6 percent, respectively, in the two years. Stocks suffered the same malaise. From its January 11, 1973, peak, the Dow Jones Industrial Average fell to a trough of 577.60 on December 6, 1974, a drop of 45 percent. Dividends, which rose in 1973 and fell only by a hair in 1974, failed to curb the decline. At 6.12 percent, the Dow's 1974 yield was the highest since 1950. The Dow's price-earnings ratio, which had reached an apex of 15.2 in 1972, bottomed out at 6.2 in 1974. No comparably low valuation had been observed since the Great Crash of 1929.

An Ordinary Man

The White House was occupied by an accidental President during the Very Good Year of 1975. Gerald Ford had been tapped for the vice presidency in 1973 upon the resignation of Spiro "Nolo Contendere" Agnew. (Agnew, facing bribery allegations, pleaded "no contest" to charges of income tax evasion.)

As House minority leader, Ford had won the admiration of his fellow Republican congressmen for his decency and fairness. Intellectual prowess was another matter. Lyndon Johnson once instructed an aide

to talk Ford out of his opposition to the Model Cities program by using toy blocks to explain the legislation to the "little baby boy." The
Wall Street Journal's assessment was hardly less deprecating:

> The Michigan congressman isn't a creative man. Rather he is a
> pleasant but plodding party wheelhorse who often speaks and ap-
> parently thinks in clichés.

Even Richard Nixon, who chose Ford to succeed Agnew, reportedly disdained his immensely loyal Vice President. In fact, Ford's con-
spicuous lack of brilliance may have been one of his chief qualifications
for the number-two slot, in Nixon's mind. The Democrats would have
to think twice about trying to oust the President if it meant replacing
him with Ford.

When Nixon stepped down, he was succeeded by a man with a limited grasp of economics. (In fairness, the same statement would apply
to most Presidents of the twentieth century.) On April 22, 1966, Ford
had convened a press conference to denounce "Johnson inflation,"
calling on LBJ to "apply the brakes." When news arrived, on May 3,
that automobile sales had fallen during the first two weeks of April,
Gerald Ford charged that the Democratic President had applied the
brakes too hard. Challenged to specify which "brakes" LBJ had
slammed on, Ford cited a hike in interest rates five months earlier. Not
only was that action by the Federal Reserve outside the President's authority, but Johnson had protested it. Then, when automakers reported record sales in the final two weeks of April, Ford compounded
his loss of credibility by renewing his attack on "Johnson inflation."

A Hard Rain's A-Gonna Fall

> Sometime in 1975—probably by late year—the worst financial col-
> lapse since the early 1930s will occur. For the first time in history,
> runaway inflation will precede—and overlap—a full-scale depres-
> sion. This is inevitable, and no man or government on the face of
> this earth will prevent it from happening.

So read the lead copy of an advertisement for the *Capitalist Reporter* that appeared in the March 2, 1975, *New York Times*. It was a
pitch well calculated to induce readers to subscribe to the magazine
focused on "the incredible opportunity to be gained from economic
collapse." Conditioned by the harsh economic winds of 1973–1974,

Americans responded enthusiastically to prophecies of continuing and worsening travails.

Some of the *Capitalist Reporter*'s moneymaking schemes truly were incredible. Others were merely outlandish. Among the choice concepts were the following:

- Traveling from coast to coast for $60.
- Buying dried food for half the normal price.
- Obtaining free animals from the federal government to stock an exotic pet store.

Editorial director Patrick W.H. Garrard even boasted that his magazine was the only one printing inside information about black market activities. This provided readers a rare opportunity to capitalize on chronic shortages.

"If ever there was a need for such a publication," wrote Garrard, "it's surely right now." On the assumption that a financial debacle was imminent, there was no disputing this view. ("The worst IS about to happen," proclaimed the *Capitalist Reporter*.) But the survivalists' doomsday scenario proved to be a classic case of forecasting via the rearview mirror. One month after the advertisement ran, the recession hit bottom. Just as Garrard claimed, financial opportunity was all around, during the worst of times, in the unlikeliest places. The least likely of all, considering the calamities that the 1973–1974 crisis seemed to foreshadow, was the stock market.

The Sun Was Shining Everywhere

The 1975 rebound rally began with a steep drop in interest rates. As unemployment figures continued to look worrisome, the Federal Reserve began to ease up on its effort to restrain money supply growth. September 1974, as it turned out, marked the cyclical peak in inflation.

Trouble in the banking system gave the Fed a second reason to deemphasize its goal of restraining monetary growth. Long Island–based Franklin National Bank, the nation's 20th largest, collapsed in October 1974. It was the biggest U.S. bank failure up to that time.

Although Franklin had been on the skids for some time, the immediate cause of its demise was a $40-million loss on foreign exchange transactions. Seven Franklin executives later pleaded guilty to engaging in unauthorized trading. In the latter stages of its existence, the bank had come under the control of Michele Sindona. A produce-transporter-turned-financier and sometime investment adviser to Pope Paul VI, Sindona was accused of misappropriating $45 million from Franklin. A month before he was to stand trial in 1979, he disappeared. His family insisted that he'd been kidnapped by a leftist group called the Proletarian Committee of Subversion for Better Justice, but the U.S. attorney's office simply listed him as missing. Sindona resurfaced a couple of months later, with a leg wound that a doctor said could have come from a bullet.

The Franklin National debacle was one of several prominent bank failures during 1974. News of a $30-million loan loss precipitated a deposit drain and failure at a subsidiary of Beverly Hills Bancorp, known as the "Bank of the Stars." Also going belly-up was U.S. National Bank of San Diego, controlled by Richard Nixon's friend and financial backer, C. Arnholt Smith. Hundreds of southern Californians were reportedly so unnerved by these events that they withdrew their savings from local banks and secreted the funds in cookie jars and beneath potted plants. No full-scale bank run developed, but Americans' "confidence in banks was at its lowest ebb in 40 years," according to *Business Week*'s Thomas C. O'Donnell.

To head off any possible financial panic, the Fed threw open its discount window. From a cyclical peak of 8 percent in November 1974, the Fed cut the discount rate in stages to 6 percent in June 1975. This ensured that banks could fund themselves in the open market and lend to corporations that were unable to roll over their commercial paper. By good fortune, interest rate reductions by major European central banks made it easier for the United States to shift course.

Commercial banks quickly picked up the cue. Four times during January, they lowered the prime lending rate by one-quarter point, leaving it at 9½ percent by month-end. The Dow industrials responded with a 14 percent rise, the largest one-month increase in 35 years. Four more reductions in the prime followed in February, bringing the base lending rate to 8½ percent. After three additional reductions, the prime reached a mid-March low of 7¼ percent before backing up a quarter-point to 7½ percent. By then, the 1973–1975 recession, one of the most severe since the end of World War II, was over.

Suddenly, the investment climate was friendly. Inflation was receding as a threat to financial assets. According to U.S. Treasury figures, the price level rose by only 1.5 percent during the first three months of 1975, down from 2.6 percent in the final three months of 1974.

The easing of inflation had several sources. For one thing, business had been caught off guard by the most severe economic downturn since the Great Depression. Companies moved swiftly to rein in inventory levels by cutting prices. Automakers offered rebates to consumers and even construction costs showed signs of declining. Meanwhile, the threatened oil shortage gave way to a temporary glut. That lessened the appeal of energy stocks but boosted autos and motels. Food shortages around the world appeared to abate, driving down prices of food commodities and further easing inflationary pressures.

Even as the inflation threat ebbed, the fear that recession would turn to depression began to fade. Late in March, the House and Senate passed a $22.8-billion tax cut aimed at slowing the economic slide. Speculators began turning their attention to smaller-capitalization stocks, a classic sign of exuberance.

Report for Duty When It's 12:01 in Honolulu

Spearheading the rally-sparking interest rate cut was a man William McChesney Martin reportedly had hoped wouldn't succeed him as Federal Reserve chairman. Arthur F. Burns was just the sort of academic economist, albeit one with outstanding credentials, that Martin had labored to keep out of central bank decision making.

Burns reciprocated the feelings. Promised the Fed chairmanship by President-elect Richard Nixon, he was obliged to bide his time as head economic counselor until Martin's term expired. It nettled the former Council of Economic Advisers kingpin that after almost 20 years on the job, the incumbent Fed chief was unwilling to resign early. "Martin will be sitting in that chair right up to midnight, Hawaii time, of his last day in office."

During Martin's chairmanship, as in that of Marriner Eccles and, later on, Alan Greenspan, the Fed's independence was repeatedly questioned and challenged. Burns's tenure likewise fueled the debate. "Some critics of Burns's performance," wrote economist John P. Cullity in a biographical sketch, "have argued that he engineered the sizable expansion of the money stock in order to ensure the victory of President Nixon in the fall 1972 election." *Fortune* claimed that the Fed stupefied monetary historians during that period by accelerating the growth of the money supply, even though recovery from the 1970–1971 slump was already well underway. Burns pointedly denied the magazine's insinuations about politicking on Nixon's behalf. The Fed chief also raised eyebrows in 1971 when he accepted appointment as head of the Committee on Interest and Dividends under Nixon's wage-price controls program. Burns never explicitly mentioned in testimony before Congress concerning this role that it potentially conflicted with his Fed duties. By committing himself to hold down interest rates, he effectively promised to expand the money supply.

A New York State of Mind

Stock investors saw bright horizons in 1975, but the financial picture was far from rosy in the center of the financial markets. New York City had dug itself so deeply into debt that in early March the major commercial banks balked at extending any more credit. With a payroll coming due and two loans maturing on March 14, insolvency threatened.

Just a week before New York would have defaulted, the banks relented. They agreed to purchase $537 million of bond-anticipation notes, which in turned enabled the city to buy some time. The bankers put a high price on relief, however. In light of the large credit risk they were taking, the lenders demanded an interest rate of 8.69 percent.

The rate on the notes smashed the city's previous record borrowing cost of 7.79 percent, set in October 1974. In the interim, interest rates in the U.S. had trended lower, but a Chemical Bank spokesman commented, "The syndicate feels that the rate reflects the current market conditions." The politicians saw it differently. "This is an outrageous stickup," blustered city council president Paul O'Dwyer. Controller Harrison Goldin complained that New York *State* fiscal problems, which he deemed unrelated to the city's situation, had created an "unwarranted climate of suspicion in the marketplace." Matthew J. Troy, Jr., chairman of the city council's finance committee, demanded an investigation of possible collusion by the lenders to exploit New York's financial weakness. "The banks," cried Troy, "make Jesse James look like an amateur."

New York State's constitution appeared to preclude matters coming to such a pass. In reaction to the fiscal shenanigans of Mayor William Marcy Tweed, amendments were adopted in 1884 that restricted borrowings by local governments. To begin with, debt was limited to 10 percent of the value of taxable property. In addition, borrowings were permitted only for capital projects, while borrowing to finance operating deficits was prohibited. Finally, the term of a debt could not exceed the probable useful life of the project that it financed.

Mayor John Lindsay found these restrictions "archaic." By this he meant that limitations on borrowing interfered with his ability to run billion-dollar annual deficits. The photogenic mayor deftly maneuvered around the constitutional barriers, doubling the city's debt during the eight fiscal years ending June 30, 1974. In one dodge, Lindsay diverted borrowings from the requisite capital projects to the operating expense of a job training program. A compliant city legal counsel deemed it a *social* capital item.

Hizzoner also found a clever way around the estimated-useful-life limitation on debt maturities. The state constitution permitted short-term borrowing for such purposes as paying bills for a few months, until regular tax receipts came in. By law, these short-term notes had to be repaid within one year. Lindsay wasn't deterred, however. He borrowed a billion dollars, not to meet temporary cash needs, but to cover the city's annual budget deficit. The next year, when by law the sum had to be repaid, he borrowed *two* billion. One billion repaid the outstanding note, while the second covered the new year's deficit. In year three, New York City issued $3 billion of notes. Lindsay's pyramid scheme collapsed when the short-term borrowings reached $6 billion.

The political system's responses to the fiscal crisis were predictable. On one front, New York's leaders proposed to remedy the ills brought on by excessive borrowing by borrowing even more. No matter that the city's 10 percent debt cap had been reached. The restriction didn't apply to public corporations, so a Municipal Assistance Corporation promptly came into being. Its mission was to raise additional funds on the strength of the city's sales tax revenues. (Although the end run around the debt limitation was tricky, an appeals court voted 4–3 that such plans should be upheld unless patently illegal.) Abraham Beame, successor to John Lindsay, pursued the other obvious course of seeking a federal bailout.

Secretary of the Treasury William Simon didn't respond warmly to New York City's plea for help. He argued that it would undermine the Constitution's federalist principles for Washington to ride to the rescue. (The Ford Administration's commitment to principle was perhaps reinforced by the fact that the petitioner was a predominantly Democratic city little loved around the country.) Simon proposed a novel alternative to bailing out Gotham: "We're going to sell New York to the Shah of Iran," he announced. "It's a hell of an investment."

In the Merry Month of May

May 1, 1975, was a watershed for the U.S. securities industry. The New York Stock Exchange abandoned the rule of fixed-rate commissions, adopted at its founding in 1792. At first, the novel practice of price competition had limited impact. Heavy trading volume, courtesy of the bull market, offset the pressure on profit margins. In time, however, the passing of the clubby old days led to the demise of many inefficient brokerage houses.

Ironically, the securities industry's shakeout was ultimately a product of excessive prosperity. During the 1960s, expanding trading volume had made it extremely lucrative to execute trades at the traditional, nonnegotiable rates of around 1 percent. Seeing that the brokers were becoming rich at their expense, the increasingly powerful institutional investors pressed for abolition of the fixed-rate system.

With a push from the Securities and Exchange Commission, the brokers began to open the door to competition. First, commissions on trades of more than $500,000 were made negotiable. Sizable discounts quickly became available. Encouraged by these results, the SEC ordered all commissions to become negotiable by the beginning of May 1975.

May Day was to be remembered, according to James Gipson of Batterymarch Financial Management, with about as much fondness as the U.S. Navy reserved for Pearl Harbor Day. It marked the end, Gipson wrote, of "generations of preaching the rigorous virtues of competitive capitalism while practicing the pleasurable vices of monopoly and price fixing."

At first, some of the major institutional brokers announced that they would cut their previous commission rates by no more than 8 percent. Business swiftly dried up at those houses. Within a few days, 50 percent discounts to institutions became commonplace. Cuts of as much as 90 percent off the old scales were not unusual.

On small trades by individuals, brokers tried to hold the line or even raise rates. But soon the little guy was able to obtain discounts by accepting certain restrictions. Before long, discount brokerage shops appeared, catering to individuals who simply wanted execution without such frills as investment advice. Among the early entrants in the new category was Muriel Siebert, the woman pioneer who'd been rejected for lack of a college degree when she first sought employment on Wall Street.

Inevitably, *Newsweek* paid homage to Calvin Coolidge by labeling the age of negotiated rates a "new era." For once, the phrase was apt. From now on, the securities business had to learn to control its costs of clearing trades and to merchandise its services.

I'd Say That I Had Spring Fever

During the spring, the Fed continued to reduce the discount rate. Banks lowered the prime rate to 7¼ percent in May and to 7 percent

in June. Toward the end of June, however, signs began to appear that
the Federal Reserve was moving rates back up. The Dow nevertheless
made a new high of 874.14 on June 26, marking a rise of nearly 42
percent in just half a year.

On July 1, Heinz Biel noted in *Forbes* that the market had become a
trifle wobbly, even fluctuating violently on occasion. But not to worry,
said Biel. Strong resistance was predictable at this stage, producing a
healthy correction that would forestall major excesses in the future.
Little noticed amidst the hesitancy of the broad averages, Biel pointed
out, were new highs by many secondary stocks of good quality. Strong
demand for bonds and utility stocks cinched the case for continuation
of the rally. "In my experience," Biel declared, "these are bullish indications for the stock market."

As it turned out, however, the Dow was within three weeks and 1
percent of its 1975 peak.

Who's Laughing Now?

Gerald Ford was generally regarded as a decent man, a welcome relief
in many ways from his immediate predecessors. The public saw in him
neither a wheeler-dealer on the order of Lyndon Johnson nor a tricky,
gloomy character of Richard Nixon's peculiar stamp. Regrettably,
Ford had an aptitude for lubricating the wheels of politics with folksy
humor that was more on a level with Nixon's than with Johnson's.

Here's how gag writer Bob Orben wrote a joke for Gerald Ford to
tell on himself, playing off his comparatively low pre-Presidency public
recognition.

LADY: (*As President Ford passes her in a hallway.*) You look familiar.
FORD: (*Helpfully.*) Jerry Ford?
LADY: No, but you're close.

Here's how it tripped off Ford's tongue in a speech in Indianapolis:

LADY: You look familiar.
FORD: I am Jerry Ford.
LADY: No, but you're closer.

Smack Dab in the Middle

"Gifted, determined, ambitious professionals have come into investment management in such large numbers during the past thirty years,"

wrote Charles D. Ellis in the July/August 1975 issue of *Financial Analysts Journal*, "that it may no longer be feasible for any of them to profit from the errors of all the others sufficiently often and by sufficient magnitude to beat the market averages."

Ellis was not alone in perceiving that it had gotten tougher for smart people to make superior profits in stocks. The following year, the *Financial Analysts Journal* published this statement in an interview with a noted investment expert:

> I am no longer an advocate of elaborate techniques of security analysis in order to find superior value opportunities. This was a rewarding activity, say, forty years ago. . . . But in light of the enormous amount of research now being carried on, I doubt whether in most cases such extensive efforts will generate sufficiently superior selections to justify their cost. . . .

The self-proclaimed convert to the "efficient market" school was none other than Benjamin Graham, the father of securities analysis. To be sure, Graham's most renowned disciple, Warren Buffett, appeared to go on defying the odds for many more years. But Graham, shortly before his death, concluded that the era of ferreting out unrecognized bargains was over.

Princeton economist Burton G. Malkiel has hailed Graham's capitulation. He regards it as a vindication of the academic theory that markets work too smoothly to permit investors to profit from fundamental analysis. In contrast, money manager and *Forbes* columnist Kenneth L. Fisher regards Graham's 1976 statement as evidence that he "was simply old and unable to keep up with the times." After all, says Fisher, didn't computer testing begin to "poke all kinds of holes" in the efficient markets theory shortly after Graham embraced the idea?

The fact is, most of the hole poking has focused on whether there are identifiable patterns in the movement of stock prices. Examples include seasonal biases (such as the "January effect") and persistently superior risk-adjusted performance by low-P/E stocks. These nonrandom patterns shouldn't exist if the stock market digests information with absolute efficiency. But identifying a pattern in the behavior of groups of stocks or in the market doesn't indicate one way or the other whether Graham-style company evaluation makes money.

In reality, the profitability of fundamental analysis is a difficult, if not impossible, proposition to test. Each company represents a unique situation, rather than a data point that submits readily to quantitative analysis. Certainly, a fund manager who claims to rely on fundamental analysis may demonstrate superior performance for a time. Without a record of every trade, however, we can't be certain that the index-beating returns genuinely came about through brilliant stock picking. The true source may have been astute market timing or simply luck. Perhaps the real answer is that fundamental analysis makes money, but only for a few very smart people.

Graham's 1976 assessment was that over time, it had become hard for even the isolated genius to get a leg up by studying a company's financials. His basis of comparison was the environment of 60 years earlier, when he entered the investment business. Not long before he came to Wall Street, *Munsey's Magazine* had proposed to help investors by publishing a schedule of U.S. Steel's properties. It turned out to be a much larger task than the author had initially supposed. The company itself said that it had no such tabulation. Wading into this sea of ignorance, Graham became one of the first to exploit valuable information disclosed in corporations' regulatory filings. By poring over such documents, he uncovered idle assets that could be distributed to shareholders. He uncovered the level of subsidiaries' unconsolidated earnings, which were the subject of speculation to other investors.

As the years passed, Graham's innovative methods became standard practice, partly because he was generous in sharing his knowledge. Additionally, New Deal securities law reforms required essential financial data to be more widely disseminated. In short, Ben Graham was not behind the times when he questioned the continued effectiveness of fundamental analyis. On the contrary, he was acknowledging that the old ways might not work, in light of changed conditions.

Summertime

By summer, interest rates were clearly on the rise. During July, the prime rate rose in two steps to $7\frac{1}{2}$ percent. In August, the prime receded to $7\frac{1}{4}$ percent and the market staged a brief rally. The upturn fizzled after Labor Day, however, with the New York City fiscal crisis getting the blame. September saw the prime climb to 8 percent.

Anything You Don't Say May Be Held against You

On October 29, Gerald Ford rebuffed New York City's appeal for a federal bailout. It was bad news for bondholders and a setback for

Mayor Abraham Beame. And the complex financial dimensions of the story presented a major problem for the editors of the *Daily News*. The ordinary front-page subjects of New York's picture newspaper— sex and crime—were easy to summarize in lurid headlines of five or six words. How could the format accommodate a fiscal crisis?

Managing editor William Brink and his staff spent the entire afternoon vainly groping for the right phrase. Joe Kovach, who was responsible for headlines, rejected every idea. Finally, with the deadline imminent, Brink cried in desperation, "What do you want to say— 'Drop Dead'?"

"That's it!" Kovach exclaimed. Editor Michael O'Neill concurred. A short while later, the newsstands trumpeted the latest development in New York's intricate maneuverings to put its financial house in order:

FORD TO CITY: DROP DEAD

No matter that the President hadn't said any such thing. It was a catchy phrase that wasn't easily forgotten. A year later, Gothamites still "remembered" that Gerald Ford had told them to kick the bucket. He lost New York State in the 1976 election, and with it the presidency. The *Daily News*'s hyperbolic headline was widely regarded as a factor in Ford's defeat.

Wrapping Up

Interest rate pressure eased during the final quarter of 1975. The average federal funds rate fell from 6.16 percent to 5.41 percent. Banks lowered the prime in October from 8 percent to $7\frac{1}{4}$ percent, where it ended the year after a brief backup to $7\frac{1}{2}$ percent in November. During the fall, New York City's fiscal crisis put a damper on stock prices. Finally, however, promises of federal aid eliminated its depressing influence. Toward the tail end of the year, auto stocks helped propel a renewed surge. (For the year, General Motors advanced from 29 to 59.)

The vigorous rally of 1975 occurred during the most severe U.S. economic contraction since the 1930s. April marked the low point of the recession, yet full-year earnings per share for the Dow industrials declined by 24 percent from 1974.

Aside from the downward trend of interest rates, the biggest thing going for the market in 1975 was the depressed stock price level of

1974. The rebounding Dow gained a remarkable 38.32 percent. Total return for the Standard & Poor's 500 measured 37.21 percent.

By Next Year Our Troubles Will Be Far Away

Two weeks before the start of the magnificent 1975 bull market, *Barron's* convened a panel of market experts to gaze into the year ahead. Here are a few highlights of what they saw:

Edson Gould, technician and author of bimonthly Findings & Forecasts*:*

"It will be years before we get another roaring bull market. Way off in the 'Nineties, I'd say. But we could get a very decent recovery."

Walter Mintz, partner in investment management firm Cumberland Associates:

"The probabilities are that we will have an up market this year. But there's no reason to look for a wild bull market."

Irving Komanoff, stock trader with Herzfeld & Stern:

"I see a major opportunity to buy stocks which in my opinion stand a good chance of doubling and tripling in 1975. . . . As far as I'm concerned, it could be one of the greatest opportunities to make money we've had in the last five or six years."

Robert Wilson, hedge fund manager:

"I'm less bullish than Irving, but I'm bullish. . . . Even so, I wouldn't put nearly all my money in stocks because we are on the edge of a precipice. There are liquidity problems relating to oil, Eurodollars, and the banking system, and things could get very bad."

All in all, the pundits had widely divergent opinions going into the Very Good Year of 1975. One way or another, 1975 seems to have been destined for high volatility. Perhaps if a few breaks had gone the other way, the more dire prophecies would have been fulfilled. As it turned out, though, extreme financial conditions in 1974 paved the way for a sensational rally, much in the manner of the Panic of 1907.

∽ 1995 ∽

*W*hat can't be denied is the crucial role played by foreign investors, especially central banks, in bringing down U.S. interest rates and sending the bond market into orbit.

—RANDALL W. FORSYTH, *Barron's*

*R*obert Rubin wouldn't want to go down as the Treasury secretary who bailed out Mexico and let Uncle Sam fail.

—ROGER LOWENSTEIN, *Wall Street Journal*

A mutual fund will do as well as the market in general, which is not brilliant at all, but you are not going to lose your shirt in it unless you get some crazy [fund] management that buys derivatives.

—PHILIP L. CARRET, Carret & Company

A Fairly Bad Year

Even though the stock market rose slightly in 1994, it's not inaccurate to call the Very Good Year of 1995 a rebound rally. On February 4, 1994, Federal Reserve chairman Alan Greenspan caught most investors badly off guard by suddenly raising short-term interest rates for the first time in five years. Up to that point, stocks had been rising. In fact, the Dow Jones industrials came within a hairbreadth of cracking the 4000 mark for the first time. But when Greenspan spied a danger of renewed inflation, he resolved to obliterate it in the bud. The Dow promptly plummeted 96 points, a one-day drop of 2.4 percent. Over the course of 1994, the Fed boosted short-term rates by a total of 2½ percentage points.

Greenspan's shift in policy crushed the bond market, as 30-year Treasury yields rose from 6.35 percent to 7.88 percent. Long-term government securities posted their worst total return since 1967, according to Ibbotson Associates. "More money has been lost in the bond market since October 1993 than was lost in the stock market in

1987," estimated Salomon Brothers debt strategist Greg Parseghian, alluding to the stock market's October crash of seven years earlier. Bond buyers, who just one year earlier had eagerly assumed the risk of buying very long-dated issues to obtain the highest rates, turned gun-shy. "If 1993 was the year of the 100-year bond," said Morgan Stanley debt syndicate manager Mark Seigel, "1994 was the year of the one-year note."

Interest rate–sensitive stocks got hammered, as well. Dow Jones's financials group fell by 6.6 percent. Utility share prices declined by 13.7 percent, led by the electric power companies' 18.0 percent drop.

Celebrated hedge fund manager Michael Steinhardt was down roughly 28 percent in 1994. His huge, highly leveraged bet on falling rates, which had generated sensational returns in the preceding years, turned around and bit him. The even more celebrated George Soros managed to stay marginally in the black. But because he failed to maintain the 60-percent-plus annual returns that he had racked up in 1991–1993, the market drastically reduced his fund's premium over net asset value. Recent buyers consequently got whacked by approxi-mately 20 percent. Between losses and withdrawals, hedge fund assets shrank by 25 percent in 1994, according to *U.S. Offshore Funds Direc-tory* publisher Antoine Bernheim.

Along with the home-grown problem of rising interest rates, rum-blings south of the border caused unease among the *americanos*. Mex-ico had shone especially brightly in the excellent 1993 performance of international emerging markets. An Indian uprising in the state of Chiapas got 1994 off on the wrong foot, however. In March, the pres-idential candidate of Mexico's ruling party was assassinated under cir-cumstances not well explained. Talk of a turn from oligarchy to a more open and responsive political system was beginning to ring hollow. Mexico's Very Bad Year ended in a full-fledged financial crisis after the new administration mismanaged an attempt to avoid the currency de-valuation that traditionally accompanied presidential changeovers. In-stead of adjusting smoothly to current foreign exchange market conditions, the peso plummeted on a widespread loss of confidence. Mexico paid dearly for its heavy reliance on "hot-money" foreign in-flows. (Unlike direct investments in productive assets, short-term money-market holdings could be readily converted to cash, which in turn could be pulled out of the country quickly.)

In December, Federal Reserve chairman Greenspan indicated that he still saw little evidence of economic slowdown. His comments im-plied that the interest rate tightening launched in February was not yet at an end. Despite all, the Dow Jones Industrial Average scratched out a 2.1 percent increase during 1994. The trailing-12-months price-earnings ratio slid from 25.6 to 15.0, however. Investors weren't displaying much optimism about the stock market's near-term prospects.

Think of All You'll Derive

The surprise 1994 surge in interest rates devastated financial institutions that had speculated in derivatives. These instruments were so named because their returns were "derived" from the performance of underlying investments, such as stock or bond indexes, currencies, and commodities.

Although frequently invaluable in hedging price risk, derivatives could also be used to multiply the gain on an astute speculation. As the users should have realized, derivatives also multiplied the losses on wrong guesses about the direction of prices. In the months following the February 1994 rate shock, huge trading losses were reported from many unlikely quarters. Several major corporate treasury departments, where the traditional task was to oversee ultralow-risk cash-equivalents, turned out to have been stretching for extra yield by buying risky derivatives. As a result of losses in the innovative instruments, Orange County, California, eventually became the largest municipality in history to file for bankruptcy.

Even professionals had a hard time providing a succinct definition of the "D-word." Nevertheless, it was now an established part of the Wall Street lexicon. The proof was that investment banks put some of their brightest people to work trying to come up with another term for the highly flammable paper.

Mortgage-backed securities dealers protested if anybody applied the term "derivative" to the instruments they created by slicing and splicing underlying pools of assets. They had a valid point. To be sure, a leveraged portfolio of mortgage-backed esoterica wiped out money manager David Askin's clients to the tune of $600 million in 1994. But the reason Askin's portfolio imploded was not that its performance was derived from the behavior of other assets; his difficulties arose from interest rate swings and, he maintained, pressure from his lenders.

It was dawning on investors that financial institutions and even industrial corporations faced large risks that weren't well understood. Derivatives weren't even the entire story. As 1995 began, bulls had to allow for the possibility that Wall Street's financial engineering would leave the system in a bind.

Bet He's Glad He Didn't Say, "Or I'm a Monkey's Uncle"

Mexican officials were extremely persuasive when they insisted that they could defy tradition by not devaluing the peso in December 1994. Still, skeptics abounded among money managers, leading to many contentious discussions with Mexico's backers on Wall Street.

One brokerage firm's economist grew impatient hearing the argument, which ultimately proved correct, that economic pressures were leading inexorably to a fall in the exchange rate. Using the Spanish equivalent of "period," he closed off debate with the words, "Mexico isn't going to devalue its peso. *Punto.*"

Once the currency debacle hit, wags ceased calling the economist by name, instead referring to him as "Punto." This disparagement was "not very nice," commented the victim.

The Wayward Wind

It couldn't be said that President Bill Clinton was shoring up investors' optimism at the outset of 1995. His political fortunes were at a low ebb. The centerpiece of Clinton's legislative initiative, health care reform, had disintegrated. In November, his party had lost control of both houses of Congress. Furthermore, the opposition had the edge in generating fresh ideas, which Clinton hadn't yet begun to co-opt as successfully as he would later on. To compound matters, the President's ideological malleability created misgivings among voters of all stripes.

Despite a presidential tradition of shifting with the winds, Bill Clinton seemed to stand out as a political opportunist. Peace candidate Woodrow Wilson became a revered figure by leading America into World War I. Cold warrior Richard Nixon was reviled by many who nonetheless extolled his diplomatic overtures to Communist China. Ronald Reagan, apotheosized as an unyielding foe of intervention in the free market, was formerly a liberal Democrat. And like Clinton, Reagan had a reputation as a ladies' man, yet cloaked himself in the mantle of family values. Perhaps because his reputation was fresher, Clinton proved less successful than Reagan in putting over the virtue act. Remarkably, "Slick Willie" managed to stand out for insincerity within a peer group of professional politicians. There was irony in this, for if any other President was more studied in his efforts to convey sincerity, history hasn't recorded the fact.

Ironic, too, was the intense personal antipathy that Clinton inspired among Wall Streeters, in light of perceptions within his administration.

Social welfare advocates groused that the chief's policies were geared entirely to the bond market's expected response. Other critics charged that Clinton shifted too minutely with vagaries of the public opinion polls. His extraordinary recovery and reelection in 1996 merely reinforced the impression that he was far better at campaigning than in displaying leadership once he got into office.

In Clinton's defense, it must be noted that Wall Street ritually denounced his Democratic predecessors as tax-and-spend liberals, as well. Still, his seeming lack of a philosophical center perhaps justified suspicions that he'd eventually backslide from his avowed commitment to fiscally sound policies.

At the end of the day, too, The Man from Hope probably just flat-out struck a portion of the citizenry as un-Presidential. His notorious appetite for Big Macs and fries was not as endearing a foible as Reagan's addiction to jellybeans. Probably few voters believed that no previous President had ever strayed from the strict path of marital fidelity. None before Clinton, however, had been taped on the telephone with a purported paramour, likening a political rival of Italian extraction to a mafioso. Undoubtedly mortifying for many, as well, was Clinton's decision not to deflect a question on an MTV broadcast about whether he wore briefs or boxer shorts. ("Usually briefs," he replied, prompting a manufacturer of boxers to ship him a hundred pair of its product. "Frankly, we're scared to think about what President Clinton looks like in briefs," remarked the company's marketing director.) Donning dark glasses and playing the saxophone on the *Arsenio Hall Show* achieved its desired effect of bringing Clinton down to the common people's level, but may have overshot.

Even if Clinton's bearing had awed the public, it mightn't have made any difference to the stock market. A well honed Elvis impression clearly wasn't going to help, however. At a low point in his political fortunes, Bill Clinton might have found some solace in believing that he was the most accomplished saxophone player among key U.S. economic policymakers. But, alas, he had to take second chair in that category.

Hear Me Talkin' to Ya

Federal Reserve chairman Alan Greenspan had originally planned a career in music. Doubling on clarinet and sax, he attended New York's Juilliard School, a cradle of virtuosos. Greenspan's talent carried him as far as a professional stint with the Henry Jerome swing band. Also in the band's saxophone section was Leonard Garment, later a key aide to Richard Nixon. Concluding that he didn't have the chops to advance beyond his sideman status, Greenspan segued into a successful career in economic consulting.

When he became head of the Council of Economic Advisers under Gerald Ford, Greenspan was 48 years old. Perceiving that proficiency in tennis was essential to the political dimensions of the job, he took up the game. Despite his late start, he developed into a strong player. "As economists are prone to do," he later joked, "I've been extrapolating, and I've concluded that I'll join the professional tennis tour at 104." Realistically, though, Greenspan would have been no match for his predecessor, William McChesney Martin. Martin was good enough to reach the second round of the Men's Nationals on three occasions. (His father-in-law, incidentally, was Dwight Davis, donor of the Davis Cup.)

One of Greenspan's disconcerting tactics on the court was switching from lefty to righty on critical points. It was a fitting, if unintended, homage to Harry Truman's celebrated wish for a one-handed economist, who wouldn't forever be saying, "On the one hand, but on the other hand." As Fed chairman, Greenspan immersed himself in details of the "real economy" of goods and services, as distinct from financial markets. Former Bank of England governor Robin Leigh-Pemberton kidded him about making comments along the lines of, "The information that I have from the vacuum cleaner industry in the state of Iowa indicates that the economy is moving up." Greenspan's Fed reign has also been noted for continuing a venerable tradition of disguising the direction of monetary policy through obfuscation. "If I seem unduly clear to you," he once remarked, "you must have misunderstood what I said."

Let's Make a Deal

Analysts searching for bullish economic signs at the start of 1995 had to fall back on the free-market agenda of the new Republican majority in Congress. With great fanfare, House speaker Newt Gingrich planned a hundred-day push to begin to enact the "Contract with America," the package of reforms on which the GOP had campaigned in November. (Democrats quickly dubbed the pact the "Contract on America.")

Not everybody regarded the Gingrich agenda as bullish for the financial markets. House Republicans had vowed to cut taxes, but if government spending didn't also come down, the federal deficit would rise. (At least, that's how the arithmetic worked for everyone except supply-side economists.) Escalating inflation was a likely result, which would force the Fed to keep ratcheting up interest rates. Perhaps this explained why key Republican Senators, including majority leader Robert Dole, hadn't signed the Contract with America.

In any case, proposals to overhaul the economy couldn't be quick fixes for the stock market. Back in the Hundred Days of 1933, it was Franklin Roosevelt's currency tinkering that resuscitated securities prices in the short run, rather than his longer-range social reforms.

Where the Money Was

Early in 1995, Mexico's financial problems produced unwelcome ripple effects in the United States. On January 3, Chemical Banking disclosed a $70 million pretax loss on peso trading that it called unauthorized. The bank had procedures in place to prevent such problems. Trader Victor Gomez, who subsequently pleaded guilty to charges of conspiring to defraud the bank, was supposed to run a "matched book." But instead of neutralizing his risks with offsetting positions, said the prosecutors, he entered fictitious trades in Chemical's computer. Evading controls was to become a recurring theme of 1995. The aggrieved institutions invariably blamed "rogue traders," never suggesting that their own vigilance might have been lax.

Meanwhile, a political squabble was developing in Washington over efforts to assist Mexico. President Clinton argued that the United States would serve its self-interest by lending a hand to a major trading partner. Objectors in Congress countered by citing the "moral hazard" problem. A bailout, they claimed, would encourage other developing countries to regard Uncle Sam as a safety net and consequently overextend themselves financially.

The critics also charged that rescuing Mexico would also rescue U.S. investment banks and mutual funds. These financial institutions had earlier profited from their emerging markets speculations. They, rather than U.S. taxpayers, should now bear the losses. Further fueling political resistance was a protectionist sentiment that Mexico was not only stealing U.S. jobs with low wages, but was seeking to fund the operation in Washington, to boot.

Clinton and Treasury Secretary Robert Rubin mounted a massive effort to win congressional support for a Mexican aid package. Alan Greenspan was persuaded to help, despite his reservations on moral hazard grounds and even though his lobbying on Capitol Hill raised concerns in some quarters about the Fed's independence. The Republican leaders in both houses, Senate majority leader Robert Dole and House Speaker Newt Gingrich, both backed Clinton. Still, the political backlash against Mexico proved uncontainable.

Opponents of a bailout were stunned on January 31 when Clinton made an end run around his adversaries. Abandoning his proposed $40 billion package, the President found financing that didn't require congressional authorization. The Treasury's exchange stabilization fund, previously used to manage the dollar's value in world markets, was tapped for $20 billion. Meanwhile, the International Monetary Fund exercised an "exceptional clause" in its charter to extend $10 billion of new loans to Mexico, on top of $7.8 billion okayed in the preceding week. Other nations were hit up for $12 billion of short-term credit. European leaders, accustomed to being consulted on major economic initiatives, were no less stunned by the audacious plan than Clinton's domestic adversaries.

Treasury Secretary Robert Rubin commented, apropos of tapping the exchange stabilization fund for long-term loans to a foreign country, "It's fair to say this is unique." But it was legal. Greatly relieved congressional leaders endorsed Clinton's clever maneuver. It extricated the legislative profiles in courage from the dilemma of believing that Mexican relief was economically necessary, but knowing that many constituents thought otherwise. Clinton had bypassed the traditional separation of powers with a dodge worthy of Franklin Roosevelt himself.

The financial markets embraced Clinton's stratagem warmly. U.S. stocks and bonds rallied, while the dollar strengthened. Mexican equities registered their biggest one-day gain since 1988 and the peso immediately recovered 10 percent of its recent loss.

A Tight Lid

Even though 1995 turned out to be a banner year for investors, the monetary picture initially didn't seem especially reassuring. Federal Reserve chairman Alan Greenspan offered no hope that his preemptive strike against inflation was over. The central bank, he said a bit later, was building sandbag dikes to restrain a flooding river. The metaphor recalled a 1955 description of monetary policy by William McChesney Martin:

> We have a moving stream—the money stream. We want the money in the stream to grow as the river bank can hold it. We don't want it to overflow the banks.

New York Congressman Maurice Hinchey wasn't impressed by Greenspan's allusive imagery. In reality, claimed Hinchey, the "flood" of inflation had been nothing more than a trickle. Replied Greenspan, "I put my scuba stuff on, so I got a pretty good look at it."

On February 1, far from beginning to wind down its antiinflationary effort, the Fed tightened once more. The central bank boosted by half a point both the discount rate (to 5¼ percent) and the federal funds rate (to 6 percent). Greenspan's decision had been widely expected, however. Nearly a month earlier, Dave Kansas had written in the *Wall Street Journal*, "Many economists believe the Fed will tighten credit again, perhaps as early as January 31." In fact, after the fed funds rate was hiked to 6 percent, an American Bankers Association panel of economists predicted that it would rise to 6½ percent by midyear. The well anticipated February 1 Fed action barely caused the stock market to blink.

As it turned out, January 30 marked the year's low point for the Dow Jones industrials. The index closed that day at 3832.08, then went on to make 69 new highs during 1995. From the trough to the 5216.47 peak on December 13, the Dow rose by 36 percent. A sharp reversal of Fed policy provided the inital impetus.

Afterburner

Back in 1954, *Forbes* columnist Lucien Hooper had foreseen better times for the cigarette makers. Their problem, he contended, wasn't all the scare talk about lung cancer. Rather, it was negative tone of backbiting advertisements that dwelt on health concerns. The picture would brighten, Hooper felt sure, once tobacco companies returned to emphasizing the pleasure of smoking.

Over the next four decades, millions of Americans vindicated Hooper's prediction that they'd keep on smoking. During the same period, however, the courts became increasingly sympathetic to smokers who sued the cigarette manufacturers over their health problems.

Finally, in 1995, a federal judge in New Orleans okayed class action on behalf of "all nicotine-dependent persons in the United States" who purchased cigarettes from any major supplier. By the *Wall Street Journal*'s estimate, this class potentially included the majority of the country's 50 million or so smokers. Analysts estimated that successful lawsuits could wipe out the combined net worth of market leaders Philip Morris and RJR Nabisco.

Greenspan Loosens the Screws

On February 23, Federal Reserve chairman Greenspan told Congress that he perceived no need for further increases in interest rates. In fact, he indicated that the Fed was prepared to begin lowering rates if the economy showed any sign of sliding into recession. The Dow Jones Industrial Average jumped 30.28 points in response to Greenspan's statement, to close above 4000 for the first time ever.

The Fed chief caught investors by surprise with his suggestion that growth was decelerating. The *Wall Street Journal* greeted the rally with skepticism, warning in its headline that the Dow's sojourn above 4000 might be brief. Market watchers, according to the *Journal*, said a correction was "inevitable." Even a month after Greenspan's comments, Bear, Stearns senior economist John Ryding disputed the view that the Fed had completed the interest rate tightening that began in 1994. During the fourth quarter of 1994, he noted, gross domestic product had grown at a 4.6 percent annualized rate, exceeding most forecasts. In a similar vein, Alan Abelson of *Barron's* pointed to signs of strength in housing. He also fretted that German interest rate cuts would have no lasting effect on the foreign exchange markets, potentially obliging the Fed to raise U.S. rates in order to shore up the dollar. All in all, Abelson thought the prospects for even one more quarter of large advances in the stock indexes were "problematic."

Aside from the near-term outlook for growth, though, Greenspan had other reasons for considering the possibility that rates had risen far enough. Monetary restraint, in his view, was necessary partly because of the federal government's chronic lack of fiscal restraint. Accordingly, the new Republican majority in Congress moved swiftly to assure the Fed chairman that its proposed tax cuts would be responsibly offset by spending cuts. "The majority is one hundred percent committed to decreasing the size and scope of the federal government," House Budget Committee chairman John Kasich told him. In at least a symbolic endorsement of that sentiment, the House overwhelmingly approved a balanced-budget constitutional amendment on January 26. Greenspan knew that the White House vehemently opposed the measure and he presciently worried that a dangerous impasse might develop over the budget. On balance, though, the deficit problem appeared to be lessening, rather than worsening.

Ultimately, the bears were vanquished. By July, the Federal Reserve had begun taking interest rates down. Before 1995 was over, the Dow cracked 5000.

All I Know Is Just What I Read in the Papers

On the same day that the Dow Jones Industrial Average first breached the 4000 mark, Lotus Development fell 1¼, to 43½. The drop occurred after company officials ridiculed the "silly" rumor reported in *USA Today* that the software producer was a takeover target.

A little more than three months later, on June 5, Lotus chairman Jim Manzi received an 8:25 A.M. call from Louis V. Gerstner, Jr. The IBM chairman informed Manzi that in five minutes he would launch a $60-a-share hostile takeover bid.

Manzi formulaically announced that the board of directors would consider IBM's bid in conjunction with other options. Realistically, though, there wasn't much considering to be done. IBM's bid represented an 85 percent premium over Lotus's recent share price of 32½ and the proposed acquisition raised no obvious antitrust flags. Shareholders were less than ecstatic with the performance of Lotus, which had traded as high as 85½ in 1994. Accordingly, analysts correctly predicted that it would all be over quickly. Within a week, Lotus became the latest victim of silly takeover speculation.

The Case of the Unauthorized Autobiographer

The John and Francis Baring Company was founded in 1763. After helping to finance Britain's Napoleonic wars and the Louisiana Purchase, the merchant bank was renamed Baring Brothers and Company. Barings went on to fund the construction of the Panama Canal and to become banker to the British royal family.

In 1989, the firm hired a 22-year-old clerk named Nick Leeson. It took Leeson less than six years, during which time he rose to head the Singapore office's futures trading operation, to bankrupt the 232-year-old company. In March 1995, Barings was sold to Internationale Nederlanden Groep for one pound.

Predictably, the venerable institution's demise was blamed on unauthorized trading. An inquiry by the Bank of England concluded, however, that "a serious failure of controls and managerial confusion within Barings" also contributed to the debacle. The firm made an elementary blunder in control systems by putting Leeson in charge of both trading and clearing. This fatally flawed managerial structure helped the plucky young trader to bury his trading losses in an error account, where they remained undetected by auditors and regulators.

As Leeson recounted in his prison autobiography, *Rogue Trader*,

the clerical systems at Barings were fully worthy of an outfit that commenced business in 1763. One of his early assignments was to dig the
firm out of a £100-million bookkeeping hole it had created through
chaotic handling of bond certificates. Such an uncontrolled environment made it almost inevitable that somebody would exploit the system and be branded a "rogue trader."

Higher and Higher

As winter melted into spring, the stock market soared to one record
high after another. The averages shook off bad news and kept climbing.

For investors who may have pinned their hopes on radical fiscal reform, the Senate's rejection of the balanced-budget amendment on
March 2 was a disappointment. Nor did it sound reassuring when, on
April 19, the U.S. dollar fell in European trading to 1.3440
deutschemarks. That was the dollar's lowest level against the mark
since the end of World War II. The yen exchange rate stood at 79.85,
down by more than 36 percent since the month Bill Clinton entered
the White House. For some time, pronouncements by various administration officials had been suggesting that the greenback's exchange
rate would be held down to help the trade balance. Japan, struggling
to climb out of a recession, was meanwhile trying to restrain the yen,
which made it all the more unattractive for Clinton to let the dollar
appreciate.

Meanwhile, the dread D-word continued to make headlines. Piper
Jaffray ageed to pay $70 million to holders of a bond mutual fund that
had flourished, then foundered, as a consequence of derivatives use.
Orange County was forced to seek extensions on its maturing debt,
while Wisconsin's state investment fund disclosed a $95-million trad-
ing loss.

The Dow Jones Industrial Average took it all in and blithely continued rising. Before March was over, the index had closed above 4100
for the first time in history. Bond prices soared as well, taking long-
term government yields below 7 percent. By April 10, the Dow had
cleared 4400.

Dream a Little Dream

"I didn't have any really big motivation in my life," investor Kirk
Kerkorian recalled, as he neared the 70-year mark. "First it was simply
to earn enough to get something to eat, then enough to buy a car."

The junior high dropout and onetime amateur boxer exceeded these modest dreams by a healthy margin. As a young man, he cleared rocks off the Metro-Goldwyn-Mayer lot for 40 cents an hour. Many years later, after making his first fortune in the airline business, Kerkorian bought a controlling interest in the film studio. In 1968, he built the world's largest hotel—the 1568-room International in Las Vegas. Five years later, his 2100-room MGM Grand on the Las Vegas Strip succeeded to that title, which later passed to his new MGM Grand, a 5005-room affair.

By 1995, *Forbes* estimated Kerkorian's net worth at $2.5 billion and ranked him 23rd on its list of America's wealthiest people. In that year, he heightened the drama of the bull market by attempting the second largest U.S. takeover ever, a run at Chrysler. With a $23-billion price tag, the hostile bid ranked behind only Kohlberg Kravis Roberts & Company's 1989 acquisition of RJR Nabisco. The battle for Chrysler mesmerized investors, much in the manner of William Durant's boardroom struggle with General Motors 80 years earlier. Having satisfied his youthful ambition of buying a car, the 77-year-old Kerkorian was now looking to buy a car manufacturer.

Or was he? Many observers suspected that Kerkorian merely hoped to make a killing on the 9.8 percent stake that he'd acquired in 1990. His takeover bid seemed poorly planned, neglecting the rather important matter of arranging financing. Kerkorian's initial purchase of a substantial minority position, much less his later attempt to acquire the entire company, struck some as foolhardy. Analyst Thomas Galvin of C. J. Lawrence, Morgan Grenfell called the news of the billionaire's 1990 toehold in Chrysler "the craziest thing" he'd ever heard. About the closest Kerkorian had previously come to the automobile business was being dubbed the "Avis of Vegas" after buying the Flamingo Hotel & Casino in the late 1960s. (The sobriquet alluded to the number-two-ranked auto rental company's longstanding advertising slogan. Its point was that Kerkorian was only the second most famous Las Vegas recluse with a background in airlines and gambling, behind Howard Hughes.)

Not everybody dismissed Kerkorian as crazy when he launched his Chrysler bid. "This man is a barracuda," said one securities analyst. "He is not going to let you go until he has bitten off what he came for or swallowed you whole." The self-effacing native of Fresno, California, brushed off such accolades. "I'm just a small-town boy who got lucky," he insisted.

It wasn't luck, however, that secured Kerkorian a valuable ally in his battle with Chrysler's board of directors. Another small-town (Allen-town, Pennsylvania) boy who made good, Lee Iacocca, was indebted to Kerkorian in connection with his reluctant retirement as Chrysler's chairman in 1992. Kerkorian had used his leverage as the company's largest shareholder to induce the directors to grant his friend Iacocca a bigger options package than they'd intended.

Lee Iacocca brought both stature and color to Kerkorian's deal. His accomplishments were legendary, in part (some groused) be-cause of his penchant for hogging all the credit. At Ford, the cigar-chomping executive won acclaim for introducing the wildly successful Mustang. In 1978, Henry Ford II famously fired Iacocca from the Ford presidency on the stated grounds that he just didn't like him. Within months, Iacocca bounced back as president (later chairman) of Chrysler. He proceeded to steer the third-ranked car-maker out of almost certain bankruptcy with the help of a federal loan guarantee. Iacocca became a national celebrity, who was even mentioned as a U.S. presidential prospect, through television com-mercials in which he urged, "If you can find a better car, buy it!"

The Lee Iacocca saga also included a bizarre incident in 1987. A few days after his 70th birthday, Henry Ford II lay dying in a Detroit hospital built by, and named in honor of, his grandfather. On Septem-ber 15, he'd been diagnosed with Legionnaires' disease, a form of viral pneumonia. Ford's physicians had been obliged to perform a tra-cheotomy to facilitate administration of oxygen. Still, family members held out hope that he'd recover. In fact, the man who'd pulled Ford out of its post–World War II swoon and crafted it into a modern cor-poration gamely clung to life until September 29.

On September 18, the Reverend John Mericantante III, associate pastor of the Immaculate Conception Church in Hialeah, Florida, strode into Ford's cubicle in the intensive care unit. There he adminis-tered the last rites of the patient's adopted Roman Catholic faith. Challenged to explain this appalling intrusion, the priest offered a vari-ety of stories: His father had been a Ford regional manager in New England. He'd been asked by a member of the Ford family—whom he refused to name—to perform the sacrament. One thing was clear, however. Father Mericantante had traveled to Detroit to participate in the wedding of Lee Iacocca's daughter, Lia. Apparently a friend of the Iacocca family, he'd been chauffeured to the Henry Ford Hospital in a Chrysler limousine. Nevertheless, Lee Iacocca denied any role in the grotesque sendoff of the man who'd sacked him nine years earlier.

Joining Kirk Kerkorian's hostile takeover bid hardly embellished

Iacocca's reputation. *Automotive News* publisher Keith Crain commented, "Now Iacocca has stunned the world again, and in the blink of an eye he destroyed all the goodwill that he built up over almost five decades." Stung by Kerkorian's criticisms of his management record, Chrysler chairman Robert Eaton struck back fiercely. He hotly contested the insurgents' assertion that the company was excessively cautious in husbanding cash in anticipation of the next, inevitable downturn in auto sales. The raiders were simply angling to enrich themselves through a quick distribution of cash, charged the defenders of Chrysler's conservative financial policy. Iacocca took an especially heavy blow when the board blocked him from exercising the options that Kerkorian had fought to obtain for him in 1992. The former chairman's participation in the takeover bid, claimed the directors, violated the conditions under which his options had been granted.

Kerkorian and Iacocca carried on their faltering campaign into early 1996 before accepting a truce. They agreed to steer clear of Chrysler for the next five years, with Kerkorian promising not to boost his by then 13.6 percent holding above 15 percent. In return, Chrysler agreed to pay Iacocca half of what his options had been worth in 1995. Kerkorian, for his efforts, obtained a seat on the Chrysler board.

Short People

Investors liked the market in 1995 and they loved technologically oriented growth stocks. By early June, computer disk storage systems manufacturer Iomega was up by more than 400 percent from the beginning of the year. Peripherals maker U.S. Robotics had better than doubled. Then there was America Online, a provider of electronic mail, conferencing, and other services. Defying critics of its accounting practices, the company sported a year-to-date gain in excess of 40 percent. All of this was great news for shareholders, but it spelled disaster for short sellers. The stocks they regarded as speculative bubbles were heading up, along with names that had solid reasons to rise.

Even when their instincts were right, the soaring market punished the short sellers. On June 4, for example, the *Wall Street Journal* reported that some major shareholders of Presstek were unloading. The printing-equipment producer's shares promptly fell by more than 10 percent. Following that drop, however, Presstek was still up by 42 percent on the year, leaving the shorts massively underwater. While this was going on, the company later revealed, the Securities and Exchange

Commission was studying "the adequacy and accuracy of statements made by the company and others." At the time (April 1997) that this tidbit was disclosed, Presstek's shares were down by nearly 75 percent from their peak. Short sellers paid dearly, however, for smelling a rat too early.

In a similar vein, America Online's accounting proved to be aggressive, just as the short sellers had contended. Ultimately, the company wrote off $314 million of deferred costs. The company's cumulative profits since inception were wiped out several times over. In effect, management conceded the bears' argument that America Online had been understating the huge cost of enticing subscribers. The short sellers' vindication, unfortunately, didn't occur until October 1996. Meanwhile, America Online's stock soared almost uninterruptedly from the low 20s in June 1995 to a peak in the mid-60s in April 1996. The shorts were fighting the tape and the tape was getting the better of it. (In fairness to America Online, even after its share price plunged to the mid-20s in October 1996, it remained above the level at which the shorts had first targeted it.)

According to investment consultant Harry Strunk, 9 of the 20 short-selling funds that he'd monitored two years earlier were out of business by the middle of 1995. Ten of the 11 survivors, Strunk reported, had lost money during the first four months of the year. Other sources indicated that unlike most of its peers, short seller Kodiak Capital was up slightly on the year. The main reason, though, was that its cash position stood at a whopping 60 percent.

That risk-averse strategy held no appeal for one of the best known short sellers, James Chanos. He resolutely remained short a variety of technology, medical, and restaurant stocks. Through April, stout Chanos was reportedly 30 percent in the hole. For the full year, calculated Michael R. Long of Rockbridge Partners, short sellers as a group hemorrhaged a total return of –15.53 percent. That represented an almost incomprehensible 53-percentage-point underperformance of the S&P 500. As in previous bull markets, the short sellers' focus on fundamental value proved a debilitating handicap during 1995.

How Low Can You Go?

In Japan, a stubbornly strong yen was impeding the country's effort to pull out of its deepest recession since World War II. Corporate bankruptcies were rising and in the just-ended fiscal year, the nation's four leading brokerage houses had lost nearly a billion dollars on their securities holdings. Investors expected the Bank of Japan to attack the problem by lowering interest rates, but they were surprised by the size of the cut that occurred. The central bank cut the discount rate by three-quarters of a percent to a postwar low of 1 percent.

By drastically reducing the yields on yen-denominated instruments, the Bank of Japan had given investors a huge incentive to shift their assets to other currencies. The dollar was one beneficiary. With pressure coming off the currency just a bit, the odds increased that the Fed would halt its crusade against inflation. Greenspan insisted that interest rate cuts would have to be preceded by a federal deficit reduction, but the economic statistics were beginning to suggest that any further rate hikes might precipitate a recession. So, with a little help from Tokyo, U.S. securities prices renewed their climb.

Japanese investors didn't cheer their government's stimulus package, however. They complained that the plans included no targets for public spending cuts. Additionally, officials were vague on future efforts to deregulate business. True, the government vowed to implement a previously announced five-year deregulation program in just three years. But accelerating that plan, said Salomon Brothers economist Jeffrey Young, amounted to "multiplying zero by a larger number." In any event, the Bank of Japan took the still more drastic step of cutting the discount rate to 0.5 percent.

Everything Old Is New Again

William Simon last figured in this chronicle of Very Good Years in 1975. As secretary of the Treasury in that year, he facetiously recommended selling New York City to the Shah of Iran. It would violate sacred American principles, Simon contended, for the federal government to bail out the financially distressed municipality.

Readers may have inferred that Simon was an uncharitable soul, but nothing could be further from the truth. In his spectacularly profitable return to the private sector, Simon became justly renowned as a philanthropist. But it was evidently not a desire for still wider fame or honor that motivated his good works. In January 1995, Simon wrote to the Foundation for New Era Philanthropy, offering to become an anonymous donor.

Anonymous donors were the key to New Era Philanthropy's success. The organization had been founded in 1989 by John G. Bennett, Jr. A medical school dropout who had migrated into administration of a substance abuse program and then fund-raising, Bennett initially offered the following proposition: Twenty charitably inclined individuals would deposit $5000 each with New Era for six months. At the end of that period, their donations would be matched by an unidentified philanthropist. They could then give $10,000 each to the nonprofit causes of their choice. The plan was as successful as it was simple. After two rounds, the "New Concepts in Philanthropy" program upped the number of individual participants from 20 to 50.

New Era worked the beneficiary side of the street, as well. Charitable institutions that deposited money with the foundation were promised multiple rather than mere one-to-one matches. For example, the Young Life International Service Center, a Colorado-based ministry involved in summer camps, placed $2.5 million with New Era to obtain an $8.5 million match. "Sort of hard to turn down, wasn't it?" commented the group's president.

The requirement that the funds be held for six months struck some contributors as odd. Bennett, however, explained that New Era needed to earn interest on the deposited sums in order to cover its operating expenses. Pressed on the matter on another occasion, he said that the six-month provision was a nonnegotiable condition established by the anonymous donors. Charities that stood to receive matching gifts didn't pursue the issue further. As Bennett presented the story, they had been specially selected on their merits to participate in the program. The potential beneficiaries worried that rude questions might jeopardize their elect status.

Religious charities, which didn't qualify for grants from many secular foundations, were particularly attracted to New Era. It helped that Bennett was known to be passionately involved in church activities. Further strengthening the faith connection was J. Douglas Holladay. Formerly President Ronald Reagan's liaison to Protestant groups, he pulled down a six-figure income as a consultant to New Era. At Manhattan's exclusive Links Club, a monthly breakfast group frequently closed its informal proceedings with a prayer by Holladay. The get-together also afforded him an opportunity to spread the good news about a remarkable innovation in philanthropy.

Many grateful beneficiaries of New Era's gift-matching were happy to make 5 percent "thank offerings" to a Philadelphia seminary that introduced them to the program. These remittances were also referred to as "finders' fees," although the seminary's president said the recipients of the matches were not obligated to pay.

Before long, money was flowing in by the tens of millions. Propelled by visions of limitless prosperity, New Era relocated its headquarters to a tonier space and opened offices in London and Hong Kong. New Era's original anonymous donor was joined by eight more, a figure that didn't include ex-Treasury Secretary William Simon. Curiously, Bennett showed no interest in Simon's generous offer.

To Albert Meyer, that wasn't the only curious-seeming thing about the Foundation for New Era Philanthropy. For example, the organization wasn't registered as a foundation and its books had never been audited. Meyer was an accounting professor at Spring Arbor College, a small Michigan institution that had given New Era $250,000. He grew sufficiently concerned to devote his spare time for nearly two years to investigating John Bennett's operation.

Meyer became convinced through his digging that New Era Philanthropy, despite its religious trappings, was nothing more than a massive Ponzi scheme. This variety of scam is akin to a chain letter. Participants make profits through cash taken in from subsequent rounds of victims. The circle must continue to expand in order for the process to continue. Eventually, the operation grows too large to support and collapses.

Spring Arbor's administration wasn't eager to kill the golden egg–producing goose. The school's president brushed off Meyer's findings, commenting that although it paid to be skeptical, "crusading zeal" could be counterproductive. Unwilling to give up his fight, Meyer wrote to the Securities and Exchange Commission and the Internal Revenue Service, as well as the attorney general of Pennsylvania, where New Era was headquartered.

The authorities launched investigations that eventually corroborated Meyer's allegations. New Era's anonymous donors were fictitious. Bennett simply took in cash to pay off earlier rounds of donors, creating the illusion that huge matching funds were flowing in. This cleared up the mystery of why a six-month delay in disbursement of the funds was necessary. The operation's Ponzi character also accounted for its shift, in its final months, to asking charitable groups to contribute their entire endowments to the matching programs.

Additional discrepancies confirmed suspicions originally raised by Tony Carnes of the International Research Institute on Values Changes, a New York nonprofit organization. For instance, during the first few years of its existence New Era hadn't filed federal tax returns or registered as a charity with the state of Pennsylvania. Another red flag overlooked by donors and beneficiaries was the absence of an escrow account for the deposited funds. Instead, New Era held the cash in an ordinary brokerage account, which it could draw upon. Finally, it turned out that the director of ministries at John Bennett's church hadn't seen the supposedly devout fund-raiser at services in almost a year.

Confronted with suggestions that New Era wasn't on the level, Bennett insisted that its finances were completely in order. The foundation's outside auditor, Andrew Cunningham, shook his head over the insinuation that New Era's anonymous donors were imaginary. "There is so much widespread cynicism in the world," he lamented, "that people cannot accept that there's a wealthy philanthropist who has a net worth in the hundreds of millions who is willing to give away substantial amounts and get no credit for it." The following year, Cunningham pleaded guilty to abetting a wire fraud.

Bennett's denial phase didn't last long. On May 13, 1995, he assembled New Era's employees and confessed that he had fabricated the anonymous donors. Bennett offered the tearful workers no explanation for his actions. Grief counselors were quickly dispatched to the scene.

On May 15, the Foundation for New Era Philanthropy filed for bankruptcy. Against assets of $80 million, the organization claimed to have $551 million of liabilities, an inflated figure that included the promised matches of 100 percent or more. Within a few days, the SEC and Pennsylvania's attorney general sued New Era for fraud. Meanwhile, Prudential Securities had sued New Era and Bennett to recover $44.9 million that it claimed the foundation had borrowed on margin and failed to repay. Federal authorities later charged that Bennett had transferred $3.5 million of the organization's funds for his personal use.

William Simon, whose offer to join the ranks of anonymous donors had been rebuffed by Bennett, had contributed almost a million dollars to be matched. He filed a claim for both the money he had lost and the extra million of matching funds that New Era had promised him.

Simon was not the only financial sophisticate taken in by New Era's founder. Legendary investor John Templeton was so impressed by Bennett that he named him a director or trustee of 24 of his mutual funds. One of New Era's most prominent donors was Simon's former business partner, Raymond Chambers, reputedly the brains behind the duo's sensationally lucrative leveraged buyout of Gibson Greeting Cards. Also among the notable contributors, directly or through foundations, were Peter Lynch, champion manager of Fidelity's Magellan

Fund; philanthropist Laurance Rockefeller; and Julian H. Robertson, Jr., of Tiger Management, one of America's most prominent hedge fund operators.

John C. Whitehead, former cochairman of Goldman, Sachs, was another enthusiastic participant. "It may sound too good to be true," he told an interviewer before New Era collapsed, "but nonetheless it is true." Whitehead also pointed to the financial heavyweights among the foundation's supporters. "We're not naive dupes, I don't think." The onetime Deputy Secretary of State responded somewhat differently when he learned that the foundation had gone bust. "Oh, my God, I cannot believe it. I'm normally very skeptical about these kinds of things, and it's hard for me to believe that I was played for a sucker."

John Bennett's personal assets were frozen shortly after the bankruptcy filing. He later surrendered $1.2 million in property, cash, and securities and agreed not to sell the book, motion picture, or television rights to his story without permission of the bankruptcy trustee. In March 1997, Bennett pleaded no contest to federal charges of fraud, money laundering, and filing false tax returns. The plea, according to his attorneys, was "consistent with Mr. Bennett's deep religious convictions." Nevertheless, the God-fearing fund-raiser indicated that he'd withdraw it if the court would let him present psychiatric evidence that he hadn't intended to commit any crimes.

The 82-count federal indictment, in contrast, charged that Bennett had intended to defraud donors from the outset. If so, he hardly could have advertised the fact more effectively than by calling his organization the Foundation for New Era Philanthropy. As noted way back in the 1927 chapter, the phrase "New Era" expressed the then-prevalent notion of limitless prosperity, which was utterly discredited by the 1929 Crash and the Great Depression. In 1958, A. T. Miller of the *Magazine of Wall Street* perceived in the growing cult of equities "ugly parallels to the New Era of the late 1920s." Bennett might just as well have announced, "My innovative approach to charity is a bubble that's bound to burst at some point."

What's still more astounding is that even the newest New Era debacle didn't end investors' fatal attraction to either the phrase or the concept. At the conclusion of 1995, Alan Abelson of *Barron's* felt obliged to challenge the "popular notion" that America had entered "a new investment era." He quoted approvingly Merrill Lynch's Robert Farrell, who observed that "every extreme has been thoroughly justified and rationalized at the time it was being created."

In Abelson's estimation, it *did* matter that at no previous point in

the century had the S&P 500's dividend yield been lower or the equity market's aggregate value been higher, relative to gross domestic
product. Almost a year later, however, bulls were still proclaiming that
such historical valuation criteria were no longer relevant. The comments echoed William R. Biggs's in 1927 on the question of whether
changing conditions had obsolesced the old standards of comparison.
But veteran money manager Lee Cooperman of Omega Partners dissented, saying he didn't "believe in either the tooth fairy or the new
paradigm."

Still, the Coolidge period's sobriquet remained ubiquitous. As Alan
Greenspan geared up for a 1997 tightening of monetary policy, he denied that a "new era" justified prevailing securities valuations. When
interest rates began to climb, the *New Republic* chided the Fed chairman for closing his mind to the possibility that the U.S. economy had
entered a "new era." Perhaps, the weekly editorialized, the "growth
optimists" were right. These cheery economists argued "with varying
levels of plausibility" that moderate inflation was consistent with a
lower unemployment rate than in the past. Globalization made it
tougher for American companies to jack up prices, they claimed, while
productivity had risen with the help of computers. In any event, "most
(though not all)" economists believed the government's inflation statistics were overstated. The *New Republic* editorialist had to concede
one point, however: "Hard data to support the new era hypotheses remains sketchy."

Despite repeated discrediting of the assertion that "this time is different," many investors continue to set a low threshold for accepting
evidence of structural change in the economy. Phenomena observed in
previous cycles are readily conceded to be departures rather than
reprises. It's just plain tough to teach a New Era dog to recognize old
tricks.

The Fed Reaches a Turning Point

On June 29, a prosperity scare slammed the bond market. Economic
reports showed an unexpectedly large drop in initial jobless claims and
a surprisingly big gain in new home sales. Perhaps Alan Abelson of
Barron's had been right in warning that a housing boom would short-
circuit the Federal Reserve's apparent transition toward a policy of reducing interest rates. Thirty-year Treasury bonds fell by $1\frac{7}{8}$ points, a
huge move for that market. The Dow initially dropped by over 34
points, although it rebounded to finish down only 6.23.

Money market economists were split on the question of which way the Fed would go the following week. NationsBanc's Mickey D. Levy stuck to his guns in saying that further easing would be well advised. But another pundit who'd been expecting a rate cut, Prudential's Richard Rippe, now said that it was "a very close call." Steven Roach of Morgan Stanley went further out on a limb, terming a rate reduction "premature."

Before the Fed Open Market Committee convened, however, one key obstacle to a rate cut began to fade. The dollar, which had lately languished below 80 yen, began to recover. A turning point was reached when Japan and the United States achieved a breakthrough in tense auto import negotiations.

Even with the threat to the dollar fading, the Fed Open Market Committee was divided on the wisdom of lowering rates. Greenspan subsequently justified the move on the grounds that the inflationary threat had receded, as evidenced by trends in labor costs, capacity utilization, and commodity costs. Some of his colleagues nevertheless favored standing pat, while others advocated more aggressive easing than Greenspan deemed appropriate. Under the circumstances, it's hard to fault money market economists whose crystal balls proved a little fuzzy.

By July 5, however, investors had made up their minds. They concluded that interest rates were heading lower and pushed the Dow through 4600. It was anticlimactic when, on July 6, the central bank chopped the fed funds rate by a quarter-point to 5¾ percent. Less than a week later, on July 10, stocks blew past yet another Dow century mark to close at 4702.73.

Climb Every Mountain

The sound of ascending stock prices continued to be accompanied by discordant strains of trading losses. For starters, Pennsylvania-based First Capital Strategists had bad news for its client, the Common Fund. The money manager announced on July 5 that a trader's "secret and unauthorized actions" had cost the overseer of endowment funds for over 1400 financial institutions a cool $128 million. In an echo of the earlier Chemical and Barings incidents, it turned out that appropriate safeguards existed only on paper. As the Common Fund explained it, trader Kent Ahrens was supposed to exploit minor intermarket price discrepancies by buying and selling stock index derivatives. Instead (according to First Capital Strategists), he made an unauthorized bet on the direction of the market and lost big.

"Big," naturally, was a relative term. In September, Daiwa Bank topped Ahrens's loss by disclosing that trader Toshihide Iguchi had accumulated $1.1 billion of losses over 11 years. Predictably, the bank attributed the calamity to unauthorized trading. Meanwhile, the Dow cracked the 4800 level.

A rare bit of good news arrived in October. Mexico announced that it would begin repaying its U.S. emergency loan package early. After that, it was back to sour notes, including a sharp drop in technology stocks on October 9. Next came a federal budget impasse. Earlier in the year, when the subject was Mexico, a default on government debt was viewed by Clinton Administration officials as a scenario too awful to contemplate. Toward the end of 1995, a default by the United States didn't appear completely beyond the realm of possibility. The market responded by blasting through the 4900, 5000, and 5100 thresholds on the Dow, all during the second half of November.

Le Vieux Carret

Alert readers may have noticed that a promise made way back in the 1927 chapter hasn't yet been fulfilled. Phil Carret, the *Barron's* staffer who wrote so authoritatively on financial statement analysis, was supposed to be reintroduced in a subsequent chapter. What happened to him after almost 70 years?

The answer is that at age 98, Carret (pronounced "car-RAY") was still putting in a 40-hour week. (Upon turning 100, he cut back to three days a week.) Besides being the world's oldest practicing money manager, he had also acquired "by far the best long-term record on Wall Street," according to his friend and fellow prodigy Warren Buffett.

Phil Carret founded the Pioneer Fund in 1928 and managed it for the next 55 years. During that span, he compiled a compound annual return of 13 percent, outperforming the S&P 500 by four percentage points. The February 1995 issue of *Mutual Fund* magazine named Pioneer number-one in total performance among U.S. funds in operation since 1929.

What were the secrets of Carret's success? One key was to avoid buying on margin. "If you don't borrow money, you can't go broke," he reasoned. Carret also emphasized the importance of having a "money mind." This meant an aptitude for spotting a product that was popular, or likely to be, and figuring out how to turn it into an investment opportunity.

One time, for example, Carret became intrigued by a fancy soap he found in a hotel. It turned out that Neutrogena was manufactured by a public company in Los Angeles. He bought the stock, which split six times in a period of eight years. Carret sold a lot of stock along the way, taking hefty profits and ending up with a few thousand shares at an average cost of about one dollar. Late in 1994, Johnson & Johnson acquired Neutrogena for $35.25 a share.

Carret cited the long-run appreciation of Warren Buffett's Berkshire Hathaway as proof of the folly of selling too early. In 1995, with the stock at $29,000 a share, he reported that he'd bought it a decade earlier at 400. (Carret's son, also a money manager, told an interviewer that his father's cost basis was 200. The discrepancy may have reflected Carret's modesty, his son's filial pride, or a series of purchases at varying levels. According to the price record, Carret couldn't literally have bought Berkshire Hathaway only a decade before 1995 as low as 400, but precision isn't really the point.)

One company that Phil Carret didn't care to invest in was a favorite of Buffett's, Coca-Cola. This was also the stock that made Hall of Famer Ty Cobb rich. Despite such endorsements, the money manager whom Buffett called "the Lou Gehrig of investing" couldn't justify Coca-Cola's lofty price-earnings multiple. Besides, said Carret, "I don't happen to like the damn drink."

Default Is Not in Our Stars

After cutting interest rates on July 6, the Federal Reserve remained on the sidelines until December. Alan Greenspan perceived that the economy had passed its maximum point of recession risk. Therefore, he indicated, investors shouldn't expect any further monetary easing in the near term. The market now turned its attention to the emerging federal budget crisis.

In May, the House and Senate Budget Committees had approved plans to bring income and outlays in line by 2002. President Clinton was sticking to a plan for a more gradual balancing of the budget, while vetoing GOP-generated spending cuts. As Fed watcher Steven K. Beckner explained in *Back from the Brink: The Greenspan Years*, the parties dug in their heels in a way that threatened the government's ability to continue funding its operations:

Gingrich had foolishly thrown down the gauntlet earlier in the year, threatening to hold an increase in the debt limit hostage to passage of a balanced budget. This was a game of chicken the administration was quite willing to play and play to win.

The rhetoric escalated. At one point, a Clinton spokesman characterized the Republicans' efforts to slow the growth of Medicare spending as a wish to see the elderly get sick and die. House Speaker Newt Gingrich thundered that the prospect of default should be no obstacle to obtaining a balanced budget. "I don't care if we have no executive offices and no bond for 60 days—not this time." (Unlike his predecessor, John Garner, Gingrich stopped short of beseeching the assembled Representatives literally to stand up for a balanced budget.)

Speaker Gingrich confidently predicted that bondholders would understand the difference between suffering a genuine default and not getting their money on time as a result of political squabbling. Stan Druckenmiller, chief investment officer for George Soros's hedge fund complex, contended that if "a default was followed by entitlement reform, the markets would not only be forgiving, but you would have a new lower level of interest rates."

Alan Greenspan wasn't so sanguine. He warned that if the government broke its word, a cloud would hang over its securities for years to come. Paul Volcker, Greenspan's immediate predecessor as Federal Reserve chairman, chimed in that default was "hardly consistent with the requirements of a great power with international responsibilities."

In any event, time was running out. Treasury Secretary Rubin proclaimed that a "train wreck" would occur by October if Congress failed to increase the existing $4.9 trillion debt ceiling. Later, he revised his estimated doomsday to November, but he wasted no time searching for nontraditional financing sources. As in the Mexican standoff earlier in the year, it appeared likely that the administration would have to pull a rabbit out of the hat.

The newest rabbit turned out to be federal employees' pension funds. Rubin indicated he'd tap that source to keep the government running beyond November 13. (Congress and the White House had agreed to a temporary extension of the Treasury's borrowing authority through that date.) When Congress proposed to bar Rubin from drawing on the pension funds as a condition of raising the debt ceiling, Clinton nixed the deal. Rubin then told the Federal Employees Retirement System's Government Securities Investment Fund to shift $21.5 billion from special one-day Treasury securities to idle cash. He also made a technical decision that would enable him to move $39.8 billion in the Civil Service Retirement and Disability Fund from securities to cash. These gambits, Rubin estimated, would stave off default until late December. Meanwhile, on November 14, the federal government furloughed 800,000 employees.

Clinton and the Republicans worked out another stopgap measure, enabling the government to resume opeations through December 15. Republicans hoped a permanent deal could be struck by then. After all, Clinton now said he was willing to work toward a seven-year deadline for balancing the budget. It turned out, though, that he still wanted to retain considerably more spending than the Republicans. The budget would balance only if the President's more optimistic assumptions about corporate profits and interest rates were vindicated.

At midnight on Friday, December 15, government employees were furloughed once again. For once, the financial markets didn't sail right through the bad news. Instead, the Dow fell by 101.52 points on Monday.

Up until that point, the market had dismissed the budget stalemate as so much political posturing. Even after government closed down for the second time, investors didn't assume that Uncle Sam would actually default. But many *had* assumed that the Fed was on the verge on lowering interest rates again.

For one thing, a reduction would bring fed funds into line with a general decline in rates that had occurred since the Fed's last easing on July 6. Furthermore, consumer spending, production, and employment were all less than robust. Another consideration involved a possible new shock to the world financial system. The already troubled Japanese banks had been tainted by association with Daiwa's tsunami-like bond trading loss. Lenders were now increasing the risk premium on rates offered to Japanese banks. By cutting U.S. rates, the Fed might ameliorate the resulting squeeze on the institutions' margins and possible threat to their solvency.

The strongest argument of all for new Fed easing was the progress that Washington seemed to be making toward a deficit reduction. Once Greenspan was satisfied that the federal budget was on a good track, investors reckoned, he'd cease to worry that lowering rates would reignite inflation. With Clinton and Gingrich at an impasse, however, it was assumed that the Fed would refrain from cutting rates.

Nevertheless, on December 19 the Fed Open Market Committee unanimously voted to reduce the fed funds rate by a quarter of a point to $5\frac{1}{2}$ percent. Greenspan's official explanation was lower-than-expected inflation, but the action had the nice effect of halting the financial markets' slide. The government shutdown lasted six days into 1996, while a budget accord was reached only on April 24. But thanks to the Fed's long-hoped-for rate cut, stocks finished 1995 on a positive note.

How Long Has This Been Going On?

In mid-November, a new D-word—default—rose to more than a whisper. Federal Reserve chairman Greenspan and Treasury secretary Rubin both deplored the possibility that the United States would spoil its record of never having failed to meet its obligations. According to Federal Home Loan Bank of Chicago president Alex J. Pollock, however, it was too late.

"The U.S. quite clearly and overtly defaulted on its debt as an expediency during the first year of Franklin Roosevelt's presidency, an action later upheld by the Supreme Court," he wrote. Pollock referred to Congress's abrogation of gold payment clauses, discussed in the chapter on 1935. He recapitulated the congressional argument that the provisions obstructed its power, yet termed the abrogation a plain repudiation. "History makes clear," he concluded, "that if Congress cares enough about something, a default will not necessarily stand in its way."

It Was Great Fun

The Dow Jones Industrial Average reached one milestone after another throughout 1995. At year-end, the index stood at 5117.12, up from 3834.44 12 months earlier. Total return on the Standard & Poor's 500 measured 36.89 percent. It was the stock market's 10th best year since 1900.

Soaring equity prices made it exceptionally attractive for corporations to pay for acquisitions with stock. The time was ripe for companies to combine, in hopes of achieving cost savings. Consolidation promised a means of maintaining earnings momentum and propelling stock prices still higher. U.S. mergers and acquisitions soared to $458 billion, according to Securities Data Company, up 32 percent from the previous record, set just one year earlier.

It was commonly said, with justification, that equities had been in a secular bull market since 1982. Two full decades had passed since the S&P's last 35-percent-plus year, however. That was the longest such interval of the twentieth century. Did this expansion of the distance between peak returns indicate that the market was becoming steadier over time?

With regard to the 1975 Very Good Year, 17 years had elapsed since the S&P 500 topped 35 percent. The third stretch of similar duration also occurred during the latter two-thirds of the century, namely, the 19 years from 1935 to 1954. Between 1900 and 1935, the average period between 35-percent-plus years was 5.4 years. After that point (through 1995), the average span was 15 years. Furthermore, since 1958 there have been no cases of total return exceeding 40 percent.

Other statistics might tell a different story about the long-run trend of market volatility. Instead of studying the calendar years with the biggest returns, an analyst might instead focus on the size of peak-to-trough price swings over full market cycles. Alternatively, there's merit in concentrating on market crashes, as many other books and articles have done. Yet another way of gauging changes in market stability would be to measure monthly, daily, or even intraday movements.

Nevertheless, it's intriguing to consider the possibility that over time, one-year bursts of spectacular stock market performance are genuinely becoming more rare. As we shall see in the Epilogue in reviewing all 10 Very Good Years since 1900, monetary factors seem to play a consistently important role. Over time, possibly, extraordinary measures affecting credit and currency have been required less and less frequently. Alternatively, the shocks may be coming along with as great a regularity as ever, but the world's central bankers may be getting better at their job. By periodically dousing the system with liquidity, they perhaps avoid the necessity of flooding it to contain a crisis. And without such extraordinary measures, it may not be possible for stock prices to rise as swiftly in a short period as they have in the 10 best years since 1900.

How the Forecasters Fared

According to the *Wall Street Journal*, economists' opinions about the outlook were unusually divided at the beginning of 1995. Everything depended on how long and how aggressively the Federal Reserve chose to stalk the inflation menace. But even though the economic forecasts covered a wide range, it's fair to say that investors received few hints that one of the all-time blowout years was in store.

Perhaps shell-shocked by 1994's tough conditions, a number of justly well regarded money managers suspected that a longer-run malaise had set in. "It's possible," said Blackstone Alternative Asset Management president Michael Holland, "that some time from now, 1994 will be considered a watershed from the period of the 1980s and early 1990s, when money management rode a tide of rising securities prices." Roger Hertog, president of Sanford C. Bernstein & Company, said 1994 marked the first "distinct change" from "an investment nirvana" that began in 1980. For the first time since 1981, his firm took the defensive step of reallocating 10 percent of its clients' equity investments into bonds.

Within the brokerage industry, too, were students of the market who expected the bad times to continue for a while. Market strategist Michael Metz of Oppenheimer foresaw a year of investor disenchantment. The sources included:

- Disillusionment with financial intermediaries such as mutual funds.
- A vast quantity of litigation involving questionable investment practices.
- A perception of rising instability, not only in international emerging markets, but also in currencies and even in the U.S. markets.

Other strategists perceived a problem in the fact that stocks had managed a small gain in 1994, despite the catastrophe in the bond market. Fixed-income investors, so the argument went, were signaling that they expected short-term rates to rise further. That would inevitably slow down the economy, yet stock buyers' actions indicated that they thought corporate earnings would remain vigorous.

Both camps could not be right, so stock and bond prices would have to become aligned, one way or another. In the opinion of Salomon Brothers strategist David Shulman, prevailing inflationary worries precluded a bond rally. Therefore, he reasoned, a decline in equities was the more likely means of reconciling valuations in the two markets. Additional Fed tightening, Shulman argued, would seal the Dow's fate by making short-term fixed-income investments more competitive with stocks. Shulman was one of several strategists looking for a sharp correction during 1995. Others in this school included Jeffrey Applegate of CS First Boston and Katherine Hensel of Lehman Brothers. Dillon, Read's Joseph McAlinden projected a decline of about 16 percent.

Much good analysis undoubtedly went into these forecasts, but they weren't vindicated by events. Far from becoming disenchanted with the stock market, investors poured a record $116.5 billion into equity mutual funds in 1995. According to the Investment Company Institute, that shattered the previous high of $91.1 billion, set in 1993. (By some analysts' reckoning, though, the huge mutual fund inflows were explained by individual investors' shifting their money out of direct ownership of stocks.) Further confounding the pessimists, stocks and bonds both enjoyed sensational years. As the S&P produced a total return of 36.89 percent, 30-year U.S. Treasury bonds returned 34.08 percent. At last the two markets were reading from the same hymnbook, but harmony had been achieved by a means that the bears hadn't envisioned. Finally, the bears' expected correction never materialized. At no point during 1995 did the Dow drop more than two points below its 1994 year-end level of 3834.44.

In short, a large body of well informed analysts urged investors to avoid a market that was about to record its best year in two decades. This group wasn't even enthusiastic about the play-it-safe strategy of sticking to bonds, which would have been just about as good a recommendation as being heavily invested in stocks.

As noted by the *Wall Street Journal*, however, opinions varied widely at the beginning of 1995. Several prominent brokerage firm prognosticators were optimistic. Merrill Lynch's Charles Clough upped his recommended weighting in equities in January and stayed bullish. Gail Dudack of UBS Securities likewise saw a good year ahead, based partly on her expectation that capital would return to the U.S. from troubled foreign markets such as Mexico. Dudack also astutely declared a peak in interest rates, based on an apparent bottoming out in utility stocks. IDS Advisory Group portfolio manager James Weiss likewise thought interest rates had reached their zenith. He predicted that the Federal Reserve would engineer a "soft landing" for the economy, while productivity gains and overseas sales growth would buoy corporate profits. In short, there were bulls as well as bears at the start of 1995. But even those who got the economic scenario and the market direction right were generally surprised by the magnitude of the rally.

Economist Joe Carson of Dean Witter had been one of the few forecasters to foresee 1994's economic acceleration and higher interest rates. He was prescient once again in peering ahead to 1995. Carson saw a strong case for noninflationary growth. Congressional Republicans, he believed, would phase in the tax-cutting aspects of their Contract with America over several years, thereby avoiding a federal deficit buildup.

On that basis, said Carson, interest rates would come down, but first the Fed would tighten, one last time, by half a percent. This prediction proved right on the money, with the central bank concluding its preemptive strike against inflation in February. Carson had to be goaded into handicapping the stock market's prospects, but he stuck his neck out by calling for a 10 percent to 15 percent rise in the Dow.

The Dean Witter economist's forecast might have seemed bold, after an increase of only 2.1 percent in 1994, yet he proved too conservative. The actual 1995 jump was 33.5 percent. Morgan Stanley market strategist Byron Wien was a bit closer to the mark with his beginning-of-the-year call for a 17 percent rise in the Dow. "That forecast was considered almost irresponsible by clients last January," Wien later recalled. "As it turned out, I wasn't irresponsible enough."

Readers shouldn't take this retrospective assessment as an endorsement of one set of handicappers over another. In other years, the shoe undoubtedly will be on the other foot, with respect to forecasting success. The hits and misses of 1995 simply indicate that no one has yet perfected the art of reading the future.

Prognosticators didn't emphasize, if they considered at all, the possible impact on Federal Reserve policy of two events of the tail end of 1994. According to Bear, Stearns economist Elizabeth Mackay, "If you looked at the monetary numbers, liquidity clearly was being provided, in reaction to Orange County and Mexico." If, as she contended, the Fed engaged in "back-door easing" to head off larger crises, the stock market got a boost that the experts weren't counting on.

Randall W. Forsyth of *Barron's* noted another unforeseen event that had a great impact during 1995. "Early in the year," he wrote, "the U.S. dollar was in free-fall, dropping to under 80 Japanese yen, a post–World War II low." Central banks around the world came to the rescue, buying dollars to shore up the exchange rate. They invested their greenbacks in U.S. Treasuries, igniting a bond rally. Then, in the summer, the Bank of Japan began to reflate by taking short-term interest rates down almost to zero. This spurred further Treasury purchases, as investors borrowed cheaply in yen and invested in the much-higher-yielding dollar market.

Thanks to the influx of investment funds into the U.S. fixed-income market, a key event in the bears' scenario never materialized. Bond yields didn't rise, so equity investment capital wasn't siphoned off by bonds. More probably, the dive in interest rates induced investors to shift funds from low-yielding savings vehicles to stocks, in hopes of earning bigger returns.

This Is How the Story Ends

"A Very Good Year," besides being a riff that reappears throughout this book, was the title of a 1995 wrap-up in *Barron's*. "Behind the rally in U.S. stocks," wrote staff member Bill Alpert, "was a combination of expanding earnings, low interest rates, modest inflation, and a strengthening dollar."

Similar multifaceted explanations could be offered for all of this century's sensational bull markets. Nevertheless, there is value in reviewing the exceptionally strong years discussed in this book, in hopes of identifying one or more common themes. This is the objective of the next and final chapter.

∽ *Epilogue* ∽
What Causes the Very Good Years?

Some readers derive intrinsic pleasure from studying history, but investors have a practical motivation. Future opportunities may emerge from conditions that resemble those responsible for rich rewards of the past. For example, by correctly understanding why annual returns have occasionally topped 35 percent, stock market participants may learn to tell when it's about to happen again.

To anticipate the great booms, it's necessary to filter out voluminous information that has no bearing whatsoever. The trouble is, it's hard to ignore irrelevant facts to which market pundits and financial journalists assign immense significance. And to be fair, some facts that shed no light on the extremely good years may be quite useful in handicapping the market's more mundane fluctuations.

The brief analysis that follows doesn't purport to explain every 5 percent or 10 percent swing in the Dow. Recapitulating the historical experience does, however, enable investors to zero in on the circumstances that produced the maximum returns.

The Candidates

Any devotee of the financial pages can reel off several possible explanations for the great bull years. The following, which are not mutually exclusive, probably represent the most common theories:

Anticipation of a Corporate Profit Rebound
The market assesses the values of common stocks as a function of current or expected future earnings. Because investors are by nature forward-looking, they begin to bid up stocks well before the general level of corporate profits rises.

Psychology Shift
Stock prices are driven by emotion. From time to time, a wave of pessimism abruptly and inexplicably gives way to optimism. Suddenly,

price-earnings ratios seem low, impelling investors to scramble for bargains. The scrambling continues long after the bargains disappear. Prices therefore escalate, without regard to intrinsic value, until euphoria once again yields to despair.

Very Long Cycles
Deeply embedded in the structure of capitalism is a tendency for major discontinuities to occur every so many years. Probably as the result of technological upheavals, massive new wealth is created in fitful spurts.

Action-Reaction
Stocks follow a regularly recurring cycle of accumulation and distribution. Prices predictably rise and fall in response to these market technicals. Following a big downturn, a huge upturn is inevitable according to this theory.

Easing of Credit Conditions
When the Federal Reserve loosens its grip on the money supply, stock prices benefit in several different ways. For one thing, the corporate earnings outlook improves. Reduced interest rates enable companies to build up their inventories and increase their customers' credit lines. To the extent that price-earnings ratios determine stock values, a jump in earnings necessitates a jump in the index. A second, more direct impact on stock prices derives from the increased availability of loans for financing securities purchases. Finally, a drop in interest rates reduces the attractiveness of fixed-income investments, relative to equities. The logical consequence is a shift of investment capital from bonds to stocks.

Which Explanations Match the Facts?

For anybody hoping to be poised for action when the next sensational year commences, the key question is this: Which interpretation(s) best fit the years examined in the foregoing chapters? Let's consider each candidate on the basis of the evidence.

"Anticipation of a corporate profit rebound" is a plausible reason for the stock market to rally. With respect to the *biggest* rallies, however, the record is spotty. In 1958, for example, earnings per share for the companies constituting the Dow industrials *fell* by 22.5 percent. And it wasn't a simple case of the market anticipating a profit surge that occurred a year later. Not until 1962 did the Dow stocks recapture their 1957 earnings peak. Similarly, earnings declined in 1975 and remained below their 1974 level until 1978. In 1954, to be sure, per-share earnings rose by 3 percent, then by 27 percent in 1955. But if that progression accounted for the stellar stock performance of 1954, why didn't comparable gains occur around 1984, when earnings rose 57 percent?

A further difficulty with the anticipation-of-rebounding-profits hypothesis is that it's unclear how "The Market" knows what future earnings will be. Investors commonly regard the trend of stock prices as a harbinger of future economic trends, assuming that someone wiser than themselves has superior information. A logician probably would seek a simpler explanation. For example, it may be that stock prices react immediately to an event that also happens to result, with a longer delay, in rising corporate profits. One such event that immediately comes to mind is a reduction in interest rates.

There's no denying that maximum stock market performance sometimes coincides with recovery in corporate earnings. But cyclical profit recoveries occur far more frequently than 35-percent-plus annual returns on the S&P 500. A gain as exceptional as that evidently depends on other conditions.

"Psychology shift," like the alleged anticipation of earnings recoveries, is ambiguous from a cause-and-effect standpoint. Few would dispute that losing a lot of money causes investors to feel blue, while making a lot of money brings them joy. On the other hand, it's unclear how a serious analyst would even begin to prove that a spontaneous shift from sadness to joy causes the market to rise. And if the proposition could be demonstrated, there would remain the immense task of predicting these mysterious mood swings.

Investment gurus love to anthropomorphize the stock market and discuss its emotions. Getting it to lie down on a couch to be psychoanalyzed is quite another matter. Foreseeing psychology shifts must be rejected as a basis for anticipating Very Good Years, on grounds of impracticability.

"Very long cycles" are irrelevant to the present project, although they may be useful for other types of market analysis. The irregular spacing of the 35-percent-plus years—1908, 1915, 1927, 1928, 1933, 1935, 1954, 1958, 1975, and 1995—suggests that if the phenomenon reflects a cycle, it's neither a very long nor a predictably recurring one.

The "action-reaction" proposition contains at least a kernel of validity. Simply on the basis of arithmetic, the market has a head start on achieving an outsized gain if it begins the year at a depressed level. It doesn't really matter, for present purposes, whether price swings are truly driven by alternating phases of accumulation and distribution. Nor does the rebound element lose all of its usefulness because major downturns aren't invariably followed in short order by major upturns. The essential question is the converse—that is, whether Very Good Years are consistently preceded by poor market conditions.

On the whole, the record confirms that the bottom is a good place to start. The 1908 rally followed the Panic of 1907 and the 1914 war *scare* preceded the 1915 war *boom*. When the Great Crash of 1929 was followed by even greater price declines, immense upside potential resulted. Even after that potential was partially realized in the century's biggest year (1933), stocks remained low enough to permit another huge rally in 1935. At the outset of 1954, the economic outlook was sufficiently clouded to cause some analysts to predict a full-fledged depression. The Dow Jones Industrial Average had declined by 11 percent in 1953. Similarly, the Dow fell by 13 percent in the year preceding the 1958 bull market. The consumer, capital goods, automotive, and defense sectors all looked pallid in 1957. As for the circumstances leading up to the 1975 bull market, they read like the Ten Plagues. The combined forces of recession and inflation had driven the Dow's price-earnings ratio to its lowest level since 1929. Finally, the Federal Reserve's unexpected tightening of monetary policy left investors in a grim mood entering 1995, even though the Dow drifted marginally higher during the year.

The two glaring exceptions to the bounce-back pattern are the back-to-back Very Good Years of 1927 and 1928. At worst, the flat market of 1926 suggested that the ebullience of 1924–1925 had exhausted itself. Far from wallowing in despair, America had an optimistic viewpoint, thanks to the Coolidge prosperity. In light of the New Era counterexample, the action-reaction notion alone cannot explain the twentieth century's biggest annual returns. Besides, the Dow industrials declined by 15 percent or more in 13 separate years that did not precede one of the century's 10 best. Clearly, there must be something more to the story than the simple strategy of buying on the rebound.

"Easing of credit conditions" qualifies as that something more. It's a consistent theme, frequently with inflationary overtones, in the years of maximum total returns. Only the form of credit-loosening has varied. In different periods, bankers, the administrative branch, or the Federal Reserve System have taken the lead.

The 1907 panic wouldn't have ended, nor would stocks have rallied, if J. Pierpont Morgan hadn't settled the bank crisis. World War I changed from a bearish to a bullish event largely because Woodrow Wilson at long last allowed America to finance purchases by the belligerents. Contemporary observers perceived an unmistakable connection between the 1927–1928 bull market and Benjamin Strong's determination to expand credit. Paramount in his mind was the rescue of Great Britain from its disastrous return to the gold standard. Strong was undeterred by the fact that commercial loan demand was too meager to accommodate the vast increase in liquidity. As a result, margin lending mushroomed and stock prices soared to a level not seen again until 1954. The magnitude of the 1929–1932 bust suggests that Strong was applying powerful medicine, indeed. Powerful enough, in fact, to produce the century's only two instances of Very Good Years that didn't require the assistance of an initially depressed market.

Even though the prospect of currency degradation had been deemed bearish in 1932, "inflation fever" was the rallying cry of 1933. Franklin Roosevelt loosened the dollar's link with gold, while also leaning on the Federal Reserve to keep monetary expansion robust. Growth of U.S. bank reserves, as a consequence of gold inflows, was cited as a source of the 1935 rally. In that year, as well, the Supreme Court beat back a deflationary threat when it upheld abrogation of the gold payment clauses. Finally, monetary expansionist Marriner Eccles arrived on the scene just as the Banking Act of 1935 increased the Federal Open Market Committee's power.

William McChesney Martin's nondoctrinaire approach to monetary policy produced a mid-1954 easing that facilitated that year's rally. Martin's abrupt change of course in November 1957, when he surprised the market with a discount rate cut, helped to launch the 1958 upturn. Further rate-cutting sustained a bullish trend that was generally perceived to be running ahead of the business recovery.

Federal Reserve easing touched off the 1975 stock price surge, as well. It probably wasn't merely coincidental that the United States had just suffered the largest bank failure that had ever occurred up to that time. As in 1957, the Fed's change in direction was abrupt. A similarly unexpected reversal in monetary policy caught investors off guard in 1995. The Fed continued raising interest rates right up until February 1, 1995. Before the month was out, Alan Greenspan confounded many pundits by suggesting that the economy was decelerating.

(Mexico's financial crisis, which threatened to spill over to other international emerging markets, was perhaps more than an incidental factor in the background.) On a global scale, credit easing was propelled by Japan's drastic reduction in interest rates.

The Winning Combination:
Depressed Prices + Sudden Credit Easing

Looking ahead, the most likely formula for the next Very Good Year emerges from the pattern of the two most recent occurrences: Stock prices begin at a depressed level, reflecting fears that inflation-conscious central bankers will inflict more pain. Suddenly, a financial crisis reduces the price level to a secondary public policy consideration. As the Fed liquifies the system, the stock market quickly and radically adjusts to the changed circumstances. In their eagerness to prevent a meltdown, the monetary authorities unavoidably give stock investors a windfall.

When a huge volume of credit suddenly enters the U.S. financial system, whether through Fed action or as the result of some other nation's central bank policy, it must find an outlet. On several occasions during the twentieth century, capital markets have provided that outlet. In these situations, inflation has occurred in financial assets, rather than in goods and services. The phenomenon has been well documented by renowned interest rate observer James Grant, who credits the related theoretical insights to the so-called Austrian school of economics.

Lending credibility to the role of crisis-induced easing is the fact of life that Federal Reserve governors, like Supreme Court justices, can read the election returns. It in no way impugns the integrity of central bankers to acknowledge that they are part of a political system. In his sketch of William McChesney Martin, Daniel Vencill quoted with approval Seymour Harris's comment that there "are degrees of independence." Harris observed as well that "to satisfy the demand for an independent board, on the part of financial men in particular, it is important for the Federal Reserve to give an impression of a degree of independence that does not in fact prevail." The Fed isn't faced with a stark choice between supporting and opposing administration policy, noted Vencill, because its pronouncements contribute to the formulation of that policy.

All in all, it's reasonable to infer that Federal Reserve chairmen feel justified in temporarily setting aside the battle for price stability when some overriding economic concern arises. *Spotting such an overriding concern, at a time when stock prices happen to be depressed, represents the best hope for getting a jump on a Very Good Year in the stock market.*

Capable prognosticators who monitor more conventional indicators haven't consistently foreseen the 35-percent-plus annual returns. (Readers can judge for themselves, given that I've documented the pundits' record in each year's chapter.) This is not to say that tracking corporate profits and standard economic data has no value to investors. Such analysis may be essential for handicapping the market during the lapses of up to two decades between its highest-performance years.

By the same token, it's well worth the effort to be prepared for a reprise of the best returns that occurred between 1908 and 1995. Participating in such a year can offset a lot of bad stock picks in other periods. The heartening news is that while the intervals between Very Good Years are irregular, the preconditions display considerable uniformity. Perhaps, after all, investors can genuinely profit from experience.

~ *Selected Readings* ~

Articles

Alpert, Bill. "A Very Good Year." *Barron's*, January 1, 1996.

"AT&T Rockets after 3-to-1 Split." *Business Week*, December 20, 1958.

Benedict, Charles [Cecelia G. Wyckoff]. "As I See It: Revolution without Revolt." *Magazine of Wall Street*, January 21, 1933.

"Benjamin Graham." *Financial Analysts Journal*, January/February 1968.

Bentson, George J. "Glass-Steagall: Shattering the Myths." *Wall Street Journal*, April 16, 1997.

"Beware the High Yielding Stock." *Magazine of Wall Street*, January 20, 1934.

Biggs, William R. "Sound Common Stocks Yielding over 7%." *Barron's*, January 17, 1927.

Browne, Scribner. "Is It Time to Take Profits?" *Magazine of Wall Street*, December 25, 1915.

"Carret Marks 100th Year and Cuts Back Just a Little." *Wall Street Journal*, December 2, 1996.

Carret, Philip L. "The Art of Speculation: How to Read a Balance Sheet." *Barron's*, December 20, 1926.

———. "The Art of Speculation: The Romance of Buying a Bond." *Barron's*, January 10, 1927.

Carton, Barbara. "Unlikely Hero: A Persistent Accountant Brought New Era's Problems to Light." *Wall Street Journal*, May 19, 1995.

Clay, Paul. "Peace and Prices." *Magazine of Wall Street*, January 22, 1916.

Cresswill, John C. "The Redistribution of Wealth Ceases to Be a Theory." *Magazine of Wall Street*, January 6, 1934.

———. "Ruin by Efficiency? What's All This Technocracy About?" *Magazine of Wall Street*, January 21, 1933.

Dana, Loring, Jr. "The New Era of Fabulous Stock Prices." *Magazine of Wall Street*, December 29, 1928.

Dorfman, Dan, and Karyn McCormack. "A Short Seller's 1995 Hit List." *Money*, February 1995.

Dorfman, John R. "Dow Diary: Euphoria Reigned in '27 Market." *Wall Street Journal*, March 11, 1996.

————. "Dow Diary: Sputnik Launch Spooked Stocks." *Wall Street Journal*, October 7, 1996.

E.K.A. "The Business Analyst: What's Ahead for Business?" *Magazine of Wall Street*, December 25, 1954.

"Fed Accompli." *New Republic*, April 21, 1997.

"Finance: The 'Election Scare' on the Stock Exchange." *Nation*, September 24, 1908.

"Finance: The 'War Scare' in Wall Street." *Nation*, October 15, 1908.

"Financial News: Resumption of Normal Trading in Stocks and Bonds." *American Review of Reviews*, December 1914.

"Financial News: War's Effect on American Securities." *American Review of Reviews*, April 1915.

Forbes, B. C. "Facts and Comment." *Forbes*, December 1, 1953.

Forsyth, Randall W. "For Bondholders, 1995 Was Terrific." *Barron's*, January 1, 1996.

Fuerbringer, Jonathan. "New Era for Taking Market's Pulse." *New York Times*, February 11, 1997.

Gasparino, Charles. "Dow Diary: Big Board's 1914 Shutdown." *Wall Street Journal*, July 8, 1996.

Getlin, Josh. "The Birth of the Headline Heard 'Round the World." *Los Angeles Times*, July 28, 1995.

Goodman, George J. W. "Flourishing Filter-Tips." *Barron's*, December 9, 1957.

Graham, Benjamin. "The New Speculation in Common Stocks." *Analysts Journal*, June 1958.

"The Great Gold Test." *Business Week*, January 5, 1935.

Halverson, Guy. "Some Lessons Learned in 76 Years of Investing." *Christian Science Monitor*, February 27, 1995.

"Harriman and His Time." *Nation*, September 16, 1909.

Hooper, Lucien O. "Market Comment." *Forbes*, January 15, 1954.

"How to Profit from the 1975 Depression" (Advertisement). *New York Times*, March 2, 1975.

"Is the Stock Market Obsolete?" *Fortune*, February 1954.

"It Takes Healthy Nerves to Be a Football Referee" (Advertisement). *Barron's*, November 27, 1933.

Kane, W. Sheridan. " 'Ware the Tipster Sheet." *Magazine of Wall Street*, December 15, 1928.

Kaufman, Henry. "Today's Financial Euphoria Can't Last." *Wall Street Journal*, November 25, 1996.

Kelsey, W. K. "Detroit's Industrial Renaissance." *Barron's*, January 6, 1936.

Kourday, Michael. "Investing in the Younger Generation." *Forbes*, June 1, 1954.

"Leading Financial Articles: Securities Are Paying for Their Keep." *American Review of Reviews*, October 1908.

Leinbach, Arthur M. "Market Finds Gallant Adversary in Federal Reserve." *Barron's*, January 26, 1929.

Levy, S. Jay. "No Panacea." *Barron's*, December 30, 1957.

Liscio, John. "Relax, Mr. Greenspan: An Interview with Joe Carson." *Barron's*, January 2, 1995.

Long, Henry Ansbacher. "Cautious Optimism: Common Stocks Gain Favor with the Investment Companies." *Barron's*, August 4, 1958.

Lowenstein, Roger. "Graham and Dodd and Dow 6000." *Wall Street Journal*, October 17, 1996.

———. "Is U.S. Too Big to Default on Debt? The Unthinkable Is Now Debatable." *Wall Street Journal*, November 9, 1995.

Luke, Robert. "Personal Business: Wise beyond His Peers." *Atlanta Journal*, October 16, 1995.

MacDonald, Stewart. "Will Prosperity Continue?" *Barron's*, January 16, 1928.

Mitchell, Greg. "Film Clips: A Look inside Hollywood and the Movies; Democracy in Action: How the Studios Torpedoed Upton Sinclair's Run for Office." *Los Angeles Times*, October 31, 1993.

Mott, Howard Schenck. "Finance: Stock Market Manipulation and Its Punishment." *Harper's Weekly*, September 5, 1908.

———. "Finance: War Scares and Their Effects." *Harper's Weekly*, October 24, 1908.

Munsey, Frank A. "A Brief Talk by Mr. Munsey about Investments and the Business Outlook." *Munsey's Magazine*, February 1908.

———. "An Optimistic View of the Business Situation, and Its Bearing on Investments." *Munsey's Magazine*, April 1908.

———. "There Isn't Money Enough in the World To-day to Do the World's Work." *Munsey's Magazine*, May 1908.

Nelson, H. J. "The Trader Gives His Views of the Market." *Barron's*, October 27, 1958.

Noland, Joseph. "Boom and Bust in the 1920s: The Economic Lessons for Today." *Vital Speeches*, December 1, 1995.

O'Brien, Robert. "Abreast of the Market: Stocks Cross 4000 for the First Time, but the Visit There May Be Brief." *Wall Street Journal*, February 24, 1995.

"Out of the Space Age: Jobs and Profits." *Changing Times: The Kiplinger Magazine*, June 1958.

"Pepper and Salt." *Wall Street Journal*, December 31, 1932.

Pollock, Alex J. "A U.S. Default? It Wouldn't Be the First Time." *Wall Street Journal*, November 8, 1995.

Raskob, John J. "Everybody Ought to Be Rich." *Ladies' Home Journal*, August 1929.

"Raskob Radio Pool Realized $5,000,000." *New York Times*, May 20, 1932.

Rea, James B. "Remembering Benjamin Graham—Teacher and Friend." *Journal of Portfolio Management*, Summer 1977.

"Remembering Uncle Ben." *Forbes*, October 15, 1976.

Ringstad, Robert C. "Companies Showing Better than Average Earnings Improvement in 1958." *Magazine of Wall Street*, January 3, 1959.

————. "Searching for Values in Low Priced Stocks." *Magazine of Wall Street*, December 6, 1958.

"Roads: The Web Begins to Grow." *Business Week*, January 11, 1958.

Rublin, Lauren R. "The Trader: The Great Bull Market Charges on after a Record Year for All but the Shorts." *Barron's*, January 1, 1996.

Silk, Leonard. "Economics for the Perplexed." *New York Times Magazine*, March 2, 1995.

"Sir Isaac Babson." *Newsweek*, August 23, 1948.

Sobel, Robert. "Default? Never!" *Barron's*, January 1, 1996.

Stecklow, Steve. "Feeding the Frenzy: A New Era Consultant Lured Rich Donors over Pancakes, Prayers." *Wall Street Journal*, June 2, 1995.

Stern, Laurence. "Managed Recovery vs. Depression." *Magazine of Wall Street*, December 22, 1934.

"Wall Street's New Boss 'Knows the Game.' " *Literary Digest*, July 21, 1934.

"War-Horrors in Wall Street." *Literary Digest*, October 30, 1915.

Weng, Rüdiger K. "The Stock That Set Off the 1907 Crash." *Friends of Financial History*, Fall 1994.

Whyte, Joseph P. "Stock Prices and Intrinsic Values." *Barron's*, January 10, 1927.

Wyckoff, Cecelia G. "Why the Market Has Made New Records." *Magazine of Wall Street*, December 15, 1928.

————. "Women Win Investment Success thru Patience and Common Sense." *Magazine of Wall Street*, January 12, 1929.

Wyckoff, Richard D. "How the Stock Market Should Act during the Remainder of the War." *Magazine of Wall Street*, January 23, 1915.

Books

Allen, Frederick Lewis. *Only Yesterday: An Informal History of the 1920's*. New York: John Wiley & Sons, 1997.

————. *Since Yesterday: The Nineteen-Thirties in America, September 3, 1929–September 3, 1939*. New York: Harper & Brothers Publishers, 1939.

Ashby, LeRoy. *William Jennings Bryan: Champion of Democracy*. Boston: Twayne Publishers, 1987.

Barrett, Mary Ellin. *Irving Berlin: A Daughter's Memoir*. New York: Simon & Schuster, 1994.

Baruch, Bernard M. *Baruch: My Own Story*. New York: Holt, Rinehart and Winston, 1957.

Beale, Howard K. *Theodore Roosevelt and the Rise of America to World Power*. Baltimore: Johns Hopkins Press, 1956.

Beckner, Steven K. *Back from the Brink: The Greenspan Years*. New York: John Wiley & Sons, 1996.

Bernstein, Peter L. *Against the Gods: The Remarkable Story of Risk*. New York: John Wiley & Sons, 1996.

———. *Capital Ideas: The Improbable Origins of Modern Wall Street*. New York: Free Press, 1992.

Bierman, Harold, Jr. *The Great Myths of 1929 and the Lessons to Be Learned*. New York: Greenwood Press, 1991.

Brimelow, Peter. *The Wall Street Gurus: How You Can Profit from Investment Newsletters*. New York: Random House, 1986.

Brochu, Jim. *Lucy in the Afternoon: An Intimate Memoir of Lucille Ball*. New York: William Morrow and Company, 1990.

Brown, John Dennis. *101 Years on Wall Street*. Englewood Cliffs, New Jersey: Prentice-Hall, 1991.

Brownlee, W. Elliot. *Dynamics of Ascent: A History of the American Economy*. 2nd ed. New York: Knopf, 1978.

Chaplin, Charles. *My Autobiography*. New York: Simon & Schuster, 1964.

Chase, C. David. *Chase Investment Performance Digest: Performance and Rankings of the World's Major Investments*. Concord, Massachusetts: Chase Global Data and Research, 1995.

Collman, Charles Albert. *Our Mysterious Panics, 1830–1930: A Story of Events and the Men Involved*. New York: William Morrow and Company, 1931.

Columbia University, Faculty of Political Science, ed. *Studies in History, Economics and Public Law*. Volume 56. New York: Columbia University, 1913.

Commerce Clearing House. *Capital Changes Reports*. Chicago, Illinois: Commerce Clearing House, 1995.

Daniels, Josephus. *The Life of Woodrow Wilson: 1856–1924*. Will H. Johnston, 1924.

Davis, Oscar King. *William Howard Taft: The Man of the Hour*. Including a Chapter by Theodore Roosevelt (Reprinted from *The Outlook*, August 1901). Philadelphia: P. W. Ziegler Company, 1908.

Douglas, C. H. *The Use of Money*. London: Stanley Nott, 1934.

Ellis, Charles D., ed., with James R. Vertin. *Classics: An Investor's Anthology*. Homewood, Illinois: Business One Irwin, 1989.

———. *Classics II: Another Investor's Anthology*. Homewood, Illinois: Business One Irwin, 1991.

Fisher, Kenneth L. *100 Minds That Made the Market*. Woodside, California: Business Classics, 1993.

Friedman, Milton, and Anna Jacobson Schwartz. *The Great Contraction: 1929–1933*. Princeton: Princeton University Press, 1965.

Friedman, Philip. *Washington Humor*. New York: Citadel Press, 1964.

Fuess, Claude Moore. *Calvin Coolidge: The Man from Vermont*. Hamden, Connecticut: Archon Books, 1965.

Gabler, Neal. *Winchell: Gossip, Power and the Culture of Celebrity*. New York: Knopf, 1995.

Graham, Benjamin. *Benjamin Graham: The Memoirs of the Dean of Wall Street*. Edited by Seymour Chatman. New York: McGraw-Hill, 1996.

Graham, Otis L., Jr., and Meghan Robinson Wander, eds. *Franklin D. Roosevelt, His Life and Times: An Encyclopedic View.* Boston: G. K. Hall, 1985.

Grant, James. *Bernard M. Baruch: The Adventures of a Wall Street Legend.* New York: John Wiley & Sons, 1996.

———. *The Trouble with Prosperity: The Loss of Fear, the Rise of Speculation, and the Risk to American Savings.* New York: Times Books, 1996.

Harris, Warren G. *Lucy & Desi: The Legendary Love Story of Television's Most Famous Couple.* Thorndike, Maine: Thorndike Press, 1992.

Hayes, Walter. *Henry: A Life of Henry Ford II.* London: Weidenfeld & Nicholson, 1990.

Higham, Charles. *Lucy: The Life of Lucille Ball.* New York: St. Martin's Press, 1986.

Homer, Sidney, and Richard Sylla. *A History of Interest Rates.* 3rd ed. New Brunswick, New Jersey: Rutgers University Press, 1996.

Ibbotson Associates. *Stocks, Bonds, Bills and Inflation: 1996 Yearbook.* Chicago: Ibbotson Associates, 1996.

Kahn, Irving, and Robert D. Milne. *Benjamin Graham: The Father of Financial Analysis.* Charlottesville, Virginia: Financial Analysts Research Foundation, 1977.

Katz, Bernard S., ed. *Biographical Dictionary of the Board of Governors of the Federal Reserve.* New York: Greenwood Press, 1992.

Kennan, George. *E. H. Harriman: A Biography.* Volume 2. Boston: Houghton Mifflin Company, 1922.

Kessler, Ronald. *The Sins of the Father: Joseph P. Kennedy and the Dynasty He Founded.* New York: Warner Books, 1996.

Kluger, Richard. *Ashes to Ashes.* New York: Knopf, 1996.

Klurfeld, Herman. *Winchell: His Life and Times.* New York: Praeger Publishers, 1976.

Koskoff, David E. *Joseph P. Kennedy: A Life and Times.* Englewood Cliffs, New Jersey: Prentice-Hall, 1974.

Lacey, Robert. *Ford: The Men and the Machine.* Boston: Little, Brown and Company, 1986.

Leeson, Nick, with Edward Whitley. *Rogue Trader: How I Brought Down Barings Bank and Shook the Financial World.* Boston: Little, Brown and Company, 1996.

Lichtman, Allan J. *Prejudice and the Old Politics: The Presidential Election of 1928.* Chapel Hill, North Carolina: University of North Carolina Press, 1979.

Lowe, Janet. *Benjamin Graham on Value Investing: Lessons from the Dean of Wall Street.* Chicago: Dearborn Financial Publishing, 1944.

McCoy, Donald R. *Calvin Coolidge: The Quiet President.* New York: Macmillan Company, 1967.

MacDonald, J. Fred. *Don't Touch That Dial!* Student ed. Chicago: Nelson-Hall, 1979.

McHugh, Christopher M., ed. *The 1996 Bankruptcy Yearbook & Almanac.* Boston: New Generation Research, 1996.

Mackay, Charles. *Extraordinary Popular Delusions and the Madness of Crowds;* and Joseph de la Vega, *Confusión de Confusiones.* With a current perspective by Martin S. Fridson. New York: John Wiley & Sons, 1996.

Malkiel, Burton G. *A Random Walk Down Wall Street: Including a Life-Cycle Guide to Personal Investing.* 6th ed. New York: W. W. Norton & Company, 1996.

Marquis (A. N.) Company. *Who's Who of American Women: 1966–1967.* Chicago, Illinois: A. N. Marquis Company, 1967.

Maugham, W. Somerset. *The Razor's Edge.* Garden City, New York: Doubleday & Company, 1944.

Mencken, H. L. *The Vintage Mencken.* Gathered by Alistair Cooke. New York: Vintage Books, 1955.

Midgley, Wilson. *Possible Presidents.* London: Ernest Benn, 1928.

Mitchell, B. R., ed. *International Historical Statistics: The Americas 1750–1988.* New York: Groves Dictionaries, Stockton Press, 1993.

Mitchell, Broadus. *Depression Decade: From New Era through New Deal 1929–1941.* The Economic History of the United States, vol. 9. New York: Rinehart & Company, 1947.

Mooney, Booth. *LBJ: An Irreverent Chronicle.* New York: Crowell, 1976.

Morgan, Hal, and Dan Symes. *Amazing 3-D.* New York: Little, Brown and Company, 1982.

Morgan, Ted. *Maugham.* New York: Simon & Schuster, 1980.

Mulkern, John R. *Continuity and Change: Babson College, 1919–1994.* Babson Park, Massachusetts: Trustees of Babson College, 1995.

Newman, Peter, Murray Milgate, and John Eatwell, eds. *The New Palgrave Dictionary of Money and Finance.* Volume 2. London: Macmillan Press, 1992.

O'Connor, Richard. *The First Hurrah: A Biography of Alfred E. Smith.* New York: G. P. Putnam's Sons, 1970.

Odean, Kathleen. *High Steppers, Fallen Angels, and Lollipops.* New York: Henry Holt and Company, 1988.

Owens, Richard N., and Charles O. Hardy. *Interest Rates and Stock Speculation: A Study of the Influence of the Money Market on the Stock Market.* New York: Macmillan Company, 1925.

Parrish, Michael E. *Anxious Decades: America in Prosperity and Depression 1920–1941.* New York: W. W. Norton & Company, 1992.

Pinard, Maurice. *The Rise of a Third Party: A Study in Crisis Politics.* Enlarged edition. Montreal: McGill–Queen's University Press, 1975.

Quirk, William J., and R. Randall Bridwell. *Abandoned: The Betrayal of the American Middle Class since World War II.* Lanham, Maryland: Madison Books, 1992.

Reeves, Richard. *A Ford, Not a Lincoln.* New York: Harcourt Brace Jovanovich, 1975.

Safire, William. *Safire's New Political Dictionary.* New York: Random House, 1993.

Schlesinger, Arthur M., ed., Fred L. Israel, assoc. ed., and William P. Hansen, mng. ed. *History of American Presidential Elections: 1789–1968*. New York: Chelsea House Publishers, 1985.

Schorer, Mark. *Sinclair Lewis: An American Life*. New York: McGraw-Hill, 1961.

Schwarz, Jordan A. *The Interregnum of Despair: Hoover, Congress, and the Depression*. Urbana, Illinois: University of Illinois Press, 1970.

Scott, Howard. *History and Purpose of Technocracy*. Rushland, Pennsylvania: Technocracy, 1965.

Shepherd, Jack, and Christopher S. Wren, eds. *Quotations from Chairman LBJ*. New York: Simon & Schuster, 1968.

Sklar, Robert. *Movie-Made America: A Cultural History of American Movies*. rev. ed. New York: Vintage Books, 1994.

Sloan, Alfred P., Jr. *My Years with General Motors*. Edited by John McDonald with Catharine Stevens. Garden City, New York: Doubleday & Company, 1963.

Sobel, Robert. *The Big Board: A History of the New York Stock Market*. New York: Free Press, 1965.

———. *N.Y.S.E.: A History of the New York Stock Exchange 1935–1975*. New York: Weybright and Talley, 1975.

———. *Panic on Wall Street: A Classic History of America's Financial Disasters—with a New Exploration of the Crash of 1987*. New York: Truman Talley Books/E. P. Dutton, 1988.

Staley, Kathryn F. *The Art of Short Selling*. New York: John Wiley & Sons, 1997.

Stump, Al. *Cobb: A Biography*. Chapel Hill, North Carolina: Algonquin Books of Chapel Hill, 1994.

Terkel, Studs. *Hard Times: An Oral History of the Great Depression*. New York: Pantheon Books, 1970.

Thomas, Bob. *Winchell*. Garden City, New York: Doubleday & Company, 1971.

Tomkins, Calvin. *Merchants & Masterpieces: The Story of the Metropolitan Museum of Art*. Revised and updated ed. New York: Henry Holt and Company, 1989.

Train, John. *The New Money Masters*. New York: Harper & Row, Publishers, 1989.

Tupper, Allan, and Roger Gibbins, eds. *Government and Politics in Alberta*. Edmonton, Alberta: University of Alberta Press, 1992.

Weisberger, Bernard A. *The Dream Maker: William C. Durant, Founder of General Motors*. Boston: Little, Brown and Company, 1979.

Whalen, Richard J. *The Founding Father: The Story of Joseph P. Kennedy*. New York: New American Library of World Literature, 1964.

Wheeler, George. *Pierpont Morgan and Friends: The Anatomy of a Myth*. Englewood Cliffs, New Jersey: Prentice-Hall, 1973.

White, Eugene N., ed. *Crashes and Panics: The Lessons from History*. Homewood, Illinois: Dow Jones–Irwin, 1990.

Wolfe, Tom. *The Right Stuff*. New York: Farrar, Straus, Giroux, 1979.

❧ Index ❧